I Can't Help
Falling in Love
With You

I Can't Help Falling in Love With You

Growing up as a Football Addict

Greg Whitaker

First published by Pitch Publishing, 2019

Pitch Publishing
A2 Yeoman Gate
Yeoman Way
Worthing
Sussex
BN13 3QZ
www.pitchpublishing.co.uk
info@pitchpublishing.co.uk

ISBN 978 1 78531 530 5

Typesetting and origination by Pitch Publishing

Printed and bound in India by Replika Press Pvt. Ltd.

Contents

'The dyslexic dunce
who couldn't read
is having a book
published. Now, that's
a turn-up for the
books.'

Peggie Blake, 2018

Introduction

THERE was a time, not all that long ago in truth, when it was all I could think about. My life could well have been falling apart around me, and relatively speaking, at times, it was, but during those years I probably didn't notice half the time. Relationships suffered, work would often deteriorate in quality, and my health, perhaps mentally more than physically, took the brunt of it all. Like an addict craving their next hit, waiting for Saturday afternoon to come became a living hell. Football was my drug of choice and Hull City AFC was my preferred strain.

Well, this is what I imagine addiction in its simplest form to feel like. Of course, as someone who has never taken an illegal substance in his entire life and is describing a period of his existence that started at the age of seven with his father, perhaps this is where the drug analogy should stop.

Despite my tendency to overanalyse every single aspect of my life – a habit which will become more significant as this story unfolds – I have yet to come up with a better comparison. Nick Hornby's *Fever Pitch* describes football fandom better than anything else I've ever read, and a hell of a lot better than I will ever be able to. Hornby quips, for him, the process of falling in love with football was similar to that of falling in love with women: '... suddenly, inexplicably, uncritically, [and] giving no thought to the pain or disruption it would bring with it'. I agree wholeheartedly. Yet, I have come to associate my relationship with football far more with *addiction* than with love. Indeed, it's worth noting that Hornby's comparison works just as well when imagining it coming from the mouth of a heroin addict desperately trying to justify their habit.

Of course, football addiction doesn't affect everyone. Some 'fans' can happily live their lives without checking their chosen football club's Twitter hashtag every other hour. Some so-called supporters can even go shopping on a Saturday afternoon rather than committing to biweekly pilgrimages to their stadium of choice. With this in mind, football fandom can be plotted on a spectrum. At one end are those heathens who can only list David Beckham when asked to name their favourite footballer. At the other end, bearded, usually anorak-wearing, stereotypes, that can, and often will, name Hull City's entire 34-man squad that was relegated at the end of the 2009/10 season. Can you guess which side of the spectrum I fall into yet?

The topic of football spectatorship, and all the culture surrounding it, is something I have thought about a lot. Indeed, I believe it was during one particularly long 3pm–11pm shift working at an unnamed bank – my first full-time job out of university – that my mind drifted, and I began to form a theory about how supporting a football club fits into modern life. Specifically, I wanted to find an answer for why, after nearly 20 years of being truly fanatical about football myself, apathy was beginning to sink in for me personally.

Sitting on the bus home after my shift, here is what I came up with.

While people from all walks of life fill my crudely thought-up spectrum of fandom, there are four distinct subgroups in which all football fans fall into: casual football fans, fans who love football, football junkies and the disenchanted 'former' fans.

Firstly, casual football fans. These are the people who like the beautiful game; however, not enough to go to every home match. This group, admittedly my least favourite collection of people on the planet at one point in my life, will often claim to support the more successful football clubs – Manchester United, Liverpool, Chelsea, and even Manchester City more recently.

As kids they would often justify their claims of support by constantly reminding you that 'their dad', who suspiciously had a strong Hull accent and went to the local comprehensive with your mum, 'is from [insert city with successful football team] and never missed a game as a kid'. Yet, infuriatingly, these people will often be the first you see on Wembley Way, clad head to toe in black and amber, when little old Hull City reach the FA Cup Final. Sickening.

Next come the fans that love football. People who pride themselves, not only on their knowledge of the game, but also their loyalty to a chosen team. Football lovers will usually be season ticket holders, and occasional travellers to away games. These fans, of which I classed myself a part of for the vast majority of my Hull City supporting life, tend to be the happiest and most content group of supporters. They read, listen, watch, breathe and *live* football because it makes them feel part of something to which they truly belong. Football is their chosen form of entertainment, their method of socialising with their friends and their passion. I envy those who remain part of this group.

Then there are the football junkies. These are fans who have spent most of their football-supporting lives in the second of these groups but have gradually, without ever truly being able to pinpoint when the change actually happened, transitioned into football addiction. While there are many similarities between those who love football and those who are addicted to it – supporting a chosen team home and away, desperately keeping up to date with transfer rumours and religiously buying every overpriced new home shirt each season – there is one key difference. While fans who love football, as my not-so-subtle title suggests, actively enjoy the sport and everything that comes with it, paradoxically, football junkies tend to resent it. Most of the time they follow football because they feel they should. Like a religious cult brainwashes its members, the global church of latter-day soccer never allows you to leave.

Finally come the disenchanted 'former' fans. I do hesitate to say 'former' fans, as, like I've just said, football never really allows you to lose interest completely. Yet, these fans are those who are completely fed up with the modern game. They have often been through the football lover and addiction stages of fandom, and their love has turned into resentment and now, quite tragically, disinterest. Money, television, commercialisation, sanitisation, lack of atmosphere, or all of the above, have ruined football for this group, who never really know if their fanaticism will ever return. Being a Hull City fan, it's hard not to respect this group – I've experienced it first-hand. Seeing a veteran fan you've seen every Saturday for the past 20 years being told to 'earn their stripes' by their club while, at the same, having their concession ticket prices taken away after 60 years of loyal support, for example, is enough to turn anyone against modern football. However, luckily, I haven't yet reached this stage. Hopefully I will never become part of this group.

As you are reading right now, you may think you still love football. Why else would you choose to read this book? But, just for a second, humour me. Really think. Can you all honestly say you pay the extortionate prices for tickets, away travel and Sky Sports subscriptions, for example, or buy a third choice away shirt each season, because you *love* football? Love the game in the same way you love your family, or your partner, or going out with your mates, or seeing your favourite band live? If you do, I am eternally envious.

That was me once. You see, if I'd have asked myself the same question just, say, five years ago, I would have said absolutely. Outside of my family, football was my greatest love and my passion. Now I can honestly say I have fallen out of love with football. Yet, this hasn't stopped me being fanatical about the game, and about Hull City specifically.

Hi. My name's Greg and I'm a football addict.

They say falling out of love is just as easy as falling head over heels, it's just that society doesn't want you to know this when you're growing up. Disney, CBBC, Enid Blyton, and even watching Coronation Street with your parents – they will all have you believe, no matter how bad life starts to appear, we will always have the people, possessions, objects and experiences we love to help us through life.

It's all a lie.

Of course, this is no real revelation. I am not suggesting that most of the human race progress into adulthood still convinced 'love', whatever that word actually means, is always a truly unconditional emotion. Individuals, situations and locations all change, grow and develop, and with them so do human emotions. What I am particularly interested in, however, are the feelings and emotions we associate, sometimes perhaps mistakenly, with our ability to love. Enthusiasm, fascination, obsession – all words used to describe love, but all fit just as well when describing addiction.

Now, I know what you must be thinking: 'You miserable, cynical, bastard.' I'm a man damaged by rejection or a string of failed relationships, perhaps? You'd be wrong. On the contrary, as it goes, I've been incredibly lucky with many of the key relationships in my life. My father, although a key player in this story of ultimate heartbreak and apathy, is still my best friend. My sister and I, despite her being six years my senior and located 300 miles away, have always enjoyed a healthy relationship. And I still call my mum and my one surviving grandparent, Peg, a number of times each week.

I am also not afraid to admit I myself am very much in love with my university sweetheart, Bex. Straight out of university I put my faith in this feeling, upped sticks and moved to a brand-new city in order to live with her. I'm delighted to say (so far) the gamble has paid off and, quite incredibly, she hasn't yet tired of me. Although, it's worth noting, this relationship may not stand the test of time if she ever discovers I refer to her as 'my university sweetheart'.

No. In my relatively short time on this bizarre little planet, it has not been personal relationships that have had me questioning the permanence of love and everything that comes with it. It's been my relationship with my first real love – football.

I started writing this book for selfish reasons – almost as a form of cathartic therapy with the aim of better understanding my changing relationship with football, love and my home town club. Yet, I hope you, the reader, may be able to take something greater away from my story. While the memories I write about are clearly very personal to me specifically, I hope the exploration of the transforming face of football over the past 20 years, and in turn my own changing relationship with my own passion, is relatable and at least of some interest to other fans. You see, I know I cannot be the only one who, despite still being fanatical about their football team, finds themselves dreaming and yearning for past days. Days when you were a fan because you loved football and your club unconditionally, and not just because it's become a habit you cannot break for fear of missing out on an unlikely return to the glory days.

I write this introduction in the autumn of 2018. While England miraculously appear to have turned a corner under the stewardship of Gareth Southgate (who saw that coming?), Hull City are once again disappointing in the Championship, having narrowly avoided back-to-back relegations last season, and still under the turgid ownership of the Allam family. Is there any real surprise I'm feeling disenchanted?

But, who knows? Perhaps this exercise will help me fall back in love. At best I hope it will act as a strange form of rehab, helping me transition back from football addict to football lover. At worst, simply a collection of, on the whole, positive childhood memories. Seems a win-win to me. Here goes.

2001–2008

Falling in Love

'This is getting better and better and better!'

Germany 1–5 England – 01/09/2001

IN true millennial fashion my introduction to football wasn't attending a live game with a family member, but through the magic of television – Germany 1–5 England. Of course, I had been aware of football long before England travelled to Munich for their now famous World Cup qualification match – I even just about remember hearing, albeit from my bedroom, my dad and sister screaming and shouting at the TV late one night two years earlier, as Manchester United completed their treble in Barcelona. However, it was this game, just three months short of my eighth birthday, that got me hooked.

It's bizarre what tiny, often insignificant, details the human brain decides to store for life. For me, there are three specific details about this game I remember being very aware of when I was sat in the lounge watching it on the BBC with my mum, dad and sister.

First was the commentary. If commentators were to be judged in the same way as the footballers who provide them with a living, this game would represent the peak of John Motson's glittering career. The sheer enthusiasm and glee for football that oozed out of every pore, combined perfectly with Motty's almost poetic verse, truly were things of beauty that night. Even now, 17 years after the event, I have lines of this commentary etched into my brain. While some people can't help but memorise more useful pieces of information, such as historic dates, song lyrics, poetry or elements in the periodic table, my brain has a tendency to store the useless sound bites of football commentaries gone by.

'It's the Germans' turn to stand like statues!', as Michael Owen equalises.

'It's 2–1 England! A smiling Sven!', as the camera pans to an ecstatic Sven-Göran Eriksson following England's second.

'Michael Owen gets his second of the match! Oohhh, fantastic stuff!', as Owen makes it 3–1.

'Could it be five? Yes, it is!', as Emile Heskey is put through on goal to complete the rout.

Earlier this year John Motson announced his retirement after nearly 50 years in his sheepskin jacket. While many snidely commented that this announcement had come ten years too late, I could not disagree any more strongly. Motty, along with his BBC rival Barry Davies, have been the voices of football, not just for my generation, but, quite incredibly, for several generations that came before mine. Just as the late, great Kenneth Wolstenholme's 'They think it's all over, it is now!' surely symbolised the beginnings of thousands of young children's love affairs with the beautiful game in the 1960s, and, as I am reliably informed, Martin Tyler's 2012 rendition of 'AGUERRRRROOOOO!' has sold the game to the youngest generation of new fans, the moment I fell for football can be almost clinically pinpointed to a euphoric Motty announcing 'Ohhhh, this is getting better and better and better! One, two, three for Michael Owen!', as the Liverpool striker completed his hat-trick.

The second detail I vividly remember from watching this match is far more niche. If you ask any English football fan of a certain age to name England's starting XI, I wager most will be able to name all but one. The unfortunate individual history has forgotten? Nick Barmby. Yet, for me, along with Owen's hat-trick and Gerrard's screamer, the inclusion of Hull-born Barmby is something I will always intrinsically associate with this game.

I was born, raised and schooled in and around the city of Hull. Nowadays, it is going through a renaissance period following the huge success of its 2017 City of Culture year. I can, and no doubt *will*, wax lyrical about what poet Philip Larkin described as Hull's 'sudden elegances' later in this book, yet in 2001 the city was still in the middle of a decades-long slump. Indeed, as I was growing up I remember being reminded constantly that Hull only had two claims to fame: having the highest rate of teenage pregnancy in the whole of Europe, and for being named the UK's worst place to live in the charmingly titled, *The Idler Book of Crap Towns*. Consequently, it's fair to say that when my dad explained that Sven's first attempt at solving England's left-sided midfield crisis was a lad from Hull who owned a house less than a mile from our own, my seven-year-old mind was blown.

It's easy to forget Barmby was excellent in this game, too. He played a key role in two of England's goals and dovetailed perfectly with his Liverpool team-mates Owen, Heskey and Gerrard. 'Oohhh, fantastic stuff!' But more about Sir Nicholas Barmby later.

The last detail I remember about this game, and which sealed my new-found love for football, was the horribly mistaken thought that England *were* the best team in the world. Indeed, England's crop of players in the early to mid-2000s were, at the time at least, considered a 'golden generation' for the national side, with world-class players in every position. Combine this with the ever-growing popularity of international football in England, stemming from Italia 90 and fuelled further by Euro 96 and, to a lesser extent, France 98, and it's understandable I came to this conclusion after watching this game and the additional fanfare that followed.

This one Saturday evening plonked in front of the television kick-started the whole thing. The hundreds of away trips, the countless meat pies, the thousands of pounds spent on tickets and football shirts, and some of the best days of my life. John Motson, Nick Barmby and the let-down that was the so-called golden generation of English international football, I have you to thank.

Handbags at dawn

Newcastle United 4–3 Manchester United – 15/09/2001

IF I was to become a football fan, I didn't have much choice in which national team I could support. Both of my parents are English, born in Hull and Scarborough respectively, and both of their parents were also born in Yorkshire. There was to be no Tony Cascarino or John Aldridge-esque changing of national allegiances for me. I was stuck with the Three Lions. But hell, after watching them smash the old enemy 5–1 in Germany's own backyard, I was more than content with this. My next big decision though – and I don't think it's too dramatic to say one that would significantly help shape my entire life – was to be which club side to support.

After that England match I spent a few weeks flirting with a couple of different clubs. First up: Liverpool. At the time, my dad travelled an awful lot for work, with regular trips to Gibraltar sticking in my mind. I remember these trips more than any other because without fail Dad would return with a gift for each family member. These usually consisted of several cartons of Superking cigarettes for my nan, jewellery for my mum, perfume for my sister and an action figure for me. This changed in the middle of September 2001. Instead of an action figure, Dad returned with a football shirt. It was the glorious 1999/2000 *Reebok* Liverpool away shirt. Green in colour with the white and blue sash running across it – think Patrik Berger. While it wasn't my first football shirt – both my sister and I owned 1995–97 Newcastle home shirts with the Newkie Brown sponsor thanks to another one of Dad's work trips a few years previous – this Liverpool shirt was the first of which I took any real notice. I've never really asked him why he chose this shirt, but my best guess would be that he simply recognised how enamoured I had become with football, and in particular Barmby, during the few weeks between the England game and his trip to Gibraltar. Why this shirt was a few years out of date is much easier to answer. Gibraltar, in those days at least, was always a tad behind the rest of the world. Indeed, I came to love the place after Dad's regular business trips to the Rock soon transformed into annual family holidays, yet I still remember seeing the same Liverpool 1999/2000 shirt on sale in Gibraltar's Sport City football section circa 2006.

I wore the shirt religiously for a good few months, but it turned out to be my one and only Liverpool strip. I would continue to idolise Nicky Barmby, but for one reason or another I never fell for Liverpool. In under a year I had grown out of the shirt and Barmby had left Anfield for Leeds United, ending the brief connection I held with Liverpool.

Coincidentally, Leeds United was another candidate that could have filled my new-found vacancy for a football club to follow. Under the stewardship of David O'Leary and the ownership of Peter Ridsdale, the West Yorkshire club were the only Premiership side in my region and had reached the semi-finals of the Champions League the season before. I had a few friends at school who had already pledged their football allegiances to Leeds, many of them with parents who, despite being local, were disciples of Don Revie and his successful Leeds sides of the 70s. It's safe to say my father was not one of these disciples and put an end to any interest in 'Dirty Leeds' very early doors. Thank God.

Indeed, when I think back, this is the one restriction I had when picking a football club. My dad – it's worth noting a talented footballer in his own right, who turned out for Scarborough and

Doncaster Rovers as a teenager – had fallen out of love with the game himself by this point. He had religiously supported his local Scarborough FC as a kid, although admits having a soft spot for Manchester United 'almost exclusively', as he puts it, due to the 'Holy Trinity' of Best, Charlton and Law – his idols. Yet moving to university in Durham, instead of pursuing a career in football himself, took its toll, and by the mid-1970s Dad had become nothing more than a casual football fan, more interested in playing rugby each weekend than standing on the football terraces. As it turned out, my interest in football would reignite his own love for the beautiful game.

Subsequently, Manchester United represents the closest I came to supporting a different football club. Along with the handful of Leeds, Liverpool and Arsenal fans at school, the overwhelming majority of lads claimed to support Sir Alex Ferguson's Manchester United. Looking back, it's hard to blame them. As a seven-year-old taking your first steps into football fandom, United appeared perfect. By some distance the best side in England, and one of the best in Europe around the turn of the new millennium, why wouldn't you want to forge a connection with them? While the names alone were enough to seduce you – Beckham, Giggs, Scholes, Keane, Neville – the fact that they went on to become one of the greatest club sides of all time invariably guaranteed valuable bragging rights to be used in the school playground.

I remember sitting with my sister in the lounge – probably wearing my green Liverpool shirt, although this detail is unconfirmed – watching my first full Manchester United match live on TV. It was 15 September 2001 and United were away at Sir Bobby Robson's Newcastle United. The date of this match is easy to recall as I vividly remember sitting in awe watching the impeccably observed minute's silence held at St James' Park to honour those who had perished in the 9/11 terror attacks just four days earlier. Obviously, at such a young age, I didn't fully grasp the global significance of 9/11; however, the image of 52,000 typically raucous football fans standing in perfect silence before this game is something that has always stuck with me.

Like my first taste of international football, my first full club match was a classic. A cliché, I know, but this game had everything. High-flying Newcastle won the game 4–3, with goals from Laurent Robert, Rob Lee and Nikos Dabizas, as well as an own goal from Wes Brown. United responded through the sensational Ruud van Nistelrooy, who went on to score 36 goals that season, as well as strikes from Giggs and Verón. But it wasn't enough. Unlike the England–Germany match, it wasn't the unusually high number of goals that I loved about this match, it was the drama of the final few minutes.

Picture the scene: Newcastle are 4–3 up with just a few minutes to play. Toon captain Alan Shearer takes the ball into the corner in an attempt to eat up valuable seconds. The ball is played off Shearer for a United throw. United captain, and renowned hothead, Roy Keane collects the ball and, for reasons impossible to decipher when watching the game in real time, launches it at Shearer's head. As expected, the former England striker reacts and squares up to the Irishman. After a few seconds of what the commentator – possibly Martin Tyler – wonderfully described as 'handbags at dawn', Keane throws a punch at Shearer and is held back by David Beckham. The United captain is promptly given his marching orders by the referee and the game ends 4–3 to Newcastle. This wasn't just a game of football, it had become theatre, and I couldn't get enough of it.

Bizarrely, in these particular circumstances, I actually sided with United and Roy Keane – a sentence which now chills me to the bone, of course. There was something almost romantic about the famous Manchester United in this period. The so-called Class of '92 was in its mature pomp, foreign imports like Ruud van Nistelrooy and Juan Sebastián Verón were selling the Premiership as the best league in the world, and the rough and tumble of the British game was still very much alive thanks to Keane and co. This United side represented the perfect transitional bridge between the broadly traditional style of British football, seen last in the 1990s, and the birth of the modern game.

Even if this is the case, fate didn't want my journey into football obsession to start with the modern game. No, while I did follow United's results for a few seasons after watching this match, I was about to fall in love with a much more traditional form of the game, a million miles away from the riches of the Premier League.

They say you don't choose your football club, your football club chooses you. Well, on 29 September 2001 I left my brief flirtations with Manchester United and Liverpool behind me, as Hull City AFC chose me.

Fer Ark, Lawrie Dudfield and raining rust

Hull City 3–0 Halifax Town – 29/09/2001

'CAN'T Get You Out Of My Head' by Kylie Minogue was number one in the charts, Tony Blair and New Labour were a few months into their second term, and the world was still reeling following the 9/11 attacks. However, I don't remember September 2001 for any of these things. I remember it as the month my dad took me to my very first football match.

29 September 2001. Just two weeks after starting my very first Merlin football sticker album, and my flings with England, Manchester United and Liverpool, my dad decided it was time to take me to my first match. My home town club Hull City were playing Yorkshire rivals Halifax Town at the old Boothferry Park ground. Having only ever seen England internationals and Premier League, or should I say *Premiership*, matches on TV prior to this, I have to say, being pushed through the rusty turnstiles at Boothferry led to somewhat of a baptism of fire for the seven-year-old me.

It's worth noting at this point that I was an incredibly shy child. Although it wouldn't be true to say I didn't have friends at school – on the contrary, I was part of a gang of six or seven lads that are still good friends to this day – my parents were always encouraging me to be more social. Stories of me flat out refusing to exit the car outside of the birthday parties of school peers for fear of my parents leaving me are told every time I visit home to this day. It's true; I remember dreading receiving party invitations at school, and even now I can't fully explain why this was the case. My best guess – admittedly based upon nothing more than psychological knowledge picked up through watching reruns of *Frasier* – is that I felt inferior when with other people my age, particularly in a school environment, and that my parents' presence represented a safety net that I could always rely on.

Up to this point I had struggled at school. Even at the age of seven I could barely read, and my numeracy skills were not much better. By this stage my parents – perhaps ironically a school inspector and special needs teacher by respective trades – had decided to move me to a different school, luckily with my best pal at the time, Henry. However, just a month in at the time of my first trip to Boothferry, I was still well behind my fellow year 2 students and, worst of all, I knew it. Nowadays my dad claims he was never that worried about me, and that he knew all I lacked was confidence and, as I would receive much later, an accurate diagnosis of dyslexia. Yet I can't help but think my first pilgrimage to Boothferry Park with my dad was one in a long line of social activities he organised in an attempt to build up my confidence. Looking back, it worked an absolute treat.

The specific memories I have from that day are a perfect combination of old-school football clichés and strange Hull City-related trivia that only fans who visited Boothferry Park will be able to fully appreciate. After parking on a terraced street roughly a five-minute walk from the ground, and walking past the busy Three Tuns pub, I remember turning into the car park at Boothferry Park and gazing up at the North Stand. It put me in a state of awe. Admittedly, the gloss was slightly taken off this momentous moment in my life by a few minor details. Unlike the picturesque, almost sanitised, view say the Kop at Anfield or the Stretford End at Old Trafford would have provided as my first sight of a football stadium on matchday, the fact that both Kwiksave and Iceland supermarkets were built into Boothferry's North Stand made for a much less glamorous image. But this wasn't going to put me off.

The moment my eyes fixed on the huge red lettering spelling out 'BOOTHFERRY PARK' which adorned the ageing stand, I felt a tingle run down the length of my spine. This was a phenomenon that never went away during the Boothferry Park years of my Hull City supporting life. Even at night when the sign appeared to read 'FER ARK' due to a mixture of broken light bulbs, faulty electrics and, during the ground's final few years of existence, missing letters, the wonderfully out-of-date, clearly lower-league feel to Boothferry never lost its magic.

The game itself was by no means a classic. This is perhaps stating the obvious – I'm not sure it's possible for a tie between Hull City and now-defunct Halifax Town to ever be described as 'a classic', regardless of what might have happened. Nevertheless, it was a good game to represent my first step into the world of live football. Through the frequent showers of raining rust every time the ball hit the stand, and the smell of beer, chicken balti pies and fag smoke – a unique sensory experience lost from football fandom since the introduction of new stadiums and the public smoking ban – my dad and I witnessed a Hull City victory at my first time of asking. City ran out comfortable 3–0 winners on the day, with Tigers' cult hero Lawrie Dudfield having the pleasure of scoring the first Hull City goal I ever witnessed, before Sunderland loanee Michael Reddy came off the bench to score twice.

In hindsight, the make-up of the crowd is also of some interest. Socially speaking, I usually consider the start of my journey in football to have taken place very much in the modern era of the game. A post-hooligan, post-Italia 90 environment in which the game had supposedly become far more accessible for the middle classes. This is often reflected in the type of people who attend football matches today. For example, nowadays the attendances at Hull City fixtures, and that of most football grounds in the country, consist of a widely diverse pool of fans. Fans of all ages, all genders, all races and all religions. Prior to writing this book, I had come to think this had always been the case during my time in the terraces. Yet, really thinking back to my first few seasons at Boothferry Park, I would wager 90 per cent of the crowd at any given match was very white and overwhelmingly male.

Sitting in a crowded stand experiencing a live football match for the first time fascinated me. This was something I hadn't prepared myself for. Prior to the game, I was expecting a broadly similar experience to watching football on TV, perhaps with the added bonus of catching the ball if it was cleared into the stand, or collecting a few players' autographs at half-time. Of course, live football has much more to offer. I probably spent much of the game gazing around Boothferry's crumbling terraces at the 9,500 supporters who had given up their afternoon to watch fourth-tier football. I was astounded by the sheer volume of people in one place. Although in the future I would see City play at Wembley Stadium in front of a crowd nearly ten times this size, at seven years old I could not fathom that the city of Hull even contained this many people. The chats, the constant stream of swear words I had never heard before, the chain reaction of people standing up whenever the home side were on the attack, and the deafening roar that greeted each of the Tigers' three goals that day. The atmosphere was intoxicating. If the England–Germany match had successfully transformed me into a fan of the beautiful game itself, Hull City v Halifax Town introduced me to the magic of live football.

I've come to realise that as you get older childhood memories seem to become blurred in your mind's eye. Details become fuzzy, emotions less visceral and images grainier. But this process never appears to affect the memory of your first football match. Ask any football fan about their first live game and they will be able to tell you everything about that day. The season, the weather, the goalscorers, the opposition's manager. It's quite incredible. Of course, I am no different. I loved that day. I still have both the matchday programme and ticket stored away in an old shoebox in the loft of my parents' house, and, proving my point, can still name the whole Hull City starting XI off by heart to this day. (Glennon, Edwards, Whittle, Mohan, Petty, Holt, Johnsson, Whitmore, Beresford, Dudfield, Alexander and super-sub Reddy.)

In my job as a freelance journalist over the past few years, I have had the honour of interviewing a number of big personalities for certain publications and broadcasters. I've been lucky enough to talk to the likes of Steve Bruce and David Meyler face to face just days before Hull City's 2014 FA Cup Final and, away from football, politicians Jeremy Corbyn and Natalie Bennett in the aftermath of general elections. However, the most nervous I have ever been before an interview came in 2016 when I got the chance to question Lawrie Dudfield – the scorer of my first ever Hull City goal – for the Hull City Supporters' Trust website. It's illogical really. The interview took place completely via email and was published in a simple Q&A format with a readership confined to a relatively small pool of diehard City fans. Yet this article remains one of my favourite pieces of work. Lawrie was fantastic and provided a fascinating insight into his role in the start of what I labelled 'Hull City's golden generation'. Aside from the content, what struck me when I was talking to Lawrie was the raw passion he still held for the game – a passion rarely expressed by many 'media-trained' footballers nowadays. But more of that later. I explained to him about my first visit to Boothferry Park and the massive role his opening goal has had on my life. Now in his forties with children of his own, I think Lawrie really understood how much this specific match means to me, and the emotional power of football more broadly. Talking to the striker, who ironically will barely feature again in this story of football addiction, was a cathartic experience for me. At a time when I was just beginning to feel the first twinges of apathy towards Hull City, and football in general, this interview briefly took me back to where it all began, and I was reminded, momentarily at least, how I first got hooked.

Since this autumnal day in 2001 I have attended close to 500 Hull City fixtures, being a season ticket holder for the vast majority of this time. I have been a phenomenally lucky Hull City fan. Before my generation, the last 100 years or so of the Tigers' history had been fairly unremarkable. A couple of promotions to the second tier here and there, a few inconspicuous FA Cup runs, and, of course, a highly prestigious second-place finish in the 1974 Watney Cup. Though, since the day my dad decided to take me down to Boothferry to see my very first live football match, Hull City have had no less than five promotions (three of which to the Premier League), a first FA Cup Final, an, albeit very brief, excursion into European football, and a move to a state-of-the-art new stadium. But I'd like to think I'd have attended the same number of matches with my dad regardless of this success.

I remember being so surprised at how thrilling seeing live football actually was. As I've mentioned, I'm from a generation that saw many kids at school pick Manchester United, Liverpool, Chelsea or Arsenal as their team to support. There was a very real feeling of 'why would anyone want to support little old Hull City of Division 3, when you can support Manchester United, Liverpool or Arsenal from the comfort of your armchair?' People seemed to accept this and assume that going to watch Hull City every weekend must have been a horrible experience. All I needed to prove this was not the case was a cold afternoon watching two Division 3 teams from Yorkshire battling it out at a deteriorating traditional football ground.

My first football match with my dad was a fantastic moment in both of our lives, and one that fathers and sons (and mothers, daughters, grandparents, etc.) have had for generations. As this book is testament to, this day has shaped my life more than anything else, aside from my family. My confidence, my friendship group, my profession, even my choice of university can all be indirectly traced back to watching Theo Whitmore put Michael Reddy through on goal in September 2001.

I would love to have the same experience with my son or daughter one day, taking them to watch Hull City AFC, regardless of where the club finds itself.

The first cut is the deepest

England 1–2 Brazil – 21/06/02

EVERY football supporter remembers their first World Cup. Almost without exception the self-proclaimed 'Greatest Show on Earth', which comes around just once every four years, never fails to disappoint. My first World Cup came in the summer of 2002 and I was positive England were going to win it at a canter. From the second I opened my glorious 2002 England home shirt – complete with shorts, socks and tracksuit – for my eighth birthday in December 2001, World Cup fever began to take hold. Whilst the tournament, which took place in Japan and South Korea, has not gone down in history as one of football's classics, the first World Cup to be held outside of Europe or the Americas will always hold a special place in my heart. Yet, to understand the personal significance of this World Cup, I must rewind a few months.

After the success of my first visit to Boothferry the September before, my love for football had continued to grow. Between that cold autumnal day and the following February, Dad and I went to every home game City played, including a few Tuesday night fixtures. Safe to say, I was told not to use my attendance at these games as an excuse when teachers inevitably asked why seven-year-old me was struggling to stay awake at school on Wednesday mornings. Nevertheless, this was to be good practice for what was soon to become a regular occurrence, with both home *and* away games to attend on Tuesday evenings for the next decade to come.

Sadly, and for a reason I could never have foreseen, my maiden season as a football supporter was interrupted during the first few months of 2002 when my grandad became suddenly very ill, eventually passing away in the April of that year. Although he suffered from many different illnesses throughout his life – 'from malaria to gout', as my grandma, Peg, often remarks – it was a rare form of blood cancer that took him in the end. At the time doctors were reluctant to speculate on what might have caused the cancer, chalking it up to anything from age to simply dumb bad luck. Though Peg is convinced to this day that the cancer can be traced back directly to the time my grandad spent in Japan, and specifically Hiroshima, as part of his service with the RAF just months after 'Little Boy' – the uranium-based nuclear bomb – was dropped on the city. Either way, I guess we'll never find out for sure.

The death shook the entire family and made the first half of the year incredibly difficult. During this period, it felt as though my mum – an only child – was left with the job of helping my grandma cope with the loss of her husband, while my dad, who treated Grandad Fred more as a close friend rather than his father-in-law, faced the task of helping my sister Steph and I through our first proper experience of death. Indeed, this was no easy task. Grandad Fred, or 'Ba' as he was always affectionately known, had played a huge role in all our lives. Living just a two-minute walk down our street, we saw Peg and Ba daily. With both of my parents in full-time work, Ba would often be the one to pick us up from school, do any DIY jobs around our house, and play cards and dominoes with us every weekend. Steph and I were crushed. Even at the age of eight, I understood that the grieving process would take a long time to run its natural course, and I even think I was aware that different members of the family would grieve in different ways. Peg was incredibly strong and showed little raw emotion in front of Steph and I, while my mum appeared to deal with it how any child losing a parent does – slowly and in familiar stages.

It wasn't until much, much later that I finally understood how strongly Ba's death impacted upon Dad. Immediately after the death, Dad appeared to be the one holding it all together for the family. He showed very little outward emotion, organising all the difficult administration, which is inevitable after a family member passes away, and helping my sister and I understand the complex and awkward period of grief that took over the family during the following months.

Yet getting to know my father much better as an adult in recent years has highlighted just how difficult this period was for him, too. You see, Dad truly did lose one of his best friends when Ba passed away. Like the relationship my father and I share today, the pair did everything together. Almost religiously, they would spend every Thursday evening in each other's company with a big group of pals playing snooker and poker at their local social club, and when Sunday came, without fail you'd find them out on the golf course, or having a drink 'on the nineteenth', as my dad would say. Indeed, I don't think the strength of their bond really hit home until Dad took me to become a member of that same social club nine years later, on the night of my 18th birthday – fittingly enough, a Thursday. The surviving members of their group of friends, nearly all from Dad's generation nowadays, showered me with stories and tales from Ba and Dad's nigh on 40-year memberships. Whilst it might sound terribly Hallmark, it was perhaps my favourite gift that I received for my 18th.

Naturally, this landmark event in my young life impacted upon my relationship with football. After not missing a home match for the first seven months of the season, family came first and Dad and I inadvertently postponed attending live matches until the following August. Looking back, we didn't miss too much. City finished in 11th place in the old Third Division, ten points outside of the play-offs – a disappointment after such a strong start to the campaign, which ultimately saw manager Brian Little depart the club before the end of the season.

Despite this lacklustre finale to the domestic football, after a few months break, football was about to come flooding back into my life. World Cup fever, the symptoms of which had subsided somewhat during my difficult start to 2002, became visible once again as a nation's attention shifted to David Beckham's broken metatarsal and England's golden generation.

As I've already alluded to, after England's demolition of Germany less than a year previously, followed by *that* Beckham free kick against Greece that had guaranteed England's place at the tournament prior to Christmas, I didn't think there was a chance the Three Lions would not win the 2002 World Cup.

Unlike subsequent international tournaments where I have endeavoured to watch as many games as is physically possible, the time difference between the UK and Japan provided a challenge for both myself and the rest of England. Most games were broadcast during the morning on UK television, meaning work, or in my case school, prevented an all-out football-viewing marathon, the likes of which have occurred on a biennial basis ever since. This, combined with specific memories simply being lost in the annals of time, means I don't remember a large amount about the tournament. Other than England's fixtures, I do remember three iconic moments. Firstly, defending champions France being eliminated during the group stages at the expense of El Hadji Diouf's unfancied Senegal side. Secondly, the great Rivaldo of Brazil throwing himself to the floor clutching his face after Turkey's Hakan Unsal kicked the ball at the Brazilian's shin – an incident that saw the Turk controversially sent off, and Brazil winning the group game 2–1. And finally, goalkeeper of the tournament Oliver Kahn's costly mistake during the final to allow Ronaldo to score Brazil's first in their 2–0 victory.

Yet, unsurprisingly, my clearest memories are of England's fixtures. Following a mixed bag in the group stage, which saw two uneventful draws against Sweden and Nigeria sandwich the classic 1–0 victory over Argentina, England were through to the knockout stages. A 3–0 demolition of Denmark in the last 16 followed, by which time Sven's England side were starting to look the real deal. Next up for England was the mighty Brazil in the quarter-final – a game which in hindsight consisted of the two best teams in the tournament. The purists would say this fixture came two rounds too early and would have made for the perfect final that year, and it's hard to disagree. What a game it was.

I must have quite literally watched thousands of football matches during my time, but I don't think I will ever watch one in a more surreal environment than that of England v Brazil in the 2002 quarter-final. Once again, the time difference between Japan and the UK made for awkward viewing, and an argument with Mum and Dad about my attendance at school that day was inevitable. Rather than my preferred viewing environment of the lounge, sitting on the sofa next to my dad with a large mug of tea, I was forced to watch England's most important game since Euro 96 at school, in the main hall, surrounded by hundreds of other kids, half of whom didn't give a toss about football. To make things even worse, we were forced to watch the game on a television that, despite being so large and heavy it had to be wheeled around on its own special cart, had a screen not much larger than a modern-day tablet. Absolute nightmare. Nevertheless, I was determined not to let anything ruin this for me. Along with my best mates Henry, Tom and Sam – all fellow football fans – I arrived early and we plonked ourselves right in front of the cart where we remained, sat cross-legged, for the next two hours.

From the very first whistle this game felt special. We may have been 9,000 miles away from the action, but the magic of supporting our nation in a World Cup had us fixated on that tiny screen. After a few miserable months, sitting with a group of my best mates watching England play Brazil in a World Cup, knowing we should be in the classroom studying for our end-of-year exams, was pretty perfect. And the game itself certainly lived up to this excitement.

England came storming out of the blocks and unquestionably took the game to the Brazilians in the first half. This early pressure paid off as Michael Owen fired England ahead in the 23rd minute, consequently creating mayhem in the hall, as over a hundred primary school children went mad.

Admittedly, at least half of these kids didn't have a clue why they were cheering, yet the atmosphere it created will live with me forever regardless. As I sat back down, crossing my legs on the cold wooden floor, I remember thinking how this game would now be a walk in the park for England. Sven's men would see off the already wounded Brazilians, destroy Turkey or Senegal in the semi-finals, before a meeting with Germany in the final, which would, of course, result in another England thrashing – à la Munich nine months before.

Tragically, my daydream was rudely interrupted just before half-time as Brazil equalised through a very well worked Rivaldo goal. Things went from bad to worse just ten minutes after the interval when a goal was scored that still haunts my dreams to this day. With the game poised perfectly at 1–1, Brazil were awarded an innocuous-looking free kick around 40 yards out from David Seaman's goal. The buck-toothed magician, Ronaldinho, who I had no prior knowledge of before this tournament, stepped up and floated a high ball goalwards. Time seemed to slow down as the PSG midfielder's effort sailed over the ponytailed head of David 'Safe hands' Seaman and into the top-left corner of the net. While there will always be a debate over whether or not the future Ballon d'Or winner meant it, I have absolutely no doubt. Seaman was, for reasons still unknown, standing in the no man's land between his own goal line and England's surprisingly high defensive line, and Ronaldinho took full advantage of this.

England seemed to go into panic mode at this point – a trait of the national team that would become more and more common over the next 15 years. Even during the last half hour of the match, which saw Brazil go down to ten men after the match-winner Ronaldinho was sent off for an over-the-ball tackle on Danny Mills of all people, England never looked like getting back into the tie.

The final whistle went and with it the tears began. England, the side I was so confident were going to come home from Japan victorious, had crashed out of the World Cup once again. I was heartbroken. Fast-forward 16 years, thousands of matches watched, and far more emotions invested in football, and I still cannot remember being as disappointed with a result. What I remember making it even worse was the 'I told you so' look on Dad's face as he picked me up from school that afternoon. He had been burnt before and knew better. I still had a lot of learning to do.

The first half of 2002 was a horrible few months for my family. Grief lingered over our house like a black cloud we just couldn't shake off, and priorities changed as our family dynamic altered forever. I think I grew up a lot during this period. I missed attending football games with my dad, of course, but as a family we all became much closer after Ba's death. Some might say quite miraculously, England's painful and premature exit from the World Cup did nothing to deter me from the beautiful game, and come August, Dad and I, along with the very welcome addition of Steph, who wanted to see what all the fuss was about, were back at Boothferry cheering on the Tigers.

Your first experience of death stays with you forever, and in many ways, I don't believe you ever fully recover from it. Of course, it would be churlish to compare this to a football supporter's first experience of the World Cup, yet for me the two formative experiences will forever be closely entwined. I will never forget watching that exhilarating quarter-final in the summer of 2002, but more importantly, I will certainly never forget all the fantastic times I spent with my wonderful grandad, Ba.

Change

Hull City 2–0 Hartlepool United – 26/12/2002

AS summer turned to autumn and the nights began to pull in, I started to feel uneasy. Come December, Hull City AFC were to leave their home of 56 years and move into the state-of-the-art Kingston Communications Stadium a mile down the road. I'm not too sure why the idea bothered me so much. After all, I had only been attending Boothferry Park for a little over a year, and I'm convinced any normal nine-year-old supporter could not have been happier at the prospect of swapping the crumbling terraces of Boothferry for the pristine new all-seater stands of the KC.

I suppose I didn't like the idea of such a big change after I had finally got settled. Indeed, change is something I'd always struggled with, and in many ways still do. To this point, my fortnightly visits to Boothferry with Dad had worked wonders for my confidence and any change to this new routine represented a potential threat in my eyes.

Quite aside from my football-watching habits, the back half of 2002 saw a lot of change in my life. After two happy years spent in years 2 and 3, I had once again started a new school in September. Indeed, while I had progressed a great deal during the previous two years, academically speaking I was still lagging behind the rest of my friends. Heading into year 4, at the bottom of a new school that would become my second home for the next ten years, I felt my confidence start to slip once again.

As an adult it's sometimes difficult to remember just how much panic seemingly insignificant aspects of life can induce during your formative school years. In this vein, it would not be an exaggeration to say I worried about nearly everything that was going on around me, and I knew any small change usually involved being thrust out of my relatively small comfort zone. My biggest fear – a common one amongst kids this age, I'm sure – was being 'found out'. I felt as though it was my own fault that, in terms of my education at least, I was progressing at a much slower rate than my friends, and at any moment I would be exposed as the phoney I believed myself to be.

What if I fail tomorrow's spelling test again? Will I be given a dreaded 'demerit'? Why does it take me twice as long as anyone else to read our book assignment? Why don't I just 'get' maths like everyone else? Why am I not as clever as my friends?

These are the questions I would lie in bed quite literally worrying myself sick about each night. It sounds ridiculous when I look back, but as a nine-year-old at a new school, the fear of falling behind your friends or embarrassing yourself means everything. I hated this feeling, and thinking back to certain parts of this period now still sends a nasty shiver down my spine.

Although I was lucky enough to start my new school along with a large group of friends, come October half-term I would go to bed each night dreading going to school the next morning. Aside from going to the football with Dad and Steph on Saturday afternoons and Tuesday evenings, the only time I felt confident was when I was playing sport myself. While I was struggling badly in Maths and English classes, representing the school at football or rugby on a Saturday morning, and then local Sunday league football the next day, was when I was at my happiest. Naturally, as the school year went on, little by little my confidence grew. Yet it would be another few years before I believed I had finally caught up with my peers academically, if indeed this time ever did arrive at all completely.

Away from my personal life, City were also ringing the changes, and after a summer of watching the greatest players on the planet battle it out at the World Cup, my football fix was soon being filled by the delights of the old Third Division and a new-look Hull City. Former Liverpool star Jan Mølby became Brian Little's permanent replacement in the summer of 2002, and with the prospect of a brand-new stadium to move into just months away, there was a growing buzz around the side. Ironically, however, despite the Dane signing a handful of players that would go on to become Hull City legends – Ian Ashbee, Stuart Elliott and Stuart Green included – Mølby's spell in charge proved to be an unmitigated disaster. He was dismissed by October, having only managed two league wins from 17 games.

With decent money having been spent on the squad, and the move to the best stadium in the division fast approaching, chairman Adam Pearson needed to get his next managerial appointment right. Funnily enough, throughout his first spell at the club, Pearson had a bizarre track record when it came to appointing managers, seemingly always finding a way to follow a bad managerial appointment with an inspired one, before again then making another poor choice. Jan Mølby, Peter Taylor, Phil Parkinson, Phil Brown, Iain Dowie, Nigel Pearson – three good, three bad.

But more of that later. What matters at this stage is that Adam Pearson made what must be described as his most important and significant appointment to date in October 2002 when the former Leicester City and Brighton and Hove Albion manager, Peter Taylor, was announced as Mølby's successor. Taylor – or 'Peter Taylor, the man who gave David Beckham the England captaincy' as the press exclusively referred to him during his first few months in charge – was to be in many ways the final piece of the puzzle and, if you will indulge me one more metaphor, was the catalyst which finally woke the sleeping giant. While the rest of the 2002/03 season was treated as somewhat of a write-off in terms of promotion ambitions after our woefully poor start under Mølby, Peter Taylor's influence on the rest of the season built the foundations for the most successful 15 years in the club's history, which were immediately to follow. Balancing a mismatched squad, injecting a Premier League standard of professionalism into a group of players whose mentality was previously questioned, and overseeing a seamless migration from an old ground to a new stadium – Taylor's first ten months in the job were key to City's future development. Despite a forgettable season in terms of final standings in the league table, these achievements should not be forgotten.

Yet despite the lack of memorable moments on the pitch during this season, there are two games that stick in the minds of every City supporter, for obvious reasons. It would perhaps be easy to list Hull City's last ever match at Boothferry Park against Darlington in this collection of my most memorable and influential games of football, but the truth is I really did not enjoy that match at all. In 'typical City' fashion, the Tigers somehow managed to lose this game 1–0 on a horrible December afternoon. But it wasn't the result that irked me. Instead, it was the sheer amount of self-proclaimed 'City fans' that turned up at Boothferry that day. In hindsight, I had no right to feel this way. Fans from all over the UK decided to make one final pilgrimage to say goodbye to a football ground they loved, and even if they had fallen out of love with Hull City, as in some ways I have at this moment in time, they of course had the right to pay their final respects to City's former home. Yet, the cynical streak in my nine-year-old self noted that the vast majority of the crowd that day were not following the team a year previous, or even a month earlier for that matter, and this annoyed me greatly. Although I loved seeing the parade of Hull City's greatest 100 players grace the pitch pre-match – which kick-started a personal 'history of Hull City' research project over the next few months – the match itself was ruined, and my overwhelming memory of that day is a feeling of resentment that the presence of these extra 10,000 fans or so had compromised my vantage point of the pitch. For these mostly selfish and self-centred reasons, City's next home league game will always remain far more significant to me.

The official opening game at the KC Stadium was a friendly organised against the Premier League side Sunderland, in which, up for grabs was the Raich Carter Trophy – a classy nod to one of Hull City and Sunderland's greatest ever players. After the disappointment of the final game at Boothferry, City's 1–0 win represented the perfect start to a new chapter in the club's history. Special mention must go to City midfielder Steve Melton, who holds the honour of scoring the very first goal at the new stadium. Yet, in my eyes, the dawning of a new era for Hull City began eight days later when the visit of high-flying Hartlepool United to the KC marked the official first league game at the Tigers' new home.

The Christmas holidays were strange that year. Not only were they the first school holidays I had experienced in which I was expected to complete a long list of schoolwork before my return in the new year – I had of course been set extra work in both Maths and English as teachers attempted to 'catch me up' – it was also the first Christmas period without my grandad. Ba's absence, although not openly discussed at any great length that Christmas, was all too apparent and made it an unusually gloomy Christmas Day. Sat eating my chicken dinner (for some reason our family never cooks the traditional turkey dinner on Christmas Day), I remember desperately wanting to leave the table, go upstairs to my bedroom, and play on the new FIFA 2003 PlayStation game I had opened with delight that morning. I got my wish a few hours later and after the initial annoyance of finding Division Three Hull City had not been included in the game, I sat alone in my room for the rest of the evening playing match after match and waiting for Boxing Day to come.

I woke up the next morning and immediately felt nervous. I didn't know what to expect. After 18 months of watching live football at the glorious Boothferry Park, I was terrified I would somehow not enjoy the experience as much in the sanitised environment of the new KC Stadium. Safe to say, I had nothing to worry about.

Moving to a new ground is a strange experience for football fans. Going to the football each week becomes a habit, and a new ground challenges the status quo. It is the little things that don't really occur to you until the moment you are already in the car heading to the first game in a new stadium that get you. Steph, Dad and I had arranged to go to the match with some old family friends – Dad's snooker and poker pal, Phil, and his two sons Oliver and Luke, both of whom were around my age. It was only when we were halfway to the stadium did we realise we had no idea where we were going to park the car and, far more importantly in my view, where we were going to go for our traditional pre-match fish and chips. While the KC is directly next to Walton Street – an empty piece of land used every Wednesday for Walton Street market, Hull's park and ride service, and the famous Hull Fair every October – unusually bad traffic took this away as an option. In order to make our seats for kick-off, we parked our car in the same place we had for the past year, just around the corner from Boothferry, and power-walked towards the KC. Our lack of forward planning had ruled out any chance of a quick stop at the chippy, meaning on our first pilgrimage to our new home we would be sampling the KC's meat pies at half-time.

The 20-minute walk actually proved to be a lot of fun. Thousands of City fans had seemingly had the same idea as us and had abandoned their cars around Boothferry. This created a fantastic atmosphere as a wave of black and amber convoyed down Anlaby Road, all in full Christmas cheer and excited by the prospect of finding their new seats at the KC. As chants of 'City 'til I die!' and 'We all follow the black and amber team' (to the tune of 'Yellow Submarine') began, the nervous feeling I had experienced all morning slipped away and was replaced by raw excitement. This experience was to be different to the 18 months spent on the terraces at Boothferry, but from that moment on, I knew it was going to be equally as special.

For the first and last time we sat in the upper tier of KC's main West Stand. Although providing a fantastic aerial view of the entire pitch, as we queued for our pies at half-time, we all agreed that in the future we would prefer to be much closer to the action and sat with the fans who we had stood with at Boothferry.

These fans had opted for seats in the cheaper East Stand located directly opposite, and this was where the real atmosphere was being generated. Indeed, after this game we never looked back, as the East Stand became our home for the next 15 years.

Nonetheless, we didn't let our location ruin the game for us. On the contrary, the match itself was an absolute cracker. Played in front of a crowd of over 22,000 – a record attendance for the old Third Division since English football's 1992 reforms – a City XI of Musselwhite, Regan, Joseph, Anderson, Delaney, Ashbee, Green, Keates, Melton, Elliott and Alexander cruised to an emphatic 2–0 win over a strong Hartlepool side who, it is worth noting, would go on to be promoted that season. There was something special about that day. From the first to last minute the City faithful sung their hearts out and created an atmosphere the like of which I had not yet experienced as a football fan. Looking down over Peter Taylor's dugout, I remember thinking to myself that this was the first football match I had attended where the noise of the crowd was drowning out the sound of the two managers bellowing out instructions, and even the sound of the referee's whistle (interestingly enough, in this case, the whistle of World Cup Final 2010 referee, Howard Webb). When the game ended, and more than 20,000 fans remained in their seats to sing one final rendition of 'If you're 'ull City, stand up!', while the City players did the first of many laps of honour around the pitch, I knew I had been worrying for nothing. The KC would be a fitting home for my beloved City, and I couldn't wait for the next match.

While City would go on to have a mixed season in terms of results, I will always pinpoint this match as the start of the club's monumental rise up the Football League. We had a fantastic manager in Peter Taylor beginning to work his magic, the best chairman the club had had in over 20 years in the shape of Adam Pearson, and now a stadium fitting of a Premier League football club.

As the six of us walked back down Anlaby Road and passed the now locked gates of Boothferry Park, I thought to myself, 'Perhaps change isn't all that bad after all.'

The Galacticos: A footballing masterclass

Manchester United 4–3 Real Madrid – 23/04/2003

BRAZIL, 1970. Liverpool, 1975–84. AC Milan, 1987–91. Manchester United, 1999. Hull City, 2008. Barcelona, 2008–11. Spain, 2008–12.

With perhaps one glaring exception, these football teams all have one thing in common. They are all answers provided when lovers of football are asked to name their greatest football teams of all time. (I agree, reader, the inclusion of Sacchi's Milan is perhaps a bit of a stretch.)

It's an argument as old as the game itself that is had in pubs, offices and homes the world over on a day-to-day basis. Of course, it is a debate that will never be settled, but that doesn't stop the average football fan from putting their opinion forward. During my two decades as a football fanatic, and more recently in my role as a football writer, I am often asked which football team I believe to be the best ever. Utilising just the right aspects of both politics and journalism degrees, I usually manage to skirt around the issue fairly successfully, sitting precariously on the fence and never pinning my colours to any particular mast.

It is indeed an interesting and divisive topic among football supporters. While my answer will likely always involve a certain degree of fence sitting, my dad, for example, would answer in a heartbeat. Despite being totally unwavering in his belief that George Best was the greatest footballer to ever play the beautiful game, Dad would always tell me (and anyone else who would be stupid enough to ask) that the best *team* he ever watched was the great Brazil side that lifted the World Cup in 1970. Indeed, as a child, I remember watching Jairzinho, Carlos Alberto and, of course, Pelé combine to score one of the greatest goals in history – Brazil's fourth in their 4–1 drubbing of Italy in the 1970 final – on an old and very grainy VHS tape.

'That's not a bad ball for Pelé on the right side. It's Carlos Alberto ... Oh, what a great goal that was!'

Yet, coming from a different generation, I have never felt anything more than a distant respect for this great team. Indeed, when I myself feel pressured to chip in with inevitable, usually alcohol-induced, debates regarding the greatest football teams of all time, my two pennies' worth always come with a caveat. For a football supporter of my relatively young age and vintage, looking past Pep Guardiola's Barcelona side of the late noughties would be criminal.

It's true – the revolutionary 'tiki-taka' style of football has produced some of the best displays I have had the pleasure of watching in my time as a football supporter – more will be said on them later. More importantly, the clause I always insist on adding to my contribution is, while the consistency of Pep's Barcelona means they likely do represent the greatest football team during my limited time as a football supporter, they did not produce the greatest footballing *performance* I have ever had the pleasure of witnessing. That great honour goes to Real Madrid and the first incarnation of the so-called 'Galacticos'. Somehow this has always remained more significant to me.

Over the course of a decade or so, Florentino Pérez's mission to build the best and most expensive football team ever assembled went through several different phases with varying levels of success. Though, in just 90 minutes back in April 2003, I was convinced I had witnessed the greatest football team I would ever see.

The occasion was the second-leg quarter-final of the 2002/03 Champions League. The stage was Old Trafford. Sir Alex Ferguson's United side, also packed with world-class players in each position, were heading into the crucial second leg 3–1 down, and Ferguson's controversial decision to leave David Beckham on the bench had raised a few eyebrows to say the least.

For the life of me I cannot remember where we were on holiday, but my overriding memory of watching this game is being sat in a hotel room, glued to a tiny television screen with Steph. At this point, it's worth noting that it was during this period that I had started to become fascinated with the exotic Real Madrid and its team of international superstars. Indeed, several summer holidays to the Costa del Sol during the immediate years previous had seen me start an impressive collection of knock-off, yet very convincing, market stall football shirts. Consequently, when I wasn't wearing a Hull City shirt, I would be wearing one of my many national team shirts, with the name and number of Raúl, Figo, Zidane or Ronaldo blazed across my back.

Nevertheless, I had to remind myself that I still had a soft spot for Manchester United, and with the reasonable (yet ultimately incorrect) assumption that I would never have the chance to support my beloved Hull City in a European competition, supporting the British side on big European nights seemed natural.

The game got off to an incredibly high-paced start, with both sides attacking from the off – Madrid looking for the goals to kill off the tie, and United looking to start an all-too-familiar Fergie-inspired fightback. To my great disappointment, it was Real that broke the deadlock early on. Ronaldo, the player I had watched just months earlier win the World Cup for his native Brazil, fired past a hapless-looking Fabien Barthez from the edge of the box. 1–0, and seemingly all over. Despite this early blow, the dynamic of the game did not alter. After a season of watching Division Three football – which, at the time at least, lived up to the stereotypes of lots of long balls occasionally interrupted by a horrendously late tackle – watching these two magnificent football teams trade blows was a revelation. United's trademark never-say-die determination was rewarded just before half-time when Ruud van Nistelrooy's tap-in gave the home team a flicker of hope once again.

The second half began with a blitz of Madrid pressure. Moments after Luis Figo hit the crossbar with a long-range effort, a fantastically well-worked team goal was finished off by, who else but, Ronaldo to make it 2–1 five minutes into the second period. At this point I remember turning to Steph – who by this time was bored and sat texting on her Samsung flip-up mobile phone – telling her I was *still* convinced United were going to turn the game around. While my faith was to be rewarded a minute later when a Madrid own goal levelled the game once more, I was not to see United progress that night. What I did see though was an absolute football masterclass.

The last 40 minutes of the match passed in a blur as footballing ecstasy took over my body and mind. When the sensational Ronaldo completed his hat-trick just seven minutes later, it was all I could do to stop myself jumping off the hotel bed to applaud what I had just witnessed. Less than ten minutes later, the world's greatest striker was walking off the Old Trafford turf to the sound of 66,000 fans giving him an unprecedented standing ovation, along with the inevitable 'Fergie, sign him up!' chants raining down from all four corners of the Theatre of Dreams. I was still punch-drunk at this moment. I couldn't believe what I had just seen. I wasn't aware that players existed on this planet that could do such incredible things with a football.

Quite incredibly, the Ronaldo-less final half hour of the game refused to peter out. Without the Brazilian on the pitch, United regrouped and substitute David Beckham's two late goals kept Ferguson's side fighting right until the very last minute. Although, despite all of this drama, the game will always be remembered as the night Ronaldo showed English football just why he is considered one of the greatest players of all time.

It is rumoured that this one fixture was the reason Roman Abramovich decided to buy a Premier League football club.

Indeed, the Russian billionaire attended Old Trafford that night and just three months later he purchased Chelsea with the promise of building a side capable of becoming the best side in Europe. The west London club won their first Champions League title in 2012.

Like Chelsea, I owe a lot to this one match. Up until this point I had become a passionate football supporter, following Hull City each week and watching as much football on TV as physically possible. Yet it was this one Real Madrid performance that first began to tip my passion over the edge and into the realms of obsession. It was at this point I wanted not only to watch football every week, but also devote a lot of my free time to learning about the history of the game, the different footballing cultures around the globe, tactics and formations, and the greatest players and teams of all time. I wanted to know everything there was to know. This obsession has led to where I am today. I lay in the hotel bed that night not able to sleep, replaying the key moments of the match over and over in my mind. Real Madrid was the first team that illustrated to me that football could be *art*, and not just a sport. This may sound pretentious, I know, but all football supporters will remember the first time they themselves had this mind-blowing personal revelation. Even at that young age, football was fast transforming from a hobby to something that more closely resembled a religion or philosophy, and I just could not get enough.

Perhaps ironically, despite a decent level of success, history tends to look back on the first incarnation of the Galacticos in a slightly negative light. A side of individuals thrust together with fistfuls of cash, that never quite lived up to its fantastic potential. The 'project' – as it was usually labelled, rather than the traditional 'team', 'club' or 'side' – tends to be compared with the far more organic, homegrown talent of Guardiola's Barcelona, which was to appear just a few years later. These comparisons will of course continue to be drawn, with Barca's classes of 2008–11 more often than not likely to be considered the more superior team in the years to come. To a certain extent, and when using my brain ahead of my heart, I would have to agree with this. But to this day, with a wry smile, I will always reserve a somewhat trivial mention for that 2003 Real Madrid side, spearheaded by the unstoppable Ronaldo, when asked to name my greatest football team of all time.

Block E5, Seat 151

Hull City 6–1 Kidderminster Harriers – 27/09/2003

AFTER a football-less summer in 2003 – a void that was filled with a long holiday in the south of Spain, where I pounced on the opportunity to expand my collection of knock-off football shirts – come the end of August, I was more than ready for the start of the new Football League season and a fresh school year.

It was to be this year that I began to enjoy school. In September, I started year 5, and while I was still struggling with both Maths and English, the two classes I loathed the most, a large group of friends and plenty of sporting opportunities had begun to make for a compromise agreement I could just about get on board with. Indeed, academically speaking, to describe myself as a 'late bloomer' would be an understatement. My dyslexia diagnosis, which would in future years provide me with the required extra time I needed to complete homework assignments and exams to the best of my ability, was still five or six years away. This made progress slow and, in hindsight, contributed to a natural decline in my general interest towards many subjects. Despite this, my confidence continued to grow. Being half decent at sport and proving fairly popular amongst my classmates provided the injection of self-belief I needed. Indeed, these final few years at primary school set the tone for the rest of my life, both academically and socially. My grades were not progressing as well as Mum and Dad had hoped, but both often reassured me that in terms of my schoolwork, the penny *would* eventually drop, and that the only effective catalyst for this was happiness and confidence. Of course, they were absolutely right. Yet, I believed that as my parents, they were presumably contractually obliged to say these things in order to make me feel better. With one a former primary school teacher and the other a former school inspector, I should have perhaps had more faith that they knew what they were talking about. After all, Dad's mission to build up my confidence, which had begun at Boothferry two years earlier, had paid off and was starting to yield results at school in the form of a big gang of friends and participation in more social activities than I care to mention. Year 5 – 2003/04. This was to be one of the most enjoyable school years I can remember, made better only by the fact it coincided perfectly with a vintage season for City.

I have always assumed it a universally acknowledged fact that a football fan's first promotion season is always their sweetest footballing memory. Yet, having spoken to many friends and colleagues who have never supported a club outside of the Premier League, I'm starting to think this fact is perhaps a tad redundant when applied to the modern fan. If this assessment is true, I feel sorry for fans of the so-called 'super clubs'. In my very best playground logic, I stand by the philosophy that you can watch your club win as many Champions League titles on the telly as you like – give me a promotion party away at Huish Park (the home of Yeovil Town, for those of you who don't know) any day of the week! For the thousands of football fans who have spent years nobly supporting lower-league sides, I know you're with me on this. For those supporters of boring, permanently successful clubs, humour me for a minute. My first promotion season was City's 2003/04 Division Three campaign, and even if my beloved Tigers were to go on to win every other honour the game has to offer in my lifetime, this season will still always remain my favourite. Nothing compares to your first promotion season.

After half a year of consolidation following the move to the new stadium and the arrival of 'Peter Taylor, the man who gave

David Beckham the England captaincy', expectations in the city were high. The Tigers had not enjoyed a promotion season since 1985, but with Taylor at the helm, a brand-new stadium and money being spent, there were no more excuses to be made. Despite my rhetoric about a fan's first promotion season being their most memorable, the first few fixtures are a bit of a blur to me. That being said, I do vividly remember the opening day of that season. It was a sunny day in West Park, which saw four of Peter Taylor's new signings – Burgess, Price, Thelwell and Allsopp – all score, as City convincingly beat Darlington 4–1. Though, I admit I remember little of the following six or seven fixtures – a rare gap in my almost encyclopaedic knowledge of Hull City matches of the new millennium. The first game I truly associate with that magical season came at the end of September, on another gloriously sunny day at the KC. High-flying City were up against a struggling Kidderminster side, knowing it was this type of game that had seen them slip up the season before. Following a nomadic few months trying to find our preferred viewing location at the unfamiliar KC Stadium, this was the season that saw Dad, Steph and I settle in the East Stand – our home away from home for the next 13 years. Despite Dad assuring me we sat in our usual seats in the East Stand for every home game prior to this one that season, for some reason my mind always tricks me into believing this game was the start of my affiliation with Block E5, Seat 151. If it's all the same to you, I think I am going to stick with my belief that this was the first home game in our beloved E5 seats.

Dressed from head to toe in my brand-new Patrick Hull City tracksuit, the day started with the three of us walking down Anlaby Road on that baking hot September afternoon looking for a new chippy. You see, since the move to the KC, we had yet to come across fish and chips worthy of becoming our traditional pre-match lunch. Really, the problem had been that our greed and impatience had got the better of us initially, and we'd been going into the first chippies we found, most of them located at the top end of Anlaby Road, closer to the now-closed Boothferry than to the new KC. That afternoon we decided to look for sustenance far closer to the new ground. After all, we thought, if we couldn't find a chippy, the backstop plan of a meat pie inside the ground was not a terrible alternative. Parking up and walking down to the KC earlier than usual, we kept our eyes peeled. It was just as we were about to cross the road, all resigned to a meat pie lunch, that we came across just what we were looking for.

'Bloody hell, why didn't I think of this place?' Dad said, as we joined a queue of around 15 or so City fans, outside the door of Viking Fisheries. Just as much as I associate this match with the start of my favourite City season and our long-standing season ticket seats, it was on this day that our pre-match Viking ritual began. Exactly as how walking over three drains on the way to the ground, or not wearing a City shirt that the Tigers had beaten that day's opposition wearing during a previous season, had become my own personal Saturday afternoon superstitions, getting three 'matchday specials and an extra pattie' from what I still regard as the best chippy in Hull, became a pre-match essential, somehow pivotal in deciding the fate of City that day. Quite aside from the superstitious element attached to our biweekly visits to Viking, the quality of food is certainly also worth a mention. Friends, colleagues and even my girlfriend often think I am exaggerating when I moan about the quality of fish and chips from anywhere other than my home town of Hull, or Dad's native Scarborough. Yet, if you hail from a coastal city or town in the north of England, I know you'll agree with me. A sign outside Viking reads 'Simply the Best!', and I can't disagree. As my continued boycott of home games continues – a very sore point that I will come on to – I miss these little details of matchdays, and everything else that comes with being a football supporter, just as much as the games themselves.

As we walked through West Park, eating our fish and chips out of newspaper with wooden forks, the familiar pang of excitement that only attending live football matches brings hit me. Walking towards the grand main entrance of the KC's glistening West Stand, I felt the same tingle run down the length of my spine that I had first experienced outside Boothferry two years previously.

After buying the obligatory matchday programme, which I vividly remember was adorned with an action shot of Tigers' centre-back Damien Delaney, we made our way around the stadium towards the East Stand turnstiles. Unlike the digital season 'cards' used today, at this point City were still using a system which relied on books of numbered tickets for their season pass holders. At each home match a random number between one and 25 was selected and this would be the ticket you ripped out of your season pass to gain entry at the turnstile. Each week Dad and I would guess that day's number as we walked around to our turnstile. It was only years later I realised Dad's scarily accurate predicting skills were down to skulduggery – he would check the number posted to the side of the West Stand turnstiles while I went to buy my programme. Classic 'dad behaviour'. Upon going through the turnstiles, and up the long flight of stairs to the concourse, Steph and I, as always, went to the kiosk to buy a couple of bottles of Coke to share during the game. As was tradition, we would then go and meet Dad at the in-stadium bookie's booth, where he would give us a fiver each to make our own predictions for the game. If any of our three bets came in, we would always split the winnings. Of course, none of us managed to predict the outcome of this match, but after the 90 minutes we didn't care.

The match was an absolute cracker. As an avid week in, week out supporter of an average Football League club in this country, there will always be results and games that are forever etched into your memory as matches where your little club battered the opposition. Granted, as a Hull City fan, these are few and far between – Tranmere 04/05, Southampton 07/08, Fulham 13/14, Charlton 15/16 – yet on this sunny afternoon, nearly two years to the day after my first City game at Boothferry, Peter Taylor's men produced a performance and result I will never forget. City battered the Worcestershire side 6-1, with goals from Ben Burgess, Danny Allsopp, Andy Dawson, debutant Ryan France and Stuart Green. But it wasn't just the scoreline itself that impressed, it was the nature of the goals. A 30-yard screamer from left-back Dawson, an acrobatic overhead kick from big Ben

Burgess and a sublime free kick from Green. Forgetting about the profound weaknesses of City's opposition that day, up until this point this was the closest nine-year-old me had seen a City side make football look like an art in a way similar to that Real Madrid side just months earlier. In my young eyes, regardless of the opposition, Third Division Hull City were not capable of dominating performances and spectacular goals like this. I was speechless, and needless to say left the KC that evening in jubilant mood.

At school on the following Monday my best friend Tom, a season ticket holder at Manchester United, was raving about his side's battering of Leicester City. United had won 4–1 at the Walkers Stadium to remain at the top end of the Premiership that weekend. I remember, to the sound of his laughter, promising that Hull City would be in the Premiership in three years – a quite ridiculous statement. Incredibly, two of the goalscorers from City's 6–1 demolition of Kidderminster would indeed play in the Premier League for Hull City – Andy Dawson and Ryan France – with two more squad members from the 03/04 season – Ian Ashbee and Boaz Myhill – also destined to play in all four professional divisions for the Tigers. As it turned out, City would be plying their trade in the top flight against the likes of Manchester United just five years later – I wasn't too far out! It was to be perhaps the five greatest years to be a Hull City fan, and I am thrilled I spent them all with Viking fish and chips in my hands, sitting in Block E5, Seat 151, alongside my dad and sister. Marvellous.

'E I E I E I O! Up The Football League We Go!'

Yeovil Town 1–2 Hull City – 01/05/2004

Hull City 3–0 Bristol Rovers – 08/05/2004

I WILL never understand how City managed only a second-place finish that season. Despite being head and shoulders above every other side in Division Three that year, a string of poor results in the February would ultimately cost us the title. For all of Peter Taylor's qualities, and there were many, this lack of a ruthless streak was a rare blot in his otherwise pristine Hull City copybook. Indeed, history would repeat itself 12 months later when an equally dominant City side would again finish runners-up in a division we ought to have won.

Nevertheless, after 19 years without a promotion, City fans could not be too picky. Regardless of City's mid-season stutter, the campaign was fantastic from a fan's point of view. It's true, I could write a book completely dedicated to this fantastic season, and perhaps one day I will.

Aside from the Kidderminster demolition, there are just so many wonderful memories from this season – beating top of the league Swansea 1–0 at home at a sold-out KC, battering Northampton 5–1 away, and, of course, Jason Price putting three past the eventual title winners Doncaster during a 3–1 rout in front of a crowd of 23,000 at home. These games aside, it was to be the final two games of the season that would most resonate with me. They were not only good games of football, but they represent my first promotion parties as a City fan. These are the memories true lovers of football live for.

The Tigers were to play Yeovil Town away, before the visit of Bristol Rovers to the KC Stadium on the final day. As it turned out, despite both games having very similar outcomes, my two matchday experiences could not have been any more different. Every City fan knew that a victory down in Somerset would seal a long-awaited promotion, and as such tickets for the away end at Huish Park, as well as for *Tiger Travel* – the club-organised away day coach service – were at a premium. Steph and I begged and pleaded with Dad to let us go, but, for the first, and I believe last, time, he refused the away trip on the grounds that the journey was just too long. Annoyingly, on a side note, this refusal also rankles as Huish Park remains one of the few Football League grounds I am yet to visit.

Our alternative was to watch the game on a giant TV screen inside the KC Stadium's accompanying indoor sports facility, the Vulcan Arena. While I am reliably informed that away day 'beam backs' are still enjoyed by fans of a few clubs, something about the phenomenon screams early-noughties football to me. Glorious stuff.

So, there we were – 2.55pm on 1 May 2004 – sat in an indoor sports arena with thousands of other City fans that hadn't travelled, waiting for the stream to begin. I felt awful, and this wasn't just the usual nauseous feeling I often felt before big games. No, I felt guilty.

This was by some distance the most important match City had played since I had started following my home town club, and I was stuck in a sports hall watching it on a big screen, unable to do my bit from the terraces. Perhaps noticing I was not my usual excitable self, just as the match kicked off Dad tapped me on the shoulder to say, 'Here we go, pal, this is it!', and within a matter of seconds that horrible guilty feeling that had followed me all morning drained away and was replaced with white-hot excitement. This was indeed the moment City fans had waited for all season, and I was determined to enjoy it.

Clad in that season's spectacular all-black Patrick away strip – a shirt I continue to don regularly to this day and one that is easily in my top five Hull City strips – Taylor's men got off to a strong start and, to the delight of the few thousand travelling City fans as well as everyone back home inside the Vulcan Arena, went 1–0 up after just 11 minutes. One of City's great heroes from that season, and future Australian international, Danny Allsopp, was bundled over in the box and Stuart Green calmly dispatched the resulting penalty. 1–0 – Division 2 here we come.

Of course, City do not, and cannot, do anything the easy way, and after a scrappy hour or so Yeovil equalised on 64 minutes. But something about this day felt special. Not even 'typical City' – a quite amazingly predictable affliction I would come to know well over the following decade – could ruin this day. Even at 1–1 with promotion potentially delayed for another week, the City faithful, both inside Huish Park and back home in Hull, sang, 'We are going up, say we are going up!' non-stop. It was enough to send shivers down my spine as I stood helplessly willing the Tigers on. With less than 15 minutes to go, my prayers were answered.

City fans everywhere, take a moment to picture the scene with me. The ball falls to Ian Ashbee – the first and to date only player to captain one club through all four professional divisions from the bottom up – at the edge of the box. The crowd at both viewing locations falls silent. Everyone looks on as the no-nonsense, hard-tackling midfielder, not at all known for his goalscoring abilities, looks up and (as time slows down in clichéd fashion) hits a speculative side-footed shot. The Tiger Nation holds its collective breath as the ball curls beautifully into the top right-hand corner. We wait for the net to ripple for confirmation, and then … ecstasy.

As one of the most iconic Hull City goals ever hit the back of the net, Dad, Steph, me and a random man who happened to be stood next to us at that exact moment, found ourselves in a tight huddle, bouncing up and down in the pandemonium that followed. Beer flew over us from all angles and the chants of 'We are going up!' reached deafening new levels. During the two or three minutes that followed I completely forgot I wasn't actually at the game.

Fifteen minutes later, the final whistle sounded and a second wave of pandemonium ensued. It was a surreal feeling – a promotion party, albeit one hundreds of miles away from the action. Of course, if I had the chance now to go back in time and travel to Huish Park that day, I would. But the Vulcan Arena, alongside thousands of fellow fans, was not a bad second choice. While grown men, some of whom had also never seen the Tigers promoted in their lifetime, held back the tears, the party continued. The bar stayed open for an hour or so, and we stayed in the hall, praising the individual merits of each squad member of Hull City's class of 2004, shaking hands with supporters we had never met before, and singing our hearts out for the lads.

After such an exciting day, Monday signalled the start of a long week at school. At this point there were still very few City fans my age I could discuss the game with and share my excitement. This would, of course, change as City's march up the Football League continued. I remember meeting my mate and fellow City supporter, Ben, at breaktime on the Monday morning. Ben was in a different class and, despite playing Sunday league football for the same side, we didn't see a massive amount of each other at school. We exchanged our usual pleasantries, both attempting to hide our glee. It was almost as though if one of us dared to mention the weekend's events, they might prove not to have happened. After a few minutes of skirting around the issue, it was clear both of us were either too excited or too exhausted to speak. We just smiled at each other, and Ben whispered, 'See you on Saturday; the East Stand's going to be buzzing!' before sloping off.

He wasn't wrong.

I must say, although being a supporter of a Premier League club is a fantastic feeling – especially during your club's maiden season in the top flight – one thing I did miss when City reached what Steve Bruce would describe as 'the big league' was the opportunity to sing one of my favourite terrace regulars:

'E I E I E I O!
Up the Football League we go!
When we win promotion,
This is what we'll sing,
We all love you,
We all love you,
Taylor is our king!'

This chant, along with 'We are going up', epitomises the lower leagues and provided the perfect soundtrack for City's final game of the 2003/04 season. The Tigers were facing an average Bristol Rovers side that had nothing to play for, in front of a packed house at the KC Stadium. From the minute we got out of the car and headed to Viking for our usual pre-match meal, the party atmosphere was palpable. I had missed out on witnessing City's promotion-winning game at Huish Park seven days earlier and I was determined to make the most of this homecoming.

Football writers often use the term 'exhibition match' in a derogatory manner, usually when describing a competitive game that is so lacklustre it resembles a preseason friendly. Thinking back to the Bristol Rovers match, and when watching the old footage on my scratched 03/04 season review DVD, I'd describe this game as an exhibition, yet for a different reason. It's true that the Bristol players were 'already on the beach', to use another cringeworthy football cliché, and that the first half was somewhat lacking. Yet, in a real 'game of two halves' (sorry), City were magnificent in the second period. Indeed, if the opening 45 minutes could have been confused for a friendly, the second more closely resembled an exhibition match in the sense of the Harlem Globetrotters running rings around the hapless and dazed Washington Generals, to the absolute delight of the jubilant crowd. Peter Taylor's promoted men tore their opponents apart and scored three goals of genuine quality to finish the season off in style.

Price opened the scoring with a bullet header, before Damien Delaney ran the length of the pitch, exchanged a neat one-two with Jamie Forrester, and curled the ball into the top corner to double the lead. For those of you who know Delaney only as the solid and reliable centre-half of his Crystal Palace days, I urge you to watch a few of his goals for City on YouTube. 'Damo', as he was affectionately known at City, was a hugely underrated player in my eyes, and was undeniably underused by his native Republic of Ireland. Anyway, I digress. The rout was then completed by Stuart Elliott, who hammered the ball home from 30 yards to make it 3–0 to the Tigers. I wish I could describe the quality of this goal in more detail, but unfortunately, I missed it as I was joining in with a conga line that had formed at the front of the East Stand. No regrets.

To say I went home happy that evening would be an understatement. I went to bed that night in euphoric mood, my head filled with fresh images of the post-match celebrations – medals being presented, countless laps of honour, champagne being sprayed and endless renditions of Elvis Presley's 'Can't Help Falling In Love' – City's unofficial fan anthem.

These two games will forever stay with me as screenshots in time. They will remain a few of my happiest childhood memories, topped only by one or two City-related moments that were just down the line. As time has passed and I have entered adulthood, the ever-creeping frustration, apathy and even anger that I now find synonymous with supporting Hull City Association Football Club, and football more generally for that matter, have at times endeavoured to ruin my passion, and *have* succeeded in changing the face of my relationship with it significantly. When these emotions have threatened to spill over into resentment for the game, I have sat myself down and remembered the good times. Memories like these remind me that the pain, anger, frustration and anguish that come with being a modern football supporter is bearable. It is bearable because football has provided me with some of my fondest memories, and no one can take these away from me. It is for this reason I almost feel indebted to football and hope and pray that this perverted sort of loyalty I now practise will eventually pay dividends and the good times will one day return and new memories like these will be created.

As I keep telling myself, it is this hope that makes it all worth it. Of course, I'm sure an alcoholic or drug addict also justifies their next drink or hit using a similarly problematic belief system, but the prospect of fresh moments like these renders football a risk worth taking.

En-gerrrr-land, Wayne Rooney and the Sol Campbell conspiracy

Portugal 2–2 England AET (6–5 penalty shoot-out) – 24/06/2004

UNTIL 2008, and in particular England's failure to qualify for the European Championships that year, all football fans of my age still believed England's 'golden generation' would break their (then) 40-year duck and win an international tournament. I had been badly let down at World Cup 2002 – I'm still looking at you, David Seaman – but I was convinced 2004 was to be our year.

When you think back to the never-ending summers of your childhood, there are always a few that stand out in your mind's eye. The summer of 2004 was one of these summers for me. I was finishing off a good year at school with half-decent exam results, promoted Hull City were preparing for life in the newly rebranded League One, and an England squad, refreshed with the notable additions of John Terry, Frank Lampard and wonderkid Wayne Rooney, were heading out to Portugal for Euro 2004. I was about as content as a ten-year-old lad could be. Naturally, it all ended in tears.

There was something special about mid-noughties international football. If the 1990s represented a renaissance in the international game, particularly from a European and

British perspective, the noughties saw the true beginning of the commercialisation of football on the world stage. Generally, as this book will later demonstrate, I dislike and actively resist this bastardisation of a once simple, working-class sport. However, I do understand the relentless march of progress cannot be halted, and now I look back at the sheer audacity and outrageousness of the start of this period with nothing but fondness. Like parents trying desperately to justify their dreadful 1970s fashion decisions when showing old photographs to their children, I am sure one day I will champion Nike Total 90 kits, the Adidas Roteiro ball and the footballing superpower that is Greece, at all costs. Probably anyway.

England made easy work of qualifying for Euro 2004, with Turkey providing their only real challenge throughout the qualifying process. Nevertheless, Sven's men were rewarded with a difficult group stage draw for the tournament itself. Underdogs Switzerland, a potential banana skin in the shape of Croatia and reigning European champions, France, who were desperate to impress after an embarrassing World Cup display two years earlier, awaited. Despite the national concern, I remained unshaken in my belief that England would do the business and breeze through the group. Of course, as has now become an almost biennial constant in my life – one that I could accurately use to measure the unrelenting passing of time – my pre-tournament optimism was predictably and severely damaged just 93 minutes into England's campaign. France 2–1 England.

Unusually, the Three Lions dominated the first half of their opening fixture, going a goal up early on thanks to a Lampard header, which gave fans an ultimately useless sense of false hope. Not to fear, though, Zinedine Zidane was to see to that. After Beckham missed a second-half penalty that would have killed the game off at 2–0, Zizou's pinpoint free kick in the 90th minute, followed by his 93rd-minute penalty, lost England the game and, momentarily at least, broke my ten-year-old heart. Normal service has been resumed. Yet, unlike future early-tournament embarrassments, England could, and very much *did*, take positives out of this game. After the initial disappointment had passed, and the game began to be properly dissected by the pundits, I remember feeling a tad better. After all, for all intents and purposes, it appeared England had found the final missing piece destined to complete the nation's golden generation. We had indeed managed to somehow snatch defeat from the jaws of victory once again, but in the process 18-year-old Wayne Rooney announced himself on the world stage.

Although I had seen him play in an England shirt on a few occasions, not to mention in the Premier League for Everton, this was the first instance I remember sitting up and noticing Rooney. He was so exciting that evening. In the same way that Brazil's Ronaldo had me on the edge of my seat every time I saw him collect the ball and drive forward, the young Scouser, only eight years my senior, fascinated me. He played with no fear, even to the point of which he was outclassing true legends of the game amongst the French ranks. At half-time, I recall the pundits waxing lyrical about this individual performance, and by the end of the match they were describing Rooney's performance as 'world class' – a categorisation usually reserved for players well into their twenties, with trophies galore already in their cabinet. I vividly remember a typically overexcited John Motson laughing with glee as the teenager went past French legend Lilian Thuram for what felt like the twentieth time. 'HA HA HA, fantastic stuff!' And this was just the start of Rooney's Portuguese adventure.

Alas, Rooney's marvellous display could not prevent a defeat for England that their performance didn't deserve. Regardless, the pressure was now on. Dad continued to assure me that England's Euro journey would end in disappointment and warned me not to get my hopes up, despite being visibly excited himself during each of England's four matchdays. As I had two years earlier, I ignored my old man, and put the France defeat down to bad luck. Fortunately, my optimism was handsomely rewarded as during the week that followed, England created two of their better tournament performances in recent memory, as the Sven era peaked. The Swiss were up first, and were dispatched with ease. Wayne Rooney scored twice to become the youngest ever scorer in European Championship history as England won 3–0. That was more like it! Croatia were next, and going into the final round of fixtures in Group B any two of the four sides could still qualify – England needed a win.

Naturally, we did it the hard way. Dressed in their glorious red *Umbro* away shirt, complete with a cross of St George on either shoulder, England went 1–0 down after just five minutes. A long first half followed before a Paul Scholes equaliser calmed the nerves. Two more strikes from the irrepressible Rooney and a Lampard solo effort atoned for a number of trademark David James blunders, as the match finished 4–2. Sven's men were now into the quarter-finals and my belief that we were going the whole way was well and truly restored. Finishing one point behind the French saw England draw the winners of Group A – tournament hosts Portugal. The nation held its collective breath, knowing it was to be a tough match.

As far as I recall, there were only one or two days separating the Croatia and Portugal games. This is an aspect of tournament football I adore. Not only is there football to watch nigh on every day for a month, but also, unlike domestic football, you don't have the agonising week-long wait before your side's next fixture. I spent the days dossing around school in that wonderful post-exam, pre-summer holiday period that only comes around once a year, and religiously watching the rebooted *Fantasy Football League* show late on ITV, which broadcast most nights throughout the tournament. Frank Skinner and David Baddiel's antics the previous night soon became just as much a talking point at school the next day as the matches themselves, making it a must-watch. Luckily, for my tenth birthday I had been given a TV/VHS combo television, meaning I could stay up late and watch every night from the comfort of my bedroom.

Mercifully, unlike 2002, my experience watching England's second quarter-final in as many years was not to be shaped by time difference. The match was to be held at the Estádio da Luz (or the Stadium of Light, to me and you), the home of Benfica.

With a 7.45pm kick-off, I could this time watch the match in my preferred viewing environment of the lounge, sitting on the settee with Dad.

It's worth noting at this point that I have watched this match back a few times in the 15 years that have passed since the actual event, and every time I am struck with the same sense of awe when I read the two starting line-ups. Indeed, while it's true that we overrate memories from our formative years – my dad, for example, will always argue that English football in the 60s and 70s represented a golden age that will never be outshone, despite the fact that after their World Cup victory in '66, the Three Lions failed to qualify for two World Cups thanks to bang average teams and poor management the following decade – I think it's fair to say the talent on display that night vindicates, that on this one occasion, reality truly does match up with my memory of a quality game of football. Luis Figo, Maniche, Nuno Gomes, Deco and a young Cristiano Ronaldo on one side. Beckham, Gerrard, Scholes, Owen and Rooney on the other. As Motty would say, 'This is almost fantasy football!'

Of course, it's easy to point out in hindsight, but if knockout games involving England all follow a similar template, which they invariably do, this match is the master example.

- An early goal to get fans' hopes up – check.
- An early injury to a key player – check.
- A late opposition equaliser – check.
- A last-minute 'winner' (usually from Sol Campbell) controversially disallowed – check.
- A drama-filled two periods of extra time – check.
- A penalty shoot-out defeat – check.

Nevertheless, along with the Brazil game two years earlier, I do still have positive memories of watching this match. This cannot be said for the majority of England's tournament defeats since.

Sat in the lounge with an Indian takeaway Dad had insisted on, the start of the match was too good to be true. After just three minutes Michael Owen finally arrived at Euro 2004, running on to a long punt out of defence and flicking the ball masterfully past future panto villain Ricardo in the Portuguese net. As I had done in the same situation two years earlier, I began to mentally write off the remainder of the match and started to daydream about the semi-finals, a potential final, and then, naturally, David Beckham lifting the famous Henri Delaunay Trophy. And as had happened two years earlier, I was brought crashing back down to reality 25 minutes later when England's young player of the tournament, Wayne Rooney, limped off with a broken bone in his foot. Despite still being one goal to the good, for the first time in my young supporting life, my usual eternal optimism was at this point replaced with one of anxiety and pessimism – a far more common combination of emotions amongst England fans. I was right to be nervous. Utilising playmakers Deco and Figo brilliantly, much of the next hour was dominated by the hosts. 'It's coming' Dad repeated throughout the second half. 'Just you wait, we're pushing our luck now. It's coming.' He was right.

With just seven minutes of normal time remaining, substitute Postiga headed home the equaliser. I wasn't blind and I knew he was right, but Dad's 'I told you so' attitude was starting to grate. 'It's still 1–1!' I yelled in dramatic fashion, 'There's still time!'

There was indeed still time, but not for the England winner I craved. No, instead England fans were treated to yet another example of one of the greatest football phenomena of the time: the Sol Campbell conspiracy. England launched men forward, and as the clock ran over 90 minutes, a Beckham free kick was headed on to the bar by Owen, before Sol Campbell bundled in the rebound. Before I could even get to my feet, however, referee Urs Meier – both a name and face I will never forget – disallowed the would-be winner for a perceived John Terry foul on Ricardo in the build-up. With echoes of his 'goal that never was' during England's defeat to Argentina at the 1998 World Cup, you could forgive Campbell – as well as the entire English nation, if you ask me – for suspecting something underhand was going on. For a million legal reasons, I am not saying I myself buy into this conspiracy, although, can you name another international who has had *two* vitally important goals disallowed at major finals in similar circumstances?

I digress – into extra time we went and a frantic 30 minutes followed. Rui Costa's sensational strike looked to have won the game early into the second period, before a late Lampard equaliser took the game to penalties.

In a perverse way, I was glad to see the match go to penalties. With Italia 90 happening before I was born, and Euro 96 and France 98 being a little before I can remember, this was the first international shoot-out I had experienced in which I had a dog in the fight. Ten minutes later I cursed how stupid I had been and decided I never wanted to go through an England penalty shoot-out again.

Beckham and Rui Costa both smashed their penalties way over the bar, each turning to glare at a sand-filled penalty spot in disbelief, while their four team-mates all converted, taking the shoot-out into sudden death. Two spot kicks later, Darius Vassell entered the history books, next to the likes of Stuart Pearce, Gareth Southgate and David Batty, as yet another England player to have missed a decisive penalty. It was to be Ricardo, who by this time had annoyingly decided to remove his gloves in a late fit of superstition, that saved Vassell's tame effort, putting England on the edge of crashing out at the quarter-final stage of a tournament once again. Even more infuriatingly, it was the goalkeeper who stepped up to take Portugal's match-winning penalty, which he of course buried with aplomb. And with that England were out. It was all over for another two years.

I was surprisingly restrained after the match. Unlike 2002, the same level of emotion and disappointment didn't hit me this time around. Always with a wry smile on his face, Dad had warned me about how England will always let you down and not to get my hopes up, and this was the moment I began to understand. You see, while disappointment in club football is commonplace, the two-year gap between major international tournaments is enough for old wounds to heal and false hope to be built, making the international game a dangerous animal for a football addict.

After all, as my ten-year-old self often thought, why should we put ourselves through this misery and disappointment again and again, with little prospect of an emotional payout. England couldn't provide the joy of a promotion, the excitement of a new signing or the underdog anticipation of a big cup draw against a much bigger side, so why become as emotionally involved? It doesn't make any sense.

Of course, come World Cup 2006 in Germany I was back to a state of believing that England would go all the way, yet never again have I let England's performances affect me in such a way as 2002 and 2004. That's not to say I don't still look forward to international football, though. Contrary to popular opinion nowadays, I personally enjoy the semi-regular international breaks in the routine domestic season, as well as major tournaments every other year. Following a wonderful England showing at the 2018 World Cup in Russia, this is an aspect of football I have learnt to love more and more in recent years. Besides, remaining *slightly* less attached to one particular side – compared to my club-supporting responsibilities at least – does have its benefits. In particular, it enables one to appreciate the talent and ability this unique embodiment of the game has to offer, rather than limiting oneself to the single blinkered view of an underwhelming team and ignoring the rest of the spectacle. International football is a wonderful thing; why should we let a usually shambolic England side ruin it for us?

Nonetheless, for better or for worse, international football and England will *always* be secondary concerns in my own personal footballing pecking order. While for some fans England will always come first, they will never be *my* team in the same way Hull City are. In the end, it just took another smug look from my dad and a wayward Darius Vassell penalty for me to come to this realisation. I wouldn't be burnt by England again.

Away days: Pies, bets and Michael Keane

Barnsley 1–2 Hull City – 28/08/2004

AFTER recovering from my England woes, my full attention returned to City. A two-week holiday in the Costa del Sol with my family was spent dashing to the English-run newsagents in the small village of Mijas every day to buy a copy of the *Daily Mirror*. I needed to ensure I kept on top of all the football news I was missing back home, and thanks to a plethora of expats in Andalusia, English red tops were easy to come by. However, perhaps unsurprisingly, the national was pretty lacking in League One transfer news, limiting my City-related news intake to five-minute *Hull Daily Mail* round-ups over the phone with my grandma during this two-week period. What I would have done for a smartphone in the summer of 2004.

Nevertheless, one transfer story that did make the national headlines that summer was City's signing of former England international and native Hullesian, Nick Barmby. Signing on a free transfer from Leeds United and coming just two and a half years after his final England cap, this did indeed appear some coup. With the gift of hindsight, it goes without saying that Barmby would prove to be one of City's most successful signings of the period, and alongside the likes of Ashbee, Dawson and Myhill, is a club legend. Yet interestingly, at the time, the signing did have its critics. At just 30 years old, many fans questioned the stereotyped 'injury-ridden' Barmby and his motives for leaving the Premier League and seeing his wages drop by more than £20,000 per week, in favour of a one-year deal at a newly promoted third-tier side. Of course, at the age of ten, I was yet to be affected by the crippling cynicism that comes hand in hand with being a long-term football addict. As such, I was too enamoured with the signing to take any notice of the sceptics. After all, not only had I followed Barmby's career religiously from watching his part in England's famous win in Munich three years earlier, but after years of supporting City in the lower echelons of the Football League, I had dreamt of seeing an England international play in black and amber. It was a huge deal to me, and one quote the media kept using at the time has stuck with me ever since. Barmby was a player that Pelé – debatably *the* greatest footballer of all time – once described as 'up there with Zinedine Zidane, Paolo Maldini and Ronaldo'. Admittedly, down the years, Pelé's infamous abilities as a pundit have tended to illustrate a shockingly poor level of judgement for someone so talented. However, even having a player on Hull City's books that the great Pelé could even reference seemed remarkable to me. It still does now, when I think about.

Aside from Barmby mania, Peter Taylor had strengthened his squad well during that summer, losing no key players from his promotion-winning squad, and signing astutely. The likes of Aaron Wilbraham, Leon Cort, Michael Keane (no, not that one), Delroy Facey, Roland Edge and Matt Duke were all brought in to bolster the squad, and with few exceptions, all went on to play at a higher level of the game, either with or without City. Yet it was the Barmby signing that really excited me. As the midfielder was paraded in front of the press in a new Hull City shirt that appeared about four sizes too large for him, I remember willing time to speed up. The middle of August and the start of the new season could not come soon enough.

Finally, after what felt like an eternity, the season kicked off on 7 August with an impressive 1–0 victory at the KC against a decent Bournemouth side. It was as though the four-month break since City's last competitive fixture had never happened, as normal service was resumed both on and off the pitch. Steph, Dad and I continued with our biweekly fish and chip ritual and we were rewarded with a strong start to the season. City won three and lost just one of their opening four League One fixtures meaning both the mood and the expectations of the City faithful were high going into the first of many local derby games that season – Barnsley away.

At this point I should note that Steph and I begged and pleaded throughout the preseason of 2004, and only after months of this did Dad agree. At first it was only to be local away games we would travel to. However, by the end of another magical season in City's history, the three of us would be following the Tigers up and down the entire length and breadth of the country, eagerly ticking off the away grounds we had visited like twitchers fanatically listing the rare birds they had spotted. As with every aspect of this story, and to my mother's eternal annoyance, it was my initially sceptical father who wound up being the chief instigator of nearly every future away trip, having recaught the away day bug during two unforgettable local derbies at the back end of 2004. I have him to thank for hours sat in the back of his car on what felt like every motorway in England, as well as thousands of pounds spent on away tickets, and some of my best childhood memories. Sorry Mum, but I wouldn't have had it any other way.

Indeed, for a football addict, nothing is better than a good away day. Don't get me wrong, I loved my fortnightly visits to Boothferry and later the KC, and the entire matchday routine that came with it. Yet there is something inherently special about visiting unfamiliar grounds, in alien parts of the country, with the lone intention of supporting your team in enemy territory. There is also something intrinsically British about the great Saturday afternoon away trip. While it's of course true that travelling support is a footballing phenomenon that occurs all over the globe – though perhaps unfairly and stereotypically portrayed in the UK media through the visible ultras movement in countries throughout Europe and South America – the mass appeal of *ordinary* football supporters travelling to cheer on their local teams, significantly incorporating *all* levels of a vast footballing pyramid, is unique to British football. After three years of having my support of Hull City limited exclusively to home games, I got my first taste of away day football in late August 2004 at Oakwell.

Thanks to a combination of its relatively close proximity to Hull and the fact that we have often shared the same division over the past 15 years or so, I have visited Barnsley's Oakwell on multiple occasions. For one reason or another – horrific City performances, displays of shithousery from both sets of supporters in Barnsley town centre, and foul weather, to name but a few – I have never really enjoyed our visits to the South Yorkshire club, with the notable exceptions being this first visit to Oakwell in 2004, and an Ashbee and Windass-inspired classic in 2008.

Opting to find our own way down the M62 and M1, rather than taking advantage of *Tiger Travel*, the three of us got to Barnsley early and parked up right next to the travelling coaches. At the time, away supporters were permitted to park in a field next to the traditional opened-cornered stadium – an option we took advantage of, but one we would come to regret after the match. Almost instantly, my initial excitement of travelling to my first away game doubled as I climbed out of the car and looked up at Oakwell's ageing stands. Nearly two years after leaving Boothferry for the final time, the sight of the corrugated iron roofs, floodlight pylons and an aesthetic of general shabbiness once again evoked a tingle running down the length of my spine. Grounds like this have the power to remind disenchanted football fans why they fell in love with the game. But more of that later.

The match itself was in no way a classic, especially in the wider context of a fantastic season for City. I wager most City fans of my age will scarcely remember any details other than perhaps the scoreline. Yet there are three or four aspects of this game that have ensured that my first away day has remained one of my favourite matches. Firstly, and perhaps most obviously, is the result and how it came to be. City won the game 2–1, coming from 1–0 down to win in the last few minutes. Adorned in our classy sky blue centenary away strip, Michael Keane – an underrated player, yet one so left-footed I remember him falling over on multiple occasions when attempting a right-footed shot – sliced through the Barnsley backline and curled the ball into the top corner, directly in front of the away support. A wonderful goal. But incredibly, the goal itself was topped by my other overwhelming memories of this day. You see, exactly as the Irishman hit the winning shot, and just before I saw the ball ripple the back of Barnsley's net, my attention was averted by the man stood next to me. Dressed in nothing but 1990s City shorts and a battered pair of Adidas Gazelles, the middle-aged man had decided to throw his chicken balti pie – which he had purchased at half-time and not touched for the past 40 minutes – directly into the air at the precise moment the ball left Keane's boot. As the away end erupted, my eyes were drawn not to the hero of the hour Keane, as he was mobbed by a flurry of blue shirts at the advertising hoardings, but to the exploding pasty that splattered on the pitch just metres away from the action. Dad and I have often seen 'Pieman', as we have affectionately nicknamed him, at various away games in the 15 years since then, and with a mischievous smile on his face, he always gives us a nod as our paths cross. One of those silly moments regular football goers can't help but collect over years spent in the terraces, but these are the ones I have come to find often remain some of the most memorable.

But the day was to get better still. As the final whistle went, and we stood to cheer the victorious Tigers off the pitch, Dad tapped me on the shoulder and waved a small slip of paper in my face. With all the excitement and goal-induced pie launching, it had slipped my mind that Dad had placed three £5 bets before the game – one for each of us. I had plumped for Stuart Elliott to score the first goal of the game, which had gone out of the window after just 12 minutes as Barnsley snatched the opener, while Steph had gone for an ambitious punt on Ian Ashbee to score first. Dad, however, had bet smart and gone for a narrow 2–1 away victory at 12/1. As he collected his £60 winnings at the rudimentary in-ground bookies – a shed built just outside

Oakwell's rusty away stand concourse – he handed Steph and I a crisp £20 note each. You can just imagine the look on our faces. This was to become another City tradition the three of us share, and to this day when bets are placed at City matches, we split any winnings three ways.

What felt like the perfect Saturday afternoon ended in fittingly comic style as we returned to the car. As it turned out our seemingly impeccable car parking spot, directly next to Oakwell, was notoriously difficult to exit on a matchday, and this was only exacerbated by the swelled crowd brought on by a local derby at the end of August. Who knew? Subsequently, we sat stationary for an hour and a half, next to the four or so *Tiger Travel* coaches, talking about the game and what Steph and I were going to do with our winnings. Luckily, as we were still in Yorkshire, the car radio was still picking up BBC Radio Humberside on FM. The 606-style football phone-in, and regular updates and post-match interviews from inside Oakwell with long-standing Hull City commentator David Burns, alongside whichever former City pro was co-commentating that day (possibly Peter Swan), kept us entertained as the traffic thinned painfully slowly. Broadcasting from a gantry inside the old ground and presumably receiving hundreds of texts from stranded Tigers fans, Burnsy uttered the immortal line 'Come on City fans, give your car horn a honk if you're stuck in the car park after seeing your side win 2–1 today!' Cue 40 minutes of non-stop, inescapable car horns. The hordes of travelling City fans – the like of which hasn't been seen in recent years following the Allam-induced decline – obliged nobly, to the delight of Burnsy. Again, just one of those silly little details, that many City fans there that day will have no doubt forgotten, that has always stayed with me.

I must have followed City all over the country north of 150 times since that match, and with only one or two glaring exceptions have I had a more enjoyable away day. These are the moments we football addicts live for. These are the moments we miss as the disillusion with the modern game inevitably begins to kick in. These are the days I pray will come again.

Hullsborough

Sheffield Wednesday 2–4 Hull City – 08/12/2004

IF there is one experience I favour over an away day following City, it's an away day following City on a midweek evening under the floodlights. The cliché nowadays is 'but can [insert team] do it on a cold, rainy night in Stoke', yet, for my 11-year-old self, separating the true football supporters from the pretenders at school, the question was 'but do you follow City on a cold, rainy Tuesday night in Chesterfield?' Granted, it's not quite as catchy, but it ensured I was one of the three or four football-supporting elites during my final year of primary school.

My first midweek away day came in the December of 2004 and turned out to be City's most iconic win of the season – a 4–2 victory at Sheffield Wednesday. If the idyllic account of my first away day at Barnsley sounds like it could have come straight from the football lovers' equivalent of Enid Blyton, my first visit to Hillsborough would be better represented as a Hemingway or Steinbeck novel – passionate, doused in realism and at times almost bleak, yet an absolute masterpiece all the same. Indeed, it turned out to be a phenomenal night for the vast swarm of travelling City fans, but also an experience that presented an up until this point *sheltered* young football supporter with a small glimpse into the darker side of football fandom. And I loved it.

I remember the entire day like some surreal dream. With the Christmas break still about a week away, I was at school that day. I gleefully bragged to my close circle of mates – naturally all football fans – where I was going that evening, but I knew I had to be careful. It was a Wednesday bang in the middle of our school's rugby season, meaning I was expected to attend rugby training that evening. Alongside our football commitments, my primary school were big on rugby, particularly during our final year as it looked to prepare us for an intensive seven years of extracurricular rugby in high school, now just months away. If you were selected in the 30-boy squad, you were expected to attend between two and three after-school training sessions each week. Wednesday had been selected as one of these days that week.

My dad, a talented rugby player as well as footballer during his youth, was unsurprisingly keen for me to be as involved as possible and was delighted when I was selected for the squad. Indeed, it was for this reason that it came as a bit of a surprise to me when he allowed me to skip training in favour of a City match that night. As it turned out, although I continued to take my personal sport very seriously in the years to come, this set a precedent for the next eight years. City always came first.

Whatever happens for the rest of my Hull City supporting life, whether European nights are to grace the KCOM once more or if away trips to Sutton United in the National League are more likely, I will always have my favourite away day and I don't believe this will ever change. All football addicts will have their own favourite away trip etched into their memory and will jump at the chance to reminisce given any opportunity. This is that cherished memory for me – and I wager for a huge majority of the fellow 8,000 City fans that also made the journey that night.

Having spent much of the previous decade languishing in the basement division of the Football League, high-profile local derbies had been hard to come by for City. There had been the odd Humberside derby against Scunthorpe here and there, and a few ties against Lincoln, York and Doncaster. Yet, for City fans, these were small fry. After such a long period of exile at the bottom of the pyramid, the City faithful yearned for a meaningful derby against one of the local 'big boys'. Games against the likes of Leeds United, Sheffield United, Sheffield Wednesday and even, at a stretch, Middlesbrough seemed like distant memories for most fans, and for young supporters like me felt almost unimaginable. However, following their own decade of decline, come 2004 Sheffield Wednesday had found themselves playing in the third tier of English football – a long, long way from their most recent glory days of Chris Waddle, David Hirst and Mark Bright in the mid-90s. From the moment the fixtures were announced in June, the attention of City fans everywhere turned to Sheffield Wednesday away – the first big derby City had faced in years. I was never going to be playing rugby that night.

Despite (once again) starting from a sceptical standpoint when initially propositioned with the idea of travelling to an away day on a school night, Dad eventually ignored Mum's protestations and bought tickets early. It was impossible for him to refuse in reality. After all, it was to be City's biggest game of the season so far and, regardless of the fact he will swear he only agreed to go to please us kids, it was obvious Dad wasn't going to miss this match for the world. As such, on the morning of the match I had been armed with an embarrassingly transparent 'sick note', excusing me from rugby training that evening due to a long-standing 'dentist appointment'. Skipping training without good reason often resulted in surprisingly harsh punishment for kids of our age, meaning I had to be canny. With my City shirt and scarf hidden away in my backpack, the day dragged badly. I could feel a dull ache of excitement build in the pit of my stomach as the day progressed, but it was paired with pangs of fear at the thought of admitting to my coach that I was to miss training that evening. Luckily, all went to plan. I handed over my note at lunchtime and was excused without incident. Though, my cover was almost blown hours later as I exited school at the regular time. Dad's friend Phil, who had been tasked with collecting Steph and I from school and getting us to Sheffield on time, rolled up in the school driveway with four City scarves trailing behind his car, one hanging from each window. With both the changing rooms and rugby pitches in full view, I jumped into the car before I could be spotted and away we went.

Dad had been working in Manchester, or Nottingham or somewhere that day, and had decided he would meet us at the Meadowhall shopping centre. From there the four of us would take the tram from Meadowhall to Hillsborough. What could possibly go wrong?

We left Hull early, stopping briefly at McDonald's to pick up a quick bite to eat. By 5.15pm we were racing down the M62, all four City scarves waving majestically in the wind, listing our preferred starting line-ups and giving our score predictions. Our nightmare started only as we joined the M18 and were faced with bumper to bumper traffic. Phil wasn't concerned, however. He assured us that we had left plenty of time, and once we got to Meadowhall the regular trams would get us to the ground comfortably before kick-off. In reality, thanks to a toxic combination of numerous small accidents, a congested rush hour and several thousand excited City fans all hitting the road at the same time, our expected hour and a half journey took over two hours. By the time we parked up at Meadowhall and found Dad sitting on the platform waiting for us, it was 7.20. We, along with what felt like the entire away support that evening, were pushing it. Having already bought us tickets, Dad ushered us on to the next packed tram to arrive and gave us some bad news. A Wednesday fan he had got talking to on the platform while waiting for us to arrive had informed him that the tram usually takes around 35 minutes to reach the closest stop to Hillsborough, and a short walk after that. This meant the earliest we would get to the ground was around 7.55 – ten minutes after kick-off. 'It's a shame,' Dad said, 'but there's nothing we can do about it. Hopefully we won't miss too much'. He was right – it was a shame, but the rest of the evening would more than make up for it.

Although willing it to speed up, this part of the journey was actually quite enjoyable. Packed like sardines into a tiny carriage filled with City fans, the tram was almost literally bouncing by the time we reached Sheffield city centre. After all, it was the perfect opportunity to warm up our voices using the entire repertoire of City chants. If we were to be late, the least we could do was have a little fun and get in the mood. Ten minutes later came the news we had all been waiting for. As if synchronised, what sounded like a thousand Nokia ringtones activated all at once. The news filtered down the carriage like wildfire and was received with slight excitement and relief – kick-off had been put back 15 minutes due to heavy crowd congestion in and around the ground. Though, ultimately this merely provided a short period of respite rather than a full solution.

I don't remember the short walk between getting off the tram and arriving at Hillsborough's infamous Leppings Lane End, but I'll never forget the scene that greeted us upon our arrival. It was reported that 8,000 Hull City fans travelled to Sheffield that night, almost a third of the entire attendance, and as we arrived it looked as though a good 4,000 of this number were still queuing outside the West Stand turnstiles on Leppings Lane. It was absolute pandemonium. Eight o'clock came and went and the game kicked off in front of a half-empty away end. Mounted police and dog handlers were scattered around the vicinity, while helpless-looking young stewards insisted on frisking all visiting supporters and checking each bag. As an 11-year-old lad attending his first midweek away game, and standing at just 4ft 8in, I would be lying if I said I wasn't feeling intimidated at this moment. It didn't help that just days earlier I had also come across the in-depth details of the tragic Hillsborough disaster while researching for my self-taught, part-time 'degree' in English football history, which I had enthusiastically embarked on during my spare time. I have very rarely feared for my own safety while attending a football match during the past two decades, yet there were a few occasions both before and after the game at Hillsborough that night that I'm not afraid to admit shook me.

As we joined the queue and acclimatised ourselves to the pushing, shoving and occasional surge forward you come to associate with an impatient mob, I looked up at the stand. I had seen images of the ageing turnstiles on thousands of news reports relating to the various hearings, inquiries and investigations into the horrific events of 15 April 1989 – the darkest day in English football history. The traditional stand, clad in corrugated iron with the famous name of 'Sheffield Wednesday' blazoned across it, was exactly as I expected. Yet what I didn't expect was the emotions that came with it. It's an old-fashioned 1960s terrace with plenty of character – usually my favourite variety of venue for watching football – but Hillsborough's West Stand proved the exception. While most away ends of this ilk are to be celebrated as the charming and often quirky relics of English football gone by, there is something sinister and, well, just sad about the Leppings Lane End. Even after all these years there is still a profound sense of tragedy that hangs around the stand. For this reason, despite a number of unforgettable personal memories that have been created on that terrace in recent years, it isn't an away end I enjoy returning to.

The game kicked off, but all we could do as we made our way towards the bottlenecked turnstiles was try to interpret what was happening on the pitch through the sounds and reactions of the lucky bastards that had already made it inside. I am no doubt remembering with a fair chuck of bias, yet I remember the lion's share of the phenomenal atmosphere leaking from all four corners of the ground appeared to be being generated from the away fans in that opening 15 minutes. Nevertheless, after just ten minutes, which felt like an eternity creeping forwards in the bustling queues, a roar from the far end of the stadium matched by a collective groan from the other side of the West Stand's concourse indicated the home side had scored first. Seconds later, my stomach sank as the goal was confirmed by the sickening sound of Jeff Beck's 'Hi Ho Silver Lining' booming from the stadium's old speaker system, muted just in time for the Wednesday fans to *wittily* replace the words 'Silver Lining' with 'Sheffield Wednesday'. My lifelong hatred of goal music was born.

The waiting continued as the crowds outside became more and more restless. Just as we got within touching distance of the rusting turnstiles, my heart stopped as a deafening collective shout of 'HANDBALL!' reverberated from just above us, followed seconds later by a roar from the City faithful and the thuds of fists banging against the corrugated iron stands in celebration. City had been awarded a penalty, and with it a way back into the game just five minutes after going behind. It was at this moment that the four of us, fully frisked and pockets searched, finally thrust our tickets over to be checked and pushed ourselves through the ancient turnstiles. Running up the stairs into the main concourse, I felt the stand start to shake as a sea of black and amber erupted above us. Michael Keane, the barrel-chested Irishman, had placed his penalty calmly into the top left-hand corner. 1–1 – game on.

We emerged from the concourse through the tight gangway and I got my first view of the Hillsborough pitch. Swimming through the hordes of City fans, looking for our seats, or in our case our area to stand, the chants of 'KEANO, KEANO, KEANO', and 'WHO ARE YA?' rained down towards the closest Wednesday fans. Despite missing 15 minutes and the two opening goals, we had finally made it, and I was determined to make the most of it.

The match continued at the same breakneck pace throughout the first half, with chances coming at both ends. Luckily it was City that took the advantage, ensuring we hadn't gone through our nightmare journey in vain. A rapid counter-attack with 21 minutes on the clock saw battering ram Delroy Facey brush past Owls defender Lee Bullen, finding Elliott in the box, who scuffed his shot into the path of Barmby who rolled the ball home. While the away end exploded once again to the sounds of 'There's only one Nicky Barmby ...', Dad bent down to say, 'I bloody knew Barmby would score tonight; why didn't we have a bet on?!'

Despite a carnival mood already fast developing in the Leppings Lane End, City were not yet done, and the first half was about to get even better. Just two minutes before the interval, the fans' latest rendition of 'Can't Help Falling in Love' was interrupted by one of the most iconic Hull City moments of my time as a supporter. Right up there with the play-off goals of Windass and Diamé, the Premier League screamers of Geovanni, and the FA Cup heroics of Davies and Chester, this moment will live with me forever. A long hoof from the middle of the pitch was met by the head of Ryan France who flicked the ball towards Barmby just inside the penalty area. As is the case with all my memories of great City goals, time seemed to slow right down as the ball dropped over the former England international's right shoulder and was volleyed beautifully past Lucas in the Wednesday goal. To use another one of my most hated, overused clichés, slightly modified for the relevant time period, 'if Ronaldinho had scored that for Barcelona, we'd never hear the end of it!'. It was a world-class finish, and one worthy of winning any game of football. Still, as Barmby held his arms aloft in front of the now delirious away support, we knew an important second half was still to come.

We were right. The second half did not have the same pace as the hectic first, which suited Wednesday. As the half wore on, Paul Sturrock's men began to see more of the ball and, despite not creating any clear-cut chances, looked the more likely to score the next goal. This came to pass with ten minutes left on the clock when Jon-Paul McGovern smashed past Myhill to set up what could have been a nervy final period in the away end. Fortunately, the party atmosphere was restored in the away end just two minutes later after substitute Danny Allsopp broke free of a tiring Wednesday backline to slot home with ease. 4–2 the Tigers and all over. The final whistle went and was greeted with a deafening boom of appreciation from the West Stand. After over a decade of waiting, City were not only back playing the local derbies the fans had so missed for a generation, they were also winning them. What a feeling!

City fans were told to remain seated for 15 minutes and allow the home supporters to clear the surrounding vicinity before being allowed to exit. This was common at big away ties at the time, yet I remember as Peter Taylor and his team came to applaud their club's fantastic away support at the bottom of the stand, Dad told Steph and I to stay close when we left the stadium. 'I think there could well be a bit of trouble tonight.'

After 15 minutes the gates at the back of the concourse were opened and we slowly made our way towards the exit. As soon as we hit the cold night air on Leppings Lane, I began to share Dad's concern. Looking in both directions up and down the high street, police horses could be seen separating both sets of supporters. It appeared large groups of Wednesday fans had remained behind after the final whistle, making their way around to the away end. I never found out if this had been a pre-organised event, presumably between the two dwindling 'firms' of both clubs – the so-called Hull City Psychos and the Owls Crime Squad, both of which had seen their heyday in the 70s, 80s and 90s – however, a threatening atmosphere was beginning to take over. Keeping our heads down, we cautiously began to make our way back towards the tram stop. We didn't get far though. Minutes after we left the ground, mounted police had penned an unfortunate section of the dispersing City fans into a tight square. This was common practice used by police at the time and has happened during a handful of away days I have attended in the past decade. Each time, though, I question the police's logic. Here we were, maybe 3,000 stranded away supporters unable to move as the coins, bottles and bricks started being thrown. Straight away we became a sitting target. Just minutes later a large shout came from one of the mounted police officers, as a couple of hundred young Wednesday fans attempted to breach the police barricade and get to the trapped City fans. I was terrified, but strangely excited by my surroundings. I had never experienced anything like this before. Dad had told me about the horrific state of football and hooliganism in the 70s and 80s – a chapter in British football history that had put him off the game for years – yet this was my first taste of this side of football fandom. Before I knew what was happening, the barricade broke as several of the mounted police began striking fighting groups of supporters with their police batons. It was at this point that, presumably in a complete state of panic, Steph decided to make a break for it. Completely unprompted she inadvertently – and in hindsight quite hilariously – ran directly towards a fresh group of oncoming Wednesday fans. Dad, Phil and I followed in horror, trying to grab the back of her coat to yank her back. Just as the four of us were about to come within touching distance of the charging hordes, we were hit from the side by two policemen. They shoved us all into the doorway of a *KFC* restaurant, which was filled with fellow City fans. One of the officers yelled to a terrified-looking employee, ordering him to lock the door and wait for further instructions. After checking Steph was okay after her encounter with the head of a football riot, while at the same time struggling not to laugh at her stupidity, Dad decided we may as well make the best of a bad situation and celebrate a historic City win with a family bucket. 'After all', as he pointed out, 'it could be hours before the police let us out! What about that Barmby goal, ay?'.

To the absolute dismay of my mother, it was after midnight when we finally got back to Hull. Safe to say, I was a bit tired at school the following day and I think I was relegated to the substitutes' bench for that Saturday morning's rugby match. Of course, it was all worth it, though.

Six goals – four of which scored by City – were 8,000 fellow Tigers fans creating the best away atmosphere in years, one of the greatest volleys I am likely to see live, my first football riot, three more points and a celebratory *KFC* to round it all off, *and* all on a school night. This was the stuff of dreams for an 11-year-old football addict. With memories like this, it's not difficult to understand why I can't foresee any future match topping my first midweek away day, is it?

Stepping up

Hull City 1–0 Leeds United – 01/04/2006

FOLLOWING City's famous win at Hillsborough, the remainder of the 2004/05 centenary season was a dream. It's true that City should have won the title that season, but in a near mirror image of the previous year when Doncaster had pipped us to the post, it was Luton Town that were crowned League One champions. A poor run of form during the final month of the season, after promotion was already all but clinched, saw the Tigers eventually finish runners-up and a substantial 12 points behind Mike Newell's men. Though with back-to-back promotions under our belt and a season in the second tier for the first time since the 1990/91 campaign to look forward to, I have nothing but good memories from this time. Peter Taylor had built a squad that had handled the step-up from the old Third Division to League One with ease. The incredible goalscoring exploits of Stuart Elliott – who netted 29 goals that season – along with a miserly back four and a touch of genius in the shape of Nick Barmby made sure of that. Yet, the gulf in quality between League One and the Championship proved much more of a challenge.

While City were looking to hit the ground running and carry on their momentum in the Championship, I had my own 'step-up' to contend with – the start of high school in September of 2005. It's often said that your first year of 'big school' is your most difficult in full-time education. But not for me. The challenges I had faced keeping up with the rest of my classmates would indeed come back with vengeance as I edged closer to my GCSE phase, yet I remember years 7 and 8 with great fondness. I had got through my final year at primary school with my confidence at an all-time high, and I was happier at school than I had ever been before. I was determined this was to continue into my senior education. It's true, thinking back, 2005 and 2006 stick in my memory as two of the happiest years of my entire adolescence. Aside from my continuing love for football and my ever-increasing involvement with it, other aspects of my life were also fitting more comfortably into place. For the first time in my school career, I appeared to be catching up with the rest of my classmates in every subject. I was still struggling with the pace of my reading and spelling, yet this seemed much less of an issue as my grades in other subjects, notably the humanities such as History and Geography, placed me in the top half of my class. With this my confidence grew beyond all recognition, and the unusual feeling that I actually merited my place alongside my school friends took hold. For the time being at least, I no longer felt like a phoney waiting for all my weaknesses to be exposed at any moment, as I adapted to a more adult environment. The following seven years of high school would, naturally, bring with it its own set of challenges, yet other than perhaps for my sixth-form years, I would say my first few terms of high school represented my most content time spent in statutory education.

As they had for the past few years, my own personal sporting activities also played a huge role in my confidence building, and once again I have both of my parents to thank for this. It was around this time that I began to take my sporting commitments far more seriously. An average week between the ages of 11 and 18 consisted of rugby training three nights a week after school, preparing for a game each Saturday morning during the autumn and winter terms, followed by the same hectic training regime for tennis during the spring and summer months. On top of this, running throughout the entire year, I would attend football training outside of school for Sunday league side Elloughton Juniors (later Elloughton Blackburn), with local league and cup matches taking place each Sunday between September and April. As I grew older, I remember my rugby coaches trying to convince those of us who played additional football or rugby outside of school to give up our non-collegiate sport. They argued that training the amount we were and taking part in two highly competitive matches during each frantic weekend was too much on our developing bodies. Of course, I was never going to give up any additional opportunities to play football and promptly ignored the advice. While I didn't mind playing rugby as part of a team made up of my schoolmates, egg chasing never even got close to providing the satisfaction I got from playing the beautiful game. Yet, when at the age of 22 I tore my anterior cruciate ligament playing five-a-side football at university, effectively ending my contact sport career, I began to wish I had heeded my coaches' warnings a bit more. I digress.

Confidence and self-belief had always represented my two biggest challenges growing up, and I have my parents to thank for helping me overcome these common issues. Both working demanding full-time jobs, they were always on hand to give me a lift anywhere my hobbies and commitments required me to be, regardless of what was going on in their lives. Moreover, irrespective of the often appalling Sunday morning weather conditions, Dad would always be there standing on the sidelines, watching every minute of every single Sunday league fixture I ever played over a ten-year period. If it wasn't for this support, and the required push I needed to get involved in the first place, I know I wouldn't be half as confident as I am today. It's difficult to overestimate just how big of an impact these parental sacrifices can have on a child's life, and I have to say I have been incredibly lucky and will be eternally grateful for everything my parents have done for me.

By the time I was 12 I was no longer the small, scrawny specimen I had been up until this point. My virtually continuous sporting schedule mixed with puberty beginning to kick in combined to bear unforeseen benefits. I shot up in height overnight, while my voice broke and my shoulders broadened.

Not only did these changes greatly aid development in my own sporting conquests, far more importantly, it made going to the football much more fun. The occasional pangs of anxiety caused by being thrust forward during a surge outside an away ground, or not being able to see the pitch over a particularly large fan stood in front of me on the terraces and stands, were things of the past. And maybe most crucially of all, and somewhat ironically, singing 'Oh, Ian Ashbee' to the tune of Frankie Valli's 'Can't Take My Eyes Off You' sounded much less ridiculous in my considerably more manly, deeper tone of voice. Life as a teenage football supporter was good. However, for the first time in two years life was not as good for City on the pitch. Following two seasons of relative league domination, Taylor's men looked to have found their level. The City faithful had been spoilt with two magnificent promotion seasons; now it was time to get behind their team in a potential relegation battle.

Naturally the fans obliged. Having been starved of the big away days and the opportunity to see this quality of football for 15 years, everyone was determined to make the most of it, and Dad, Steph and I were no different. Although at no point in the campaign did it even cross my own mind that relegation could be a thing that happened to my beloved Hull City, Dad decided we would treat this season as if it was to be City's last at this level. I didn't miss a home game all season and attended my highest number of away matches to date. We had paid our dues supporting City on the road, travelling to lower-league grounds up and down the country – an apprenticeship all fully paid-up football addicts should experience – but now I was excited to visit some stalwarts of English football history. Maiden visits to Molineux, Bramall Lane and Portman Road followed, as well as trips to a new generation of football stadia in the form of the Walkers Stadium (aka the crisp bowl), the Ricoh Arena and Pride Park, to name but a few.

If Sheffield Wednesday had been the team City fans had looked out for the previous season, alongside all the razzle-dazzle the second tier had to offer, there was one set of fixtures every

Tigers fan was awaiting with particular interest throughout the 05/06 campaign – the trip to Elland Road on New Year's Eve, and Leeds United's return fixture at the KC Stadium in April. Quite aside from the additional excitement of the biggest Yorkshire derby for Hull City fans in 15 years, both games were also scheduled for key points in the season. A few months into the campaign it had become clear that for City this was to be a season of consolidation – one in which Championship survival in any form would suffice. Leeds United, on the other hand, were desperate for a quick return to the Premier League after a few turbulent years, and under Kevin Blackwell were expected to be there or thereabouts come May. The clichéd 'busy Christmas period' and 'end of season run-in' would define success and failure for both sides.

Disappointingly, my first competitive meeting between Hull City and bitter rivals Leeds United during the dying hours of 2005 was a colossal anti-climax for Tigers fans. City lost 2–0, with both goals coming from Jonathan Douglas either side of half-time. In reality, we put up a decent display, with the mercurial Craig Fagan and ever-present Boaz Myhill both catching the eye. It was not the result that I recall finding most disappointing, it was the away day experience. Growing up as a football fan in Yorkshire during the early noughties, and as a fan of a *then* lower-league Hull City side, I had always wondered what it would be like to be a week in, week out supporter of a 'big' Premier League side like Leeds United. Was their ground a palace compared to the ramshackle Boothferry Park? Was watching their team – traditionally full of international stars – a marked improvement on the experience City's Third Division journeymen could provide? And, was the atmosphere created by their *multitude* of supporters *much* better than anything I had ever experienced before? Well, based on my first visit to Elland Road, I had missed absolutely nothing by selecting City over Leeds United. Granted, by this time, Leeds were a club beginning to slide down a Peter Ridsdale-induced slippery slope, yet the answer to all my ponderings was a resounding 'no'.

City had continued to battle their way through their maiden Championship slog, hovering a few places above the bottom three for much of the campaign. When I look back over our squad for that season, I am quite taken aback. Taylor had remained true to his promise of once again utilising a large chunk of the squad that had won two promotions in as many years, yet this season also saw an influx of new signings brought in to bolster the ranks. This, of course, was not unexpected, though for the first time in Taylor's tenure the number of flops appeared to outweigh the few successful signings. For every effective Craig Fagan, Jon Parkin and John Welsh brought in, there was a Mark Lynch, Keith Andrews, Darryl Duffy, Curtis Woodhouse and Sam Collins that didn't quite work out. This created an unpredictable and unsettled starting line-up most weekends, which was something quite alien after the continuity of the previous two campaigns. The situation also wasn't helped by the fact that City were without their captain Ian Ashbee, who was ruled out for most of the season with a serious degenerative bone condition. But in truth Taylor managed to get the most out of the recourses he was provided with this season, and by the summer had decided he could take City no further. Subsequently, this would go on to be the former England manager's final season at the KC and, as should have been expected, after three years of long-awaited success, City suffered badly from a post-Taylor hangover the following season. Before Taylor left for pastures new at Selhurst Park, however, there was still time for one last hurrah. If I had been let down by City's away day at Elland Road earlier in the season, the return fixture at the KC more than made up for it.

It was a sunny day and unusually warm for the beginning of April. City were still scrapping for every point to ensure Championship survival was secured, while Leeds were looking to protect their place in the play-offs after their automatic promotion bid was all but over after a poor run of form.

As always, Dad, Steph and I were confident as we took our seats just minutes after devouring our ceremonial Viking fish and chip special. As it turned out, we were right to be confident.

City came storming out of the blocks with a sense of urgency and passion that appeared to match that of the expectant home support. The early pressure nearly paid off immediately when 'the Beast' Jon Parkin leathered the ball past Leeds's veteran goalkeeper Neil Sullivan from close range, only for the home support's excitement to be quelled by the linesman's flag. City's pressing did not relent, however, and Sullivan was forced into two important saves in the first half – one from a long-range Stuart Green effort and a second from the unplayable Parkin – to keep Leeds in the game. When Parkin finally did break the deadlock in the 76th minute, sending most of the 23,500 in attendance that afternoon into ecstasy, there was more a sense of relief than joy. In truth, City could have won 2 or even 3–0 that afternoon, but until the first goal was scored, the spectre of 'typical City' – likely to materialise in the form of a fluky Leeds United breakaway winner – still loomed large. Though, as Jon Parkin outmuscled Leeds stalwart Gary Kelly to score the winner, that ghost was temporarily exorcised.

As the game ended with a deafening roar from three sides of the packed KC Stadium, I was almost in tears. When Dad and I had visited Boothferry for my first City game five years earlier – funnily enough against another Yorkshire side in Halifax – not in my wildest dreams could I have predicted I would see City beat the 'great' Leeds United in a league game in under a decade's time. The thought was a ludicrous one. The season Lawrie Dudfield and Michael Reddy had put Halifax to the sword, Leeds were coming off the back of a Champions League semi-final. Less than five years later, here we were. This is why I loved football. This is why it is so addictive.

During this final month of the regular season, Peter Taylor had boldly announced that it was his belief that a few more wins would do it – Championship safety and a guaranteed highest league finish for 16 years. As it turned out, Taylor was only half correct. City did indeed ensure their Championship survival, finishing in a respectable 18th place in the second tier, consolidating after their two previous promotion seasons.

Though, they achieved this without hitting their manager's goal of a few more victories. City only won one of their final six games in April, admittedly against a strong set of established Championship sides. However, this one win meant a whole lot more than just three points. City's 1–0 victory over Leeds United on 1 April 2006 marked a sea change in Yorkshire football. After a century of Leeds United dominating the region's professional football scene, this one game turned everything on its head. The following few seasons would see a complete reversal of fortunes for the two Yorkshire clubs. For Leeds, their spiralling decline would accelerate, and they would find themselves in the third tier of English football for the first time in their history. For my beloved Hull City, the most unexpected, fairy-tale promotion was just around the corner. With it came the promised land of the Premier League, a first season in England's top flight, an FA Cup Final, and even European football. This was the moment I believe Hull City truly stepped up. This was the moment I knew my Hull City adventure would not be stopping at the Championship. This was the moment my love for football hit all new heights.

The winker, the stamper and the end of the 'golden generation'

England 0–0 Portugal AET (1–3 penalty shoot-out) – 01/07/2006

'They just know, they're so sure. That England's gonna throw it away, gonna blow it away. But I know they can play ...'

BY 2006, a decade after the Baddiel, Skinner & The Lightning Seeds classic number one, England supporters were on the verge of once again losing faith in their national side. The golden generation that had seemingly emerged following defeat at the 1998 World Cup was nearing the end of its cycle, and Sven-Göran Eriksson's reign as manager was coming to an end. If the golden generation was to live up to its hype and win a major tournament, Beckham, Neville, Owen and co needed to perform when it mattered and make World Cup 2006 count. An England side made up of more than our fair share of the world's elite footballing talent travelled to Germany – Rio Ferdinand, John Terry, David Beckham, Frank Lampard, Steven Gerrard, Michael Owen, Wayne Rooney, the list goes on – yet somehow predictably, 30 years of hurt was about to become 40.

I was lucky enough to watch England just months before Sven's men travelled to Germany. Through a work colleague, Dad managed to get hold of three tickets for England's World Cup 2006 warm-up match against Uruguay in March of that year. This was to be my first experience of going to an international match, and although I had promised I would never let myself become as emotionally invested in an England side as I had in 2002 and 2004, I must admit I was excited. Not only was I going to see my first England match, this was the first live match I had attended in which genuine world-class footballers, still playing at the top of their game, would be almost within touching distance. Don't get me wrong, I adored going to the KC every week and watching the likes of Ian Ashbee and Andy Dawson in the famous black and amber, yet going to an England international felt special. Seeing the most famous man on the face of the planet in David Beckham pull on the Three Lions and watch him do what he does best at the peak of his career felt like an honour, and it truly was. Despite two promotions in as many years, at this point I still thought seeing Hull City in the Premier League was likely a wild pipe dream, which limited my opportunities of seeing the world's best players to the very occasional cup tie and preseason friendlies. Although unexpectedly, of course, I would go on to see this ilk of footballer visit the KC to face City over the next few years, at this point I thought an England match might be my only opportunity to see this generation of English 'super talent' up close. New England shirt on, I was determined to savour every second.

With the new Wembley Stadium still a year away from completion, England internationals were still being played at club grounds up and down the country. This game was to be played at Anfield, meaning not only would I be able to tick 'attending an England international' off the bucket list, I could also add one of the most famous venues in English football history to my ever-growing list of football grounds I have attended. For a football addict like me, there is no explaining how significant 'football ground ticks' are. Last time I counted, I was somewhere in the mid to high sixties in terms of visiting the current 92 Football

League grounds, not including a number of defunct stadia and a few clubs now playing non-league football I have also travelled to.

The game itself was decent enough, yet I was a bit disappointed with the atmosphere that evening. Despite the 40,000 fans packed into Anfield – the largest attendance I had been a part of to date – international football appeared to have a completely different feel about it. Other than the occasional chants of 'Come on England', the only atmosphere being created was coming from the regular brass band that annoyingly follow England all over the world, playing 'The Great Escape', 'Self Preservation Society' and 'Rule Britannia' on repeat. Even at the age of 12, I remember thinking they should stick to the cricket.

England came from behind to win the game 2–1, with a first international goal for Peter Crouch and a 90th-minute winner from the mercurial Joe Cole. But in reality, it was an unimpressive victory. Uruguay are often labelled as football's great overachievers. A side that, despite having a population less than half that of Greater London, have historically always punched well above their weight, winning two World Cups and 15 Copa Américas. In many ways they have epitomised the polar opposite of a constantly underachieving England side. Yet the mid-2000s signified a lull for the South Americans. Despite the two Diegos – Godín and Forlán – both lining up for the visitors that cold March evening, Uruguay were still a few years away from their own second-wave golden generation, and indeed failed to qualify for Germany 2006. Other than a sensational opening goal from Omar Pouso, the South Americans spent much of the game playing the part of an average team that an England side – expected to go on to do great things in an upcoming World Cup – struggled to put to the sword.

After the match, I left Liverpool thrilled that I could now say I had attended an England game, but disappointed with the overall atmosphere and sense of apathy directed towards the national side I had experienced that evening. Both in a collective and personal sense, this was the first experience I had of a developing disenchantment or apathy with any aspect of the game. At the time it didn't seem a huge deal. Merely a small, insignificant and almost unnoticeable blip in my football-supporting life. After all, I still had my beloved Hull City to follow, and I knew that come June I would be raring to get behind England at what would only be the second World Cup I could remember. Nevertheless, both my expectations and interest level regarding the national team would not reach the heights that they had in previous years, and it would be at least another decade before they would again.

For whatever reason, the 2006 World Cup is not a tournament I look back on with any great level of fondness. It's odd, most fans of my generation love this World Cup. They talk about a tournament full of iconic games – Brazil v France, Germany v Italy, etc. – in which all the big footballing nations delivered big performances, and that ended with one of the most dramatic World Cup Finals in history. All of this may well be true; however, all I associate with this World Cup is another England let-down, a new-found hatred for Cristiano Ronaldo and the memory of one of the greatest footballers of all time ending his career in disgraceful, albeit hilarious, circumstances. Zizou, I'm looking at you.

Indeed, 2006 was the year that *that* immensely talented crop of England players had their greatest opportunity to win a World Cup. 2002 had seen an exceptionally strong Brazil team beat England in the quarters to go on and win the tournament, while 2010 would see Vicente del Bosque's Spain – one of the most technically gifted sides in history – deservedly win a first championship. 2006, on the other hand, was a much more open tournament. Prior to the tournament starting, the bookies held England as joint second favourites to win a first major tournament in 40 years, with only reigning champions Brazil ahead of them. To put that into context, eventual winners Italy were as low as fifth favourites in the listings. Add to this the fact that England's talismanic players – Beckham, Neville, Owen, Ferdinand, etc. – were all at, or nearing, the peaks of their playing abilities, and once again you are force-fed that dangerous cocktail of hope and expectation. Cautiously, I began to buy into the hype.

England had a straightforward group on paper, with Paraguay, Trinidad and Tobago, and Sweden joining Sven's men to make up Group B. Predictably, England found perhaps the most uninspiring way of finishing top of the group – stuttering in each game. In our opener against Paraguay, a game I remember virtually nothing about, England scraped a 1–0 win courtesy of a Carlos Gamarra own goal from a Beckham free kick. A win, but a shaky win at best. Next up was Dwight Yorke's Trinidad and Tobago, in which an equally nervous performance was only just enough to hand England the three points and guarantee a place in the last 16.

The Caribbean nation frustrated the Three Lions for 83 unconvincing minutes before Peter Crouch settled the nerves. Gerrard would go on to make the win appear far more convincing than it actually was a minute into injury time when his decent long-range finish was greeted with an excitable Clive Tyldesley declaring 'That's more like it!'.

The final group standings were decided by England's last group game against Sweden. Ironically, the only match in the group stage we failed to win turned out to be the most memorable. Sat in the lounge with Dad, Mum and Steph, we watched as England's World Cup curse looked to be striking again in the opening few minutes of the game as Michael Owen was stretchered off with a nasty-looking knee injury.

'Bloody hell, here we go again,' Dad said.

Uncharacteristically, this time I was not daft enough to disagree with him. Nonetheless, notwithstanding Owen's injury, the game proved a rare pleasure to watch. Although throwing the victory away in the final minute when Henrik Larsson made it 2–2, finishing top of the group and being treated to Joe Cole's goal of the tournament appeased the doubters, including myself, for the time being at least. After all, Motty's infectiously upbeat commentary made it impossible not to feel positive heading into the knockout stages.

'There's the volley … OOOOOHHHHHHHHH! It's a terrific goal for England!'

Possibly England's most uneventful last-16 tie in living memory followed, as Beckham dragged his team into another World Cup quarter-final, with a textbook free kick against Ecuador. Next up, the game that had felt inevitable since the World Cup draw had been made months before – England's most feared 2000s foe, Portugal, in the final eight.

If our Euro 2004 defeat to Portugal had followed the same old predictable template for an England side losing out in a major tournament, the 2006 incarnation would require an updated definition of 'typical England'.

For the life of me I can't remember where Steph and Mum had gone the day of this crucial quarter-final, but I remember Dad and I watched it alone at home. The day before the big match we had gone to the supermarket and stocked up on everything we needed for a day of football. Burgers and sausages were bought for a small pre-match barbeque, and a mountain of crisps, sweets and glass bottle Coke for me (lager for Dad) to keep us refreshed all evening. Unusually, Dad felt quite optimistic about England's chances. I reminded him what he had told me years before: 'England will always let you down, remember!'

He said nothing, sitting back in his chair with a look on his face as if he knew something I wasn't privy to. If anything, this just put me more on edge.

As the game kicked off, Portugal's game plan became painfully apparent. From the very first whistle, the Portuguese, led by the young Ronaldo, were doing everything possible to frustrate England's main goal threat, Wayne Rooney. Each time he received the ball, a maroon-clad swarm descended, nipping the back of his heels and clipping his ankles. As the game progressed, and Rooney's temper became shorter and shorter, it was clear something had to give.

The scrappy first half passed without too much incident – a Luis Figo-created opportunity for Tiago the only chance of note during the first half. However, the tie came to life in the second period. Just minutes after a penalty appeal was ignored following a David Beckham cross that looked to have hit the hand of Nuno Valente in the Portuguese penalty area, the captain had to be replaced due to injury. 'That could be the last time we see Beckham in an England shirt,' Dad announced.

This was something that really had not occurred to me, and for some reason upset me. Beckham had been an ever-present in the England side for as long as I could remember, and had captained the team for most of that time. I could not imagine watching England without our number seven, David Beckham, shaking hands and passing over an FA pennant to the opposing captain before the game.

I didn't have too much time to ponder England's Beckham-less future, however. Just ten minutes after Beckham limped off, the inevitable happened. After an hour of provocation and baiting from the opposition, Wayne Rooney saw the red mist descend. A scrap for the ball in the centre of the pitch saw the young Manchester United striker stamp on Ricardo Carvalho, right under the referee's nose. Though, the worst was still to come. It wasn't until a horde of enraged Portuguese players circled Rooney and the referee, pushing and shoving England's number nine, and demanding a red card, did the referee reach for his back pocket.

'IT'S RED!' Motson cried, his voice breaking.

Seconds later, the BBC cameras panned to a close-up of Ronaldo's face. As Rooney trudged off the pitch, eyes fixated on the turf, his Manchester United team-mate was caught giving a cheeky wink to the Portuguese bench. It was the signal of a mission complete, a job well done. There is no doubt that Rooney deserved the red card following his stamp on Chelsea's Carvalho. But, equally, there is no doubt that the Ronaldo-led Portuguese went out on the pitch that day with the intention of stitching up Wayne Rooney. Unfortunately, their game plan worked to a tee.

Dad's mood immediately soured. I don't think I have ever seen him more incensed by one moment in football.

'That's it. It's all over. That cheating bastard has killed it. I hope Rooney plants one on him when they're back at United. Better yet, I hope Ferguson has him rot in the stands! He is what is wrong with modern football. Cheating bastard!'

Naturally, I agreed with every word my old man said, but while it was still 0–0, there was still a chance. Incredibly, the ten men of England rallied and defended well to get through the remaining half hour of normal time and an additional 30 minutes of extra time. As it had two years earlier, England's quarter-final with Portugal would be decided by a shoot-out.

Dad and I, now on our feet and standing about a metre away from the TV, were not hopeful. Lampard stepped up first for England, trying to level after Simão had scored Portugal's first, but saw his effort saved by everyone's least favourite keeper, Ricardo. Man of the match Hargreaves scored England's second while Hugo Viana and Armando Petit's misses put the ball in England's court. Unsurprisingly, this golden opportunity was not taken. Liverpool's Gerrard and Carragher went on to see their penalties saved – making Ricardo the first player in World Cup shoot-out history to save three penalties – while Helder Postiga and (who else but) Ronaldo scored the decisive spot kicks. The cheating bastard had done it.

'It was Maradona in '86, and now it's Ronaldo,' Dad sighed, as he turned off the TV.

But as we sat in the lounge replaying what had just happened in our mind's eye, we both knew Ronaldo was just a panto villain – the scapegoat for 2006. What he did showed him to be a shit of the highest order, there is no doubt about it. But Ronaldo was not the reason England's golden generation had crashed out of yet another major tournament at the quarter-final stage. As they had for the previous five tournaments, England had bottled it.

When I saw the replays of the missed penalties, Rooney's red card and Ronaldo's wink on news reports over the following few days, I felt the old familiar feelings I had come to associate with being an England fan flood back – crushing disappointment, anger and a feeling of determination to never let myself go through the same cycle again. But I have come to understand that supporting England is like your first few relationships as a teenager. Every time you start seeing someone new, you believe they are the one. You plan your whole future together and can't see anything ever going wrong. A few months down the line, the relationship inevitably ends in tears and you make a promise that you'll never put yourself through that again. Of course, sooner or later you meet someone new. Just like with England – sooner or later the next major tournament entices you to drop your guard and you're pulled back in.

Under Sven's replacement, Steve McClaren, England failed to qualify for Euro 2008. This prompted an unwanted four-year hiatus from international tournaments, which was enough to once again allow old wounds to heal. Before the 2010 World Cup in South Africa I was itching to watch England play at the highest level once more. While only a handful of England's original golden generation would still be playing international football by 2010, the media labelled it as their last shot at reaching their potential. Though, I disagree. For me, England's golden generation officially died the day after their defeat to Portugal. It had already been announced prior to the tournament that Sven-Göran Eriksson's time as England manager would come to an end after the World Cup; however, what was not expected was David Beckham's resignation as England captain. Although he would go on to represent his country again, seeing the only man I had ever known captain England resign in tears after failing in yet another tournament seemed symbolic. Beckham, along with the likes of Paul Scholes (who had prematurely retired from international football a few years prior), Gary Neville and Michael Owen, never played at a major international tournament again. I am still convinced that growing up I should have seen my national side win a major tournament, and I'm not sure I will ever see a stronger set of individuals represent England in my lifetime. Yet, the next decade would see a much larger issue than underachievement rock the national game – a growing indifference, disillusionment and, yes, even resentment aimed at the FA's flagship team. It was to be a miserable ten years for fans of the England national team. Luckily for me, this would coincide with an extraordinary decade for Hull City.

Survival

Cardiff City 0–1 Hull City – 28/04/2007

IN order for a season to be unforgettable, the kind of season that decades later you still reference most weekends when you are down the pub with your fellow supporters, a combination of things need to happen. Firstly, the season needs to end with one, or an amalgamation, of the following:

- A title win
- A cup win (or unforeseen cup run)
- A successfully navigated relegation battle
- An unexpectedly brilliant player emerging.

Secondly, the whole fan base of the club in question needs to be 100 per cent behind their team at all times. Cups and titles can be won, relations staved off and brilliant players unearthed, yet if a fan base is disenchanted and no one cares at the time, how can you expect anyone to care in the future? This is a phenomenon that has affected Hull City fans in recent times.

Finally, there must be a specific moment or match which best represents that memorable season. One event – a result, a goal, a red card or a missed chance – that symbolises that entire season in microcosm.

Hull City's 2006/07 season is one of those unforgettable seasons for me. It was my first relegation battle and is epitomised by one goal and one result on the penultimate day of the league season. Without once more becoming too 'sliding doors' about my time as a football supporter, it could be argued that this one goal, scored by Dean Windass, made the following decade at Hull City – the most successful period in the club's history – possible. And for all you non-Hull City fans, no, it's not the Windass goal you probably have in mind.

Over the summer of 2006 everything changed for Hull City. Peter Taylor, the man that had woken the sleeping giant and guided it back to the second tier of English football where it belonged, left to take over at his former club Crystal Palace. There were no hard feelings. Taylor stated he could not take Hull City any further, and I believed him, to be honest. Judging by our first season in the Championship, for the time being at least, Hull City had found their level. Add to this the fact that Crystal Palace is a traditionally larger club than Hull City, and that Taylor is a club legend at Selhurst Park, and you would struggle to find a City fan that begrudged Taylor this genuine shot at enhancing his managerial career. Though, it's worth noting that recently Taylor has, with the benefit of hindsight, expressed some regrets at leaving City.

City moved early to appoint Taylor's replacement, announcing that young Colchester United manager Phil Parkinson would take the reins at the KC. In many ways it appeared the perfect appointment. Adam Pearson had consciously avoided the trap of employing a 'real football man' – in other words, a 60-something-year-old has-been, fresh off the managerial merry-go-round – and instead had decided to gamble and take a punt on one of the most promising young managers in the Football League. Dad and I were impressed. How were we to know the appointment would prove an unmitigated disaster?

Indeed, it proved to be a miserable autumn. Phil Parkinson's spell in charge lasted only 21 league games, consisting of 12 defeats, five draws and just four victories – echoes of Mølby's ill-fated tenure four years earlier. Aside from results not going his way and City finding themselves in the relegation places in time for my 13th birthday at the start of December, rumours of a spat between Parkinson and a few of the senior players – including

Barmby and Ashbee – ultimately made the 39-year-old's job untenable. After embarrassing defeats away at his former club Colchester and at home to Southampton, Parkinson was sacked just four days into December and was replaced by his assistant, Phil Brown.

Although we knew it was going to be a struggle, with well over half of the season remaining, Championship survival was still very much achievable. This did not stop Dad attempting to prepare me for life back in League One, however.

'We've been incredibly lucky to have seen two promotions since we started going to the football, Greg. Relegation would not be the end of the world.'

But at this point I was still refusing to even entertain the idea. After all, despite selling Leon Cort – who became City's first £1m transfer – and Stuart Green, both to Peter Taylor's Palace, I still believed our squad was stronger than the previous season. In a bizarrely similar set of circumstances to fellow City failure Jan Mølby, Parkinson had recruited extremely well. Sam Ricketts, Dean Marney and Michael Turner had all been brought in to strengthen the squad during the summer – three players that would become Premier League regulars in under two years' time. They were also joined by experienced signings Michael Bridges and Nicky Forster, both of whom would go on to make positive contributions that season, as well as Manchester City and former England full-back Danny Mills, who joined on loan.

Phil Brown had the squad to work with, he now just needed to get the senior players back onside and ensure a misfiring City side started scoring again. Both of these issues were ostensibly solved with two masterful signings at the start of 2007. Just over a decade after being sold to Aberdeen in a move that ensured City's financial stability in the 1990s, local lad Dean Windass returned on loan until the end of the season from Bradford City. He would go on to be City's top goalscorer that season with eight vital goals. In February Windass was joined by 33-year-old Arsenal legend Ray Parlour. The 'Romford Pelé', who won ten England caps during his career, made 15 starts at the back end of that season, providing a relatively young squad with a much-needed calm head in the middle of the pitch. The initially uninspiring Brown looked to know what he was doing, yet City's relegation battle would go down to the wire.

Steph had moved to Birmingham to start university in the October of that season, meaning most of that campaign saw only Dad and I attend each home game, with Mum taking up the offer of using Steph's ticket on a handful of occasions. Once again, despite the generally poor season City were having on the pitch, we upped the number of away games we travelled to. The Hawthorns, Loftus Road, Selhurst Park and the Riverside (thanks to a cold FA Cup replay) were all ticked off the list, as I experienced my first real relegation battle as a football fan. Some football addicts say that if their side is not challenging for the league title, automatic promotion or a place in the play-offs, they would rather be involved in a relegation battle to keep the season interesting. Regardless of the fact it creates a memorable season, I am not one of these fans. Even if the emotional pay-off is phenomenal when your side beats the odds and manages to survive, the journey that sees your beloved club arrive in such a precarious position in the first place tends to be a miserable one. Give me mid-table mediocrity any day.

Unfortunately, after our wretched start under Parkinson, a mid-table finish was never a possibility. The season wore on and it became clear that the dreaded three relegation places were destined to be filled by three out of a possible five teams. Luton, Southend, Barnsley and – quite hilariously, after losing out in the Championship play-off final just the season before – Leeds United were all in the mix.

Heading into the final two matchdays of the season Luton and Southend were all but relegated, while Barnsley appeared safe. The battle to avoid the final trapdoor was between City and our biggest rivals Leeds United. Our final away game of the season was a trip to Cardiff City's hostile Ninian Park; whereas Leeds, just one point behind us, were at home to Ipswich. Who would blink first?

I was gutted not to be travelling to south Wales that day. Dad had been away all week with work and understandably couldn't face a 500-mile round trip to Cardiff. I was justifiably disappointed, but as we had with the Yeovil Town promotion match three seasons prior, I was to follow the game from back in Hull. Dad pacified the situation by reminding me that there was still one game to go after this, meaning relegation may yet not be decided at Ninian Park. In order to be safe, City needed a win and hoped Leeds failed to beat a mid-table Ipswich side. This would lift City at least three points clear, with a superior goal difference all but impossible for Leeds to overhaul on the final day.

With relegation rather than promotion at stake, the club decided not to provide a live beam back at the KC, limiting our match coverage to Radio Humberside commentary. I have come to love listening to radio commentary of football matches over the years. Indeed, listening to BBC 5Live while at work, particularly for the early kick-offs during the 2018 World Cup just about kept me sane, although when you have a dog in the fight, radio is a horrible medium for a football supporter.

Not being able to see what is going on and having to put your complete trust in a usually over-chatty local radio presenter to provide every single detail of a match, particularly one of such importance, is frustrating. Luckily, Humberside's David Burns is one of the better ones.

As Dad and I sat in the kitchen – the only room in the house with an FM radio – the nerves began to build. Dad had been cautious all season when discussing City's survival chances, yet I had remained resolute in my belief that we'd stay up. Though, as the game began and the coverage bounced regularly to Elland Road for updates from the Leeds game, I started to doubt myself for the first time. In that moment, the thought of little old Hull City staying in the division at the expense of the once mighty Leeds United sounded ludicrous when I said it in my head. Our historically superior West Yorkshire rivals were surely going to pull it out of the bag and put us back in our rightful place. Sure enough, 12 minutes into the match news arrived from an annoyingly excitable BBC Leeds pundit – Richard Creswell had put Dennis Wise's side ahead. Dad and I looked at each other, mentally preparing ourselves for away days back in the lower leagues.

'Bugger,' said Dad, quite emotionlessly at half-time. 'This next 45 minutes is huge.'

After a nervous-looking first half, in which the Tigers had to defend well, Phil Brown's men came out fighting for their lives in the second period. And it paid off. With 52 minutes on the clock, 38-year-old Dean Windass scored the game's only goal in front of a euphoric travelling support. As an ecstatic Burnsy described the 11-man pile-up forming at the base of the away end, Dad and I were dancing around the kitchen chanting 'WE ARE STAYING UP!' at the tops of our lungs. It was a surreal moment and one that was about to get a whole lot better. We settled back down in our seats around the kitchen table, accepting it was going to go down to the final day of the season in a week's time, while Burnsy broke down the many different scenarios that could play out from the various different combinations of final results. The game at Ninian Park continued, where City fans had only Boaz Myhill to thank for keeping the score at 1–0. The Welsh keeper frustrated his fellow countrymen with a string of remarkable saves, keeping the Tigers in the Championship, as it stood. Then, just as Burnsy was describing his view of the fourth official reaching for his substitution board to indicate the amount of injury time to be played, there was a roar from all four corners of Ninian Park. Seconds later an irate BBC Leeds presenter cut over Burnsy.

'News coming from Elland Road ... Ipswich have equalised! Leeds United could be heading for League One and Hull City may be on the brink of a famous great escape! Can you believe it?!'

I couldn't believe it. I refused to. As Dad nearly flipped the kitchen table as he jumped out of his seat, I rushed into the lounge to put *Gillette Soccer Saturday* on the TV. There it was right in front of my eyes – 'Leeds United 1–1 Ipswich Town, Alan Lee '88'. But the drama wasn't quite over yet. Knowing what this result would mean for their side, Leeds fans stupidly decided to flood on to the pitch seconds before the final whistle, trying to get the match abandoned. Dad and I watched the scenes on Sky Sports News, while listening to updates on Humberside. Half an hour later, the pitch at Elland Road had been cleared and the final minute of the game was played. But it changed nothing. As the whistle sounded at Elland Road, Dad and I bounced around the room arm in arm. Leeds's failure to win had all but sealed their relegation. Despite not being mathematically relegated that day, Leeds accepted their fate just days later when taking a ten-point deduction for going into administration. City were safe. Another season in the Championship beckoned. What a feeling.

City fans would go on to have a survival party, of which I was part, just seven days later on the final day of the season, but by all accounts, the real party happened at Ninian Park. It's rumoured that former Leeds United chairman, Peter Ridsdale – who by this time had taken up a similar role at Cardiff after being unceremoniously forced out of Elland Road – ensured there were bottles of champagne provided in the away dressing room upon hearing that his former club had been relegated. Meanwhile the Cardiff fans, better known for scrapping with their City counterparts after league meetings, stayed behind to cheer our players off the pitch, with chants of 'Who the fuck are Leeds United?!' and 'Deano, Deano, Deano!' reverberating from all four stands.

I was gutted not to be there in south Wales that day, as I still am now, yet the experience of listening to the entire game with Dad is a different unique memory that will live with me forever. Being a football addict isn't *always* about attending every game, it's about supporting your team in the best way you possibly can in a given set of specific circumstances. This has become a much more salient issue in recent years as many diehard City fans have felt the need to boycott home matches in protest of the Allam family's ownership of the club. An unpopular stance maybe, but a justified one that no football fan in a similar position takes lightly. But more of that later.

The 2006/07 season was a special one. It was my first relegation battle, the first season I saw Dean Windass turn out in the famous black and amber, and a personal record-breaking year in terms of new away grounds visited. The following season will always overshadow its predecessor for obvious reasons, yet 06/07 is just as important in City's recent history. Surviving in the second tier at the expense of our entitled West Yorkshire neighbours was an achievement I wasn't sure would be bettered in the foreseeable future. How wrong I was. I didn't know it at the time, but I was just months away from undoubtedly *the* greatest season to be a Hull City AFC supporter.

Daring to dream

Barnsley 1–3 Hull City – 15/04/2008

I think I've made it perfectly clear by this point in my story that I despise the excessive use of descriptive clichés in football.

'That was schoolboy defending' – no Mark, I'm fairly certain a 28-year-old World Cup winner was not defending with the talent and ability of a schoolboy – don't be ridiculous.

'This could be a cricket score here today' – I don't think it could, Dion, but if Sunderland do beat Newport by five wickets I'll be sure to apologise.

'They are a team that likes to play football' – they all like to play bloody football, Gary, they literally get paid to do it.

However, in a foul act of hypocrisy, I have to admit that the memory of my greatest season as a football addict is most easily evoked by one footballing cliché I love. The 2007/08 season saw Hull City promoted to the top flight of English football for the first time in their 104-year history. What made this season so magical was how unexpected the promotion was, both among our own set of supporters and the wider footballing community as a whole. Not only was the club incredibly unfashionable – a poor city in the north of England with little footballing history – but the fact that no big money was spent to buy our success, and that even halfway through the season the Premier League still appeared a million miles away, made us a unique case. The likes of Swansea, Bournemouth and Huddersfield have all since gone on to emulate our unexpected achievement, yet City's promotion seemed, at the time at least, to be the first to shake the new-found order of the Premier League's super-elite clubs. We were the downtrodden, unremarkable, disliked northern relative and we were about to gatecrash English football's top table.

It was a season like no other. Even to this day I struggle to explain how it happened. After a mediocre start to the campaign, what I will forever associate as the greatest Hull City XI of all time, just started winning matches. Then we couldn't stop winning matches. Then, two weeks short of a year after Dean Windass scored the goal at Cardiff that kept Hull City in the second tier, the Tigers were travelling to Barnsley knowing a victory would put them in the Championship's automatic promotion places with just a few weeks of the season to go. As we are constantly reminded, a year is a hell of a long time in football, and after a truly phenomenal six months City were on the brink of the remarkable. From one cliché to another. As Dad, Steph and I travelled to Oakwell, we had already taken the advice of Hull City's newly created PR machine. We had 'dared to dream'.

However, in order to understand how important my second trip to Oakwell is in this story of football addiction, it is first necessary to rewind a few months. The summer of 2007 was a hectic one for Hull City. Six years on from saving the club from financial ruin, Adam Pearson – the man, the myth, the legend – sold the club, stating he did not have the financial backing to take it to the next level. It was a time of mixed emotions. To this day, Pearson remains a hero in Hull – now at the helm of City's Rugby League co-inhabitants at the KCOM Stadium, Hull FC. Nonetheless, as was the case when Peter Taylor had left the club 12 months earlier, his departure felt like the end of an era. Looking back, it is amazing that the news of a takeover wasn't discovered months before it happened in the June. For the entire second half of the 06/07 campaign Pearson had been repeatedly joined by a mysterious pinstripe-suited man at each home game. Passed off at the time as either an agent or a relative of Pearson's wife, no one batted an eyelid. After all, there was a relegation battle to focus on. As it turned out, the slick individual was in fact Paul Duffen – Hull City's next chairman.

By the end of July a reported £13 million takeover (a ludicrously small figure when compared to today's valuations) was complete, and after a short handover period Adam Pearson resigned from the board, leaving Duffen in charge. All I recall of the takeover is seeing Duffen, naturally in another sharp suit and with a Cheshire cat smile slapped across his face, parading around an empty KC Stadium for the TV cameras, on BBC Look North. Apparently backed by a wealthy southern property investor, Duffen made all the right noises and a promise of stability and sensible spending followed. Dad and I were impressed. This appeared to be progress, and progress done in the right way. No talk of huge spending sprees and guaranteed promotion in year one, but a sensible and apparently well-thought-out 'five-year plan' to build a side capable of challenging to win Premier League promotion. Other City fans were sitting up and starting to listen, too. Never before had the words 'Hull City' and 'Premier League' been used in the same sentence and anyone listened.

Nevertheless, the apparent air of modesty Duffen had promised went straight out of the window a few weeks later – not that the fans seemed to care, mind – as the new owner looked for his first landmark signing. Former Italian international Christian Vieri was mentioned, as was Brazilian World Cup winner Juninho, who was spotted leaving a hotel with Brown and Duffen. But nothing came of it. Instead Brown, alongside his new assistant manager Brian Horton, himself a former Hull City manager, strengthened their squad with several more humble signings. Windass made his move from Bradford a permanent one, and was joined by Brian Hughes, Wayne Brown and Richard Garcia – all of whom would go on to play key roles in this groundbreaking season.

In what was a bit of an anti-climax, however, City started the season unimpressively. Following a 3–2 home defeat against Plymouth on the opening day, it was clear further reinforcements were needed for Duffen to match his ambitions. Henrik Pedersen, who had worked with Brown at Bolton, brought much-needed experience, while just weeks later history was made when striker Caleb Folan became Hull City's first £1 million man. As summer transitioned into autumn the final two pieces of the puzzle were acquired as Duffen got his landmark signing: 34-year-old former African player of the year Jay Jay 'so good they named him twice' Okocha signed on a free transfer. As the *Hull Daily Mail* ran with the headline 'Jay Jay WeGotcha', genuine excitement started to build across the city. Even entering the autumn of his footballing career, the former PSG and Bolton man represented some coup for the Tigers. After all, the rainbow-flicking Nigerian had appeared in three World Cups and won Olympic gold in an international career that spanned over a decade. He had even followed in Nick Barmby's footsteps, earning individual praise from the great Pelé when appearing in the Brazilian's top 125 living footballers in 2004. (Though it's worth noting that Pelé once again embarrassed himself here, also naming El Hadji Diouf on the list.) Nonetheless, Hull City fans were excited, and you couldn't blame us. Duffen and co looked the real deal.

Finally, Manchester United youngster Fraizer Campbell joined on a season-long loan. The striker, who had scored an impressive 20 goals in just 31 appearances during a season under former City manager Warren Joyce at Royal Antwerp, would ease the goalscoring burden on Windass and would help to create the most unlikely of strike partnerships, with the man old enough to be his father.

Duffen's backing had enabled Brown to build a strong side, one that was now capable of gunning for the club's highest Championship finish. I remember thinking that the dizzy heights of a respectable mid-table finish were now well within our grasp, and with a world-class talent like Okocha in the side, as well as a pacey new goalscoring striker, it was going to be an enjoyable ride to boot.

Still, it wasn't until after Christmas, when I was hesitantly beginning to choose my GCSE options for the following few years at school, did the season look like it could provide anything other than the stabilising top-half pursuit Duffen had promised.

Up until Christmas, City had played some tantalising football at times and picked up some decent results, but this had been mixed with patchy form and a few heavy defeats – notably against Preston and Southampton at the start of December. Inconsistent, perhaps, but it was proving to be an enjoyable season all the same after the struggle of the previous two campaigns. A good run of form over the busy festive period saw a five-game unbeaten run, and by 1 January 2008, Phil Brown's Hull City were sitting in ninth place in the Championship, just one point outside of the play-offs. I must admit, I thought this was where our season would peak. And what a peak that would be. Indeed, a 3–1 defeat at home to promotion favourites West Brom at the start of the new year looked as though it would confirm my theory. We had made brilliant progress to reach this point, but I thought it was a bit early for a promotion charge. How wrong I was.

Incredibly, the West Brom defeat would in fact represent one of just five defeats City would suffer in the entire second half of the season. Promotion form, indeed.

Somewhat coincidentally, it wasn't until City's return fixture at West Brom at the end of February did Dad, Steph and I believe City *could* be in the middle of a promotion push.

As we left the Hawthorns after beating the eventual league champions 2–1 on their own patch, the first tentative chants of 'We are going up!' could be heard from the travelling City supporters. By the time we were back in the car, even Dad, usually the eternal pessimist when discussing City's chances, appeared uncharacteristically excited. 'This could happen, you know. We just made the best side in the division look average, and the momentum is on our side!' If Dad was 'daring to dream' I knew we really must be in with a real shot.

Promotions and cup runs will come once more to the KCOM in the future, I am sure of it, yet for City supporters of my generation and older, nothing will top the last three months of the 2007/08 league season.

The stars were beginning to align. The odd-couple strike partnership of 38-year-old Dean Windass and 20-year-old Fraizer

Campbell flourished, City started to score goals from all areas of the pitch and a defensive partnership between Michael Turner and Wayne Brown was looking the strongest in the division. Solid victories against Burnley, Scunny, Southampton, Colchester United, Leicester City and Watford in the spring pushed City into the top six, and by the time an army of City fans travelled to Barnsley on a chilly April evening promotion fever had well and truly taken hold.

If I had to choose the top five away games I have attended, this would be right up there. The game had had to be rearranged earlier in the season due to Barnsley's impressive FA Cup run that season, and as such had been selected as a bonus match to be broadcast live on Sky Sports. Despite this, 5,000 Tigers fans still made the journey that evening, knowing a win would see their side move into the top two with just three fixtures remaining. The atmosphere inside the away end was something else. After a good half hour of pre-match chanting aimed specifically at the Sky Sports cameras, consisting of 'Can you hear us, can you hear us, can you hear us back in 'ull?!' and 'Peter Beagrie is a wanker, is a wanker!', the main event kicked off, and the atmosphere reached new heights. Not since Hillsborough three and a half years earlier had I experienced such an atmosphere. The away end was bouncing from the very first minute and, adorned in our gorgeous 2008 all-amber home shirt, City responded on the pitch.

When Fraizer Campbell was fouled in the box with 23 minutes on the clock and Dean Marney stepped up to take the spot kick, the away end went silent for the only time that evening. I held my breath. With confidence oozing out of every pore, Marney slotted home with ease. 1–0! 'We're going up, we're going up! You're not, you're not!'

As Dad and I bounced up and down arm in arm in the away end, we knew that was this game won. The confidence generated by this most unlikely of promotion charges seemed to, temporarily at least, overpower the mysterious phenomenon of 'typical City'.

Moments into the second half this theory was confirmed as captain Ashbee scored what I can only describe as *the* most comprehensive header I have ever seen. Connecting with a Marney corner, as the ball bulleted off Ashbee's head it looked as though it would break the back of the net. Cue absolute pandemonium in Oakwell's away end. 2–0! 'WE ARE GOING UP, SAY WE ARE GOING UP!'

'We might win the bloody title at this rate!' Dad shouted in disbelief, as the euphoric players gathered in the same spot Michael Keane had celebrated scoring his League One winner four years earlier.

The cherry was well and truly placed on top of the cake with just eight minutes to play when Brown threw on substitute Windass to see the game out. In typical Deano fashion he immediately latched on to Campbell's clever back-heel and smashed home with his very first touch. 3–0! 'DEANO, DEANO, DEANO!'

As the veteran striker stood in front of the travelling support, chest puffed out and hands cupping each ear, I knew City were going up. This was the moment. Nothing was getting in our way, and it felt as though it was just meant to be.

Barnsley went on to score a consolation late in the game, but I barely even noticed. After Windass had killed the game, the away end had gone into full party mode. The final whistle went and it was confirmed – Hull City were sitting in second place in the Championship, our highest position of the season.

I remember the three of us heading back to the car – this time not parked on the field next to Oakwell – and being greeted by the Mackem tones of Phil Brown giving his post-match interview on Humberside. 'That's the seventeenth time it [the Championship's top position] has changed hands; hopefully there will be another one before the end of the season.'

There was to be one or two twists in the tale before the end of the season, including a number of lows as well as incredible highs, but this game signalled the real start of *the* most magnificent month to be a supporter of Hull City. Phil Brown was 'daring to dream', and now so was the rest of the Tiger Nation.

Que será, será ...

Watford 0–2 Hull City – 11/05/2008
Hull City 4–1 Watford – 14/05/2008

WE had left Oakwell convinced we were bound for the Premier League. 'Typical City' was a thing of the past and the phenomenal run we were on meant that nothing was going to stop us. Indeed, City had sat second in the league, automatic promotion in our own hands, with just three games to go. Naturally, we didn't go on to do it the easy way. But thinking back, I think we did it the best way.

Just four days after the iconic win at Barnsley an injury-struck City side, featuring a wildly out-of-position David Livermore at centre-half, lost 2–0 at Bramall Lane. It was perhaps the most depressing away day I have attended, but I kept the faith. Seven days later and Dad and I were rewarded with a vital 2–1 win at home against fellow promotion chasers, Palace. In a game in which Windass suffered a nasty gash on his leg after a clash with Shaun Derry, Ian Ashbee rescued the three points in the 85th minute with his second towering header in as many weeks. But ultimately it wouldn't be enough. A long trip to Ipswich proved fruitless on the final day of the season, as a 1–0 defeat courtesy of an Alan Lee header confirmed City's fate. If the Tigers were going to reach the Premier League, they would have to do it through the play-offs. In truth, the real damage had been done at Sheffield United two weeks earlier. As it turned out, even a win at Portman

Road wouldn't have been enough, as Stoke's draw with Leicester City cemented their automatic promotion along with champions West Brom. It was to be the play-offs for City.

There's no doubt about it, I was disappointed as the final whistle went and with it our shot at automatic promotion. Yet what upset me more was the reaction of City's players. To a man they looked heartbroken. A group of players, many of whom I had watched pull on the black and amber shirt in the lower divisions, devastated that their shot at the big time might have passed them by.

'Whatever happens, it's been a hell of a season,' Dad reminded me. 'Brown deserves a knighthood. We could well have been playing in League One right now.'

He was right, of course. We'd come such a long way in a short space of time. But even at this moment, I was confident we were still going to do it. Now it was Brown's job to convince his players of the same.

Leaving Portman Road we frantically searched for news of other incoming results. Having finished third, City would face the team that finished in sixth place – away in the first leg, home in the second. Initially a rumour spread around the exiting City fans that it was Wolves that had scraped into the final play-off spot. By the time we reached the car and put 5Live on the radio, it was announced that City would in fact play Watford. As it turned out, the Hornets had pipped Wolves to the post, seizing the final play-off position on goal difference by a single goal. Dad, Steph and I were relieved. All three of us had agreed prior to the game that day that if the play-offs did beckon, Watford would be our opponents of choice.

'I guess we're off to Vicarage Road next week, then. 2–0, easy,' Dad said excitedly as we began our long drive back to Hull. I wish he'd put money on it.

The following week was horrible. I couldn't concentrate on anything other than City. School was particularly difficult, and it didn't take much for my teachers to notice that my mind was elsewhere. I suppose I wasn't too subtle, to be fair.

'Whitaker! Look where you are going, man! I can't wait for this Hull City nonsense to all be over – it's got your head all over the place!' yelled one of my rugby coaches, as I absentmindedly walked into him in a corridor. 'Sorry, Sir,' I murmured, as I bit my lip to stop myself going on an ill-advised rant about why this was the biggest week in Hull City AFC's history, and with it one of the biggest weeks for the city of Hull in decades. A midweek after-school detention was the last thing I needed with the Wednesday evening second leg less than a week away.

Dad too suffered from a similar unease. 'I caught myself listing my starting XI for Sunday during a meeting today,' he chuckled. 'Luckily when someone asked me a question, I think I got away with it. I'm good at winging it, but it was a close call!'

When Sunday finally arrived, we got up early, had a quick breakfast and set off for Watford. The match was due to kick off at 12.30pm, so Steph had arrived back from university the night before in order to drive down with us. It was a beautifully sunny Sunday morning and the drive down to Hertfordshire was a pleasure. Every other car and coach on the motorway seemed to contain fellow City fans, all as excited and apprehensive as us.

There was something comforting about the thought of half of all City season ticket holders convoying down to Watford for their side's biggest match in decades. Indeed, this wasn't only the most important City fixture I had ever attended, it was one of the most important in living memory. I thought about all the thousands of City fans that had come before me. The ones that had travelled all over the country, year in, year out, with not a great deal to shout about. How amazing a first ever trip to Wembley would be for them. A big result at Vicarage Road that day could almost make that dream a reality.

We got to the ground with plenty of time to spare and spent the half hour before kick-off leisurely walking around to the away end, nervously nodding and waving to fellow fans we recognised, and grabbing lunch at a shabby-looking burger van opposite our turnstile. By the time we'd found our seats at 12.20pm the nervous energy that was so obvious outside the ground had vanished and was replaced by an atmosphere built from excitement and expectation. It suited the gloriously sunny day perfectly. Just seconds before kick-off my mobile phone exploded with incoming messages. Apparently half of Hull had seen me, Dad and Steph on Sky Sports's pre-match coverage, chanting and dancing alongside five City fans dressed from head to toe in Tiger costumes. My 15 seconds of fame.

City started the game anxiously. After four minutes the away end fell silent and my heart sank. Direct from a Jobi McAnuff corner the absolute battering ram that is Danny Shittu headed home to put us behind before the game had even got going.

'Bollocks!' Dad yelled, clapping his hands against the seat in front of him as the gigantic centre-half wheeled away in celebration.

But the disappointment was mercifully short-lived. For reasons that are still unclear, referee Kevin Friend brought the Watford celebrations to an abrupt halt seconds later.

Relief washed over me. I was hot like the feeling you get when you wake from a nightmare and realise it was all just a dream. City had pushed their luck early and got away with it; I prayed we wouldn't push it again.

'We've got away with one there, I reckon,' Steph whispered as the mocking jeers and whistles rained down from the away end. 'We need to take the game to them!'

She was right, we did. And just five minutes later, we benefited from doing just that. After a loose pass from would-be hero Shittu, Campbell charged into the box before picking out Barmby, who slotted home. 1–0!

As the former England international sprinted towards the City dugout, the away end rioted. The contrast of emotions from just minutes earlier was incredible. From losing everything to winning the jackpot, us City fans now knew it was going to be our day. Fifteen minutes later, we could practically smell the burgers and hot dogs on Wembley Way as Windass doubled our lead.

The head of Campbell met a Dawson cross and the ball ricocheted off the crossbar, only for Windass to react first to tap into a gaping goal.

'E I E I E I O! Up the Football League we go ...'

As the players jogged into the tunnel at half-time, I don't think I had ever felt happier than I did in that moment. I felt drunk with joy. If you could bottle the feeling a young football fanatic experiences when his traditionally underachieving team – a club that he has followed from the lowest of the low – is suddenly on the brink of achieving something remarkable and unexpected, there would be no need for booze, nicotine or drugs in this world. Depression and unhappiness would be a thing of the past, and I think there is a good chance world peace would instantly break out. Dramatic, maybe, but this feeling – one I have been lucky enough to experience on several other occasions in my life – is like nothing I can accurately describe. It's what an alcoholic lovingly describes to the bar tender as he orders another bottle, and the junkie to his dealer as he buys his next fix. But who knew football could make us feel like this? Is there any wonder why I will never be able to kick the football habit for good?

Four days after the two Hull-born heroes Windass and Barmby, helped along by an extraordinary display of goalkeeping from Boaz Myhill, had sealed a first leg 2–0 win, a sellout crowd would fill the KC Stadium for the most important match in its short history. The 'tinpot', fourth-tier club I had first watched under the raining rust of Boothferry were now just 90 minutes away from a first ever trip to Wembley Stadium and, even more remarkably, just 180 minutes away from the Premier League. If the previous week had been difficult, the three days after Vicarage Road were murder. Wednesday evening could not come quickly enough.

Viking fish and chip special in hand and wearing my vintage 1992 tiger print home shirt, the three of us walked through West Park as a bizarre pre-match atmosphere descended. City fans knew our team were in a fantastic position and were, in theory at least, almost certain to win the tie. But still, in the back of everyone's minds, that little bit of nagging doubt was keeping the excitement from bubbling over. After all, isn't 2–0 *the* most dangerous lead in world sport? CLICHÉ KLAXON. But even 'typical City' couldn't ruin this moment, could we?

Well, safe to say we gave it our best try. Less than 12 minutes on the clock and a shaky start had led to a Darius Henderson opener. 2–1 on aggregate and a very nervous KC Stadium. Brown's men looked anxious and fidgety, and these emotions bled into the expectant crowd. We needed a goal. Then, just two minutes before what would have been an uncomfortable half-time, the killer blow. Dawson's long header into the Watford box wasn't dealt with, Garcia's loopy header looked to be heading in, before that man Nicky Barmby threw himself at the ball to force it over the line. The stadium exploded. Dad, Steph and I embraced, jumping up and down on our own little part of the East Stand we had called home for the last five years. It was 1–1 on the night, but more importantly a feeling of ease had come over the home fans, and with it the home team on the pitch. City were going to win this match. We were going to Wembley.

With 70 minutes on the clock City made absolutely sure the tie was over when Caleb Folan struck to make it 4–1 on aggregate.

'Mauled by the Tigers, you're getting mauled by the Tigers', complete with mauling actions, was the chant ringing around the KC. But there was more to come.

Richard Garcia and Nathan Doyle, the latter who was unfortunate not to score with a good effort which hit the post in the dying minutes of the away tie, snatched late goals to make a historic win even more memorable. By the time of Doyle's late strike the KC's stewards were struggling to prevent the home fans from streaming on to the pitch.

'Que será, será! Whatever will be will be! We're going to Wembley!'

The final whistle went and with it came the inevitable pitch invasion (of which I was a part). Cue the greatest post-match celebrations the KC Stadium has ever seen. The players re-emerged on the directors' balcony moments later, joined by Phil

Brown and Paul Duffen, the champagne started spraying and the party began. Naturally, Dad, Steph and I stayed until the very end. As '(Is This the Way to) Amarillo' came on over the tannoy, I was on my knees in the centre circle sobbing. I remember Dad dragging me to my feet saying. 'Cheer up! We're off to Wembley!' But that was exactly it. We *were* going to Wembley and I could not believe it. I was happier in that moment than I had ever been. I didn't know it yet, but this ecstatic feeling of joy was to be topped just ten days later at Wembley Stadium. These were the greatest days to be a Hull City fan. These are the moments football fandom are all about.

One day like this

Bristol City 0–1 Hull City – 24/05/2008

WHAT a 12 months it had been. When the unknown Paul Duffen had finalised his deal to purchase the club less than one year earlier, fans would have recognised anything other than relegation as a successful season. Now, after a spectacular six months, Hull City AFC were on the brink of the Premier League and a first season of top-flight football after 104 years of mediocrity.

Predictably the excitement was palpable. For the first time in my life it was the city's football team that drew the national media's spotlight, not the traditionally more successful rugby league sides. Hullesians camped all night, with queues circling the entire perimeter of the KC Stadium almost twice over, to secure their Wembley tickets. Fortunately, as loyal season ticket holders, Dad, Steph and I were able to get our hands on our tickets early without the nightmare of queuing. This was a time in which loyalty was still recognised and rewarded by the club.

Within days City's 40,000 ticket allocation had been snapped up. It felt as though the entire city would be travelling down to Wembley for the big match. Windass would later say in a post-match interview, 'I don't think there's anyone left in 'ull today. There might be a few houses being burgled, mind.'

If I had thought the wait between the two Watford matches had been tough, it was nothing compared to the ten days leading up to the final. Yet, this time it wasn't just my lack of focus that bothered me. Something truly nauseating also began to occur in the run-up to Wembley. Lads at school who had previously no interest in Hull City – mates that would mock me, Charlie, Ben and a few others for supporting 'Hull Shitty', while wearing the colours of Manchester United, Liverpool, Chelsea and even Leeds, throughout our school years – started turning up for school with black and amber scarves. They would talk about players they had never seen play, matches they hadn't been to and family ties with the club that didn't exist. Never in the club's history had there been such an opportunity for the city's generally uninterested masses to jump on the bandwagon, but at the first sign of a little bit of success, suddenly everyone was thanking God for *finally* rewarding their 'loyal' lifelong support.

I was struck with a weird conflict of emotions. On the one hand, I had always tried to explain to anyone that would listen how fantastic supporting my local club was. About the unforgettable memories it has created for me personally, memories that cannot be created supporting Manchester United or Liverpool from the comfort of your armchair. In this sense, seeing an almost universal interest in the club explode across the city was fantastic. And, of course, I wanted City to have as much support as humanly possible at the final. After all, anything that could provide even a slight advantage and push us closer to the promised land of the Premier League could only be a positive thing. However, on the other hand, I hated what these phonies stood for. Even now I feel childish admitting it still bothers me, but it does. Along with Dad and Steph, I felt as though I had paid my dues, travelling up and down the country, supporting City in any weather, and whatever division the club found itself in. Relatively speaking, few others could say the same. It infuriated me that now that City were briefly English football's flavour of the month, every man and his dog claimed to be lifelong Tigers fans. Of course, this is an aspect of supporting a traditionally unfashionable club going through a rare purple patch in their history I have had to learn to cope with over the past decade. During the peaks and troughs of the previous ten years these fake fans have come and gone – always the first to show their support through social media posts and

Wembley selfies during the good times, but *strangely* never to be seen when the going gets tough. Sickening definitely, but I wasn't going to let it ruin the biggest day of my football-supporting life.

We travelled down to the capital the night before the final. School had finished that day for the Whit half-term break and we had decided to make a bit of a weekend out of it. 'Win or lose, we will have a fun few days in London,' Dad said, as our Wembley tickets arrived through the post.

'Fat chance it will be a "fun" weekend if we bloody lose,' I thought.

Despite being offered a ticket, Mum had passed on the chance to join us for our Wembley adventure, instead opting for a few days in the south of Spain with Peg. This was a decision I think they both regretted a few days letter as they rang us from the famous Old London Bar in Fuengirola – the only place they could find at short notice playing the match. Instead, my uncle Phil travelled down with us in Mum's place. Phil – Peg's younger brother, making him in fact my *great* uncle – was a pleasure to have with us. A City fan his entire life, he had frequented Boothferry Park since the early 1950s and, despite having moved to Wales by this point, still travelled across the country to support his beloved City. His stories, taken from 60 years on the terraces, kept Steph and I entertained for the entire three hours we spent on the A1, with one thing in particular he said on that journey staying with me to this day. Just before we arrived at our hotel for the night, and after hours of City-related tales – from Carter to Wagstaff, Whitehurst to Deano – Phil turned around and faced Steph and I from the front passenger seat.

'I'll tell you something, kid,' he said, 'City have given me some of the best memories of my life – being picked up and passed down over the crowd to the front of the terraces at Boothferry as a kid, to taking my own lads to their very first matches. But if City do manage to win tomorrow, I think it might well be the best day of my life. I've waited 60-odd years for this. It's time.'

I felt a chill run down my spine as Phil's voice cracked and his eyes welled up with tears. At this moment in time, he was perhaps the only person on the planet more desperate for a City win than me. Luckily, we weren't to be disappointed.

The next day – Saturday, 24 May 2008, play-off final day – we all woke early. Predictably, I hadn't been able to sleep well, with a combination of excitement and nerves keeping me up most of the night. It felt like some sort of twisted Christmas morning in which I had woken up all excited for the big day ahead, but at the very forefront of my mind being very conscious of the possibility that this day could end in misery. It was a bizarre feeling.

Somewhat ironically, the Premier Inn we stayed at was in Watford. Dad had purposely looked for places to stay outside of London to avoid the outrageously inflated prices of matchday room bookings, as well as somewhere we could easily leave the car for the day outside of the capital. Watford was ideal, with the only catch being we had a half-hour train journey into London. Our plan was to head somewhere touristy to grab some lunch and kill some time before heading off to Wembley for around one o'clock.

Wearing my replica Umbro home shirt from that season, as well as my lucky City scarf that Dad had bought me at my first match against Halifax seven years earlier, I felt sick as I climbed on to the train at Watford Junction. I don't remember too much about the early part of the day other than Phil heading off to Wembley early before lunch to meet up with his two boys and young grandkids, all of whom had travelled down on the day.

By midday, Dad, Steph and I were sick of killing time and desperate to get to the ground and soak up some of the atmosphere. We had a quick bite to eat at a pizzeria somewhere off Leicester Square and then got straight on the tube and headed to the national stadium.

The sight that greeted the three of us as we stepped off the Jubilee line and walked down the stairs out of Wembley Park tube station will remain etched into my mind forever. A sea of black and amber, and red and white, flooding down Olympic Way on a baking hot May afternoon. In the distance was Wembley Stadium itself, with its famous arch glittering in the glorious sunlight. It was a beautiful image.

For a fan of any team, domestic or international, the walk down Olympic Way (or Wembley Way, as it is better known) on a matchday is always a special one. There is a deep-rooted carnival atmosphere created by the curious combination of excitement, nerves and expectation of both sets of supporters. Touts trying to sell last-minute tickets at extortionate prices, the smell of beer, burgers and fried onions, and men selling awful half-and-half scarves out of bin liners – it may not be glamorous, but it's English football fandom in microcosm.

I was never old enough to visit the old Wembley and its iconic twin towers, and this was my first visit to the rebuilt stadium, but I strongly believe it is a pilgrimage all football fanatics should make at least once. The stadium gets a lot of negative press – its cost, the atmosphere generated inside, and even its aesthetic have all been questioned since it reopened in 2007 – but I don't have a bad word to say about it. I have been lucky enough to see my club play there on four occasions, and although I haven't always left happy with the final result, I have forever exited Wembley with a smile on my face, praying that this time City fans won't have to endure another 104-year wait before their next visit to the 'home of football'.

As we made our way towards the famous ramps leading up to the stadium, stopping at regular intervals to chat to fellow City fans we knew, the feeling of sickness in the pit of my stomach began to ease up and was replaced by pure excitement as the singing began. From the moment the sea of black and amber, and red and white, split perfectly as both sets of fans climbed their designated ramps, to the minute the three of us pushed ourselves through Wembley's futuristic turnstiles, the singing didn't stop. We reached our seats half an hour before kick-off and I remember the three of us falling silent as we stood and marvelled at the sight before us. Looking up from our lower-tier vantage point, the rows of seats appeared to go on forever. It was a football stadium like none I had ever visited before and I instantly fell in love with it. Just 15 minutes later there was barely an empty seat in the place. Quite by chance, the location of our seats almost exactly mirrored that of our seats at the KC – around ten rows back from the pitch and about ten metres to the right of the halfway line. Perfect.

With just ten minutes to go until kick-off, 'Can't Help Falling In Love' started playing over the speaker system and the KC's stadium announcer Steve Jordan was sent out to warm up the 40,000 City fans. Safe to say it worked an absolute treat. By the time Jordan's Bristol equivalent was sent out five minutes later, he could not be heard over the crescendo coming from the City half of Wembley Stadium.

'AND IT'S HULLLLLLLLL CITY. HULLLL CITY AFC, WE'RE BY FAAAR THE GREATEST TEAM THE WORLD HAS EVER SEEN!'

Then the moment we had all been waiting for. The conclusion to the most successful season in Hull City's 104-year history, the climax of a magical six months. Would it end on a high or a stomach-turning low? As the players marched out of the Wembley tunnel, City's 11 clad in brand-new club anthem jackets, Dad put his arms around me and Steph and said, 'Well, here we go. This is it!'

After a few minutes of pyrotechnics and handshakes, the jackets came off and the amber shirts took their positions on the pitch. We would be attacking the goal at the far end of the stadium first, meaning any City goal in the first period would be scored right in front of the travelling Bristol fans. Wearing his lucky suit and tan shoes, the last thing I remember seeing before kick-off was a nervous-looking Phil Brown giving some last-minute instructions to the bleached-blond Dean Windass. Seconds later, and with the noise coming from both halves of the stadium reaching new deafening heights, the game was finally underway.

Looking back at that wonderful afternoon as a City fan, it's easy to forget that it was Bristol City that started the game the stronger side. It's often forgotten that early chances for both Adebola and Carle could have spoilt the party for Tigers fans before it had even started. Instead they provided the wake-up call Brown's men needed, as City dominated the remainder of the first half.

Half-chances for Barmby, Turner and Garcia all had me, and 40,000 other City fans, on our feet and holding our heads in our hands. But on 38 minutes, City made the breakthrough.

Picture the scene: Nicky Barmby breaks from his own half, looking to set up a quick counter-attack. He finds Campbell who charges into the box, looking to get himself in a position to shoot. Pushed wide towards the touchline, the young United striker looks up and chips the ball perfectly to a waiting Dean Windass. As if pulling back the hammer on an old western revolver, Windass steadies himself, aligning his body flawlessly, before drawing back his right leg and ... BANG. Before the unstoppable volley even passes the helpless Basso in the Bristol goal and hits the back of the net, the 39-year-old is already wheeling away and storming towards the City end, arms aloft.

To this day, I maintain it is the best goal I have ever seen live. As it goes, I think it still must be up there with the best goals scored at the new Wembley.

Phil Brown ran to the edge of his technical area and punched the air, while the black and amber half of the stadium went crazy.

'What a goal! And it had to be Deano! You couldn't write it!' Dad yelled, as the chants of 'DEANO, DEANO, DEANO' rained down.

Dad was right, you really couldn't have written it any better. The home town boy, desperate to return to the club where it had all started, now helping City reach the top flight at the age of 39. Unbelievable.

For whatever reason, I can only remember the second half in highlight form, as the vast majority of it still remains a blur. The snippets I do remember, however, are as clear as day. I recall a David Noble free kick just minutes after the restart being held well by Myhill and a shot from Michael McIndoe hitting the shoulder of Wayne Brown, which was greeted with optimistic shouts of 'HANDBALL!' from the Bristol end. Though, the clearest Bristol chance, and arguably the best opportunity of the entire second half, came with just minutes to go. This I remember vividly. As if in slow motion, Myhill clawed at an awkward cross that subsequently dropped at the feet of Bristol's key man, Lee Trundle. My heart sank. I knew this was the moment Bristol were going to equalise. From six yards out, the striker controlled the ball on his considerable chest and volleyed towards goal. I braced myself waiting for the net to ripple. But it never came. Seemingly out of nowhere, Michael Turner threw himself forward, deflecting the goal-bound shot over the bar. The City end let out a collective sigh of relief. However, there was still time for Gary Johnson's men to spoil the party. When the fourth official produced a board indicating an additional three minutes of injury time, the sound of 40,000 desperate City fans whistling began.

'Nothing daft now City, come on, we can do it!' Dad bellowed, as Bristol poured forward for one last attack.

With the scoreboard showing 94 minutes played, Adebola's header was punched away by Myhill and the resulting Trundle cross was caught with ease by the grateful-looking Welsh international.

'That's it, surely!' Steph squealed. Wayne Brown agreed, jumping on to Myhill's back, slapping his shaved head in appreciation.

Ten seconds later and it was all over. Alan Wiley blew the final whistle and with it Hull City were in the Premier League.

Trying to accurately describe the feelings I had at this moment would be impossible. I doubt William Shakespeare or Charles Dickens could do it justice. Windass raced on to the pitch towards the City fans before slumping to his knees and sobbing with happiness into the turf. My emotions weren't too far behind. The deafening roar of the Tigers fans that had welcomed the final whistle collectively died down momentarily. In scenes that reminded me of my first promotion four years earlier, City supporters everywhere seemed to take a minute to allow what had just happened to sink in. Supporters that had never met before that day shook hands, hugged and danced together, while grown men – many of whom wouldn't look out of place as extras in a gritty, prison-based drama – cried their eyes out. Ten minutes later, as Ian Ashbee was presented with the play-off trophy in

Wembley's famous royal box, I bawled my eyes out. I had never felt this happy.

It's strange. Without a shadow of a doubt, I'm certain this one match will always represent the high point of my football-supporting life. Ask any other City fan there that day, of any age, and I am positive the vast majority will be of the same opinion. In hindsight, I could not have picked a better time in Hull City's 104-year history to start following the club. After my first visit to Boothferry Park in September 2001 the club had been on an *almost* constant upwards trajectory. Indeed, City had taken only five years to climb from the bottom of the old Division Three to the Premier League, the third fastest climb in English Football League history. How many other football fans can say they supported the same club throughout all four professional divisions in their first decade as a fan?

With Premier League football to follow, as well as FA Cup success and an unexpected stint in European football in the not too distant future, it almost sounds churlish to say that the best it got was a Championship play-off final. But this isn't what I'm saying. You see, there was far more momentous and unforgettable experiences still to come. But, for me, this was the final moment that I remember my support of my beloved Hull City being completely and totally untainted by certain unsavoury aspects of modern football. The 2008 promotion season, epitomised by Deano's goal at Wembley, was exactly what being a football fan is all about – raw, unadulterated passion, emotion and joy. I have not experienced a feeling even close to this since. Nostalgic bias may, of course, be playing a role in this assessment, yet somehow it wouldn't matter even if it were.

Saturday, 24 May 2008 – not only the greatest and most significant day in Hull City AFC's 104-year history, but also the irreproducible high point in my own story of football addiction.

2008–2014

The Seven-Year Itch

Premier League?
We're having a laugh

Hull City 2–1 Fulham – 16/08/2008

GROWING up, my summer holidays were all identical. Without real exception, they all went something like this:

- An exciting first three weeks away from school – watching World Cup or European Championship matches every other year.
- Two weeks away on holiday with my family, usually on the Costa del Sol.
- One or maybe two concluding weeks at home in which I would dread the inevitable start of yet another school year as it crept ever closer.

However, the summer of 2008 was different. It was different because Dad and I decided it had to be different. Hull City's first match in the Premier League – the start of a maiden season in the top flight for the Tigers – was to kick off at the KC on 16 August, and there was not a chance in hell we were going to miss it.

Despite what Mum says, it's a funny story. My parents had booked our flights to Spain in the February, ready for our annual family holiday in Mijas set for the first two weeks in August. In previous years this meant potentially missing the first Hull City game of the season, depending on how weekends fell that specific year – a particular bugbear of mine, and one that became progressively more obvious as I entered my moody teenage years. After our Wembley victory in May, however, I recall Dad gleefully pointing out that the Premier League season kicked off a week later than the Football League, meaning we would be home in time for City's historic first top-tier game. Imagine Dad's horror then when in the middle of June the fixtures were revealed and it was announced that City would play Fulham at the KC Stadium on 16 August – the day we were due to be travelling home from Spain. This couldn't be happening.

Before Mum could be made aware of the situation, Dad changed our flights at the last minute, telling my mum that our two-week holiday would now be happening a week earlier than first planned. He said he was expecting to be asked to attend a 'very important meeting' at the Department for Education at short notice, likely to take place in the second week in August. Mum begrudgingly agreed. Safe to say the meeting never happened, but come three o'clock on 16 August, Dad, Steph and I were sat in our seats at the KC, Viking fish and chips in hand. Mum was livid.

I'd be lying if I said I wasn't worried about City's prospects going into that season. After all, just months earlier our play-off winning predecessors, Derby County, had finished rock bottom of the Premier League with a record low 11 points and just one win from their 38 league fixtures. While I didn't think City could possibly be that bad, the national media were less convinced.

Brown strengthened his squad considerably, bringing in the likes of Bernard Mendy, Peter Halmosi, George Boateng, and former Barcelona and Manchester City midfielder Geovanni, to name but a few, yet City's preseason outings served only to offer additional unwanted cause for concern. Brown's men lost three and drew one of their final four preseason friendlies, with a crushing 4–0 defeat away at League One Crewe and a disappointing 1–0 loss at Tynecastle both providing numerous sleepless nights. I remember at this point thinking to myself that this was the time I should be enjoying most as a City fan. For the entire preseason period at least, Hull City AFC were a Premier League side currently level on points with the other 19 best clubs in the country. This was a bubble that could not possibly be burst until reality kicked in during the first league game of the season, right?

Wrong.

A Calvin Zola hat-trick at Gresty Road stuck a premature pin in that bubble. What was initially described as City's '*kind*' opening few Premier League fixtures, against Fulham, Blackburn, Wigan and Newcastle, were starting to look a whole lot more daunting, as reality set in early.

'I just hope we don't embarrass ourselves,' Dad said, as we sat in the glorious mid-August sunshine watching 32 Premier League footballers warm up on the KC turf for the first time. 'I still think preseason can be forgotten about, though. On our day we can take a few of these stuck-up, entitled teams by surprise, I reckon.'

'I think it's fair to say we'd take 17th now,' I responded wryly.

As it goes, we would go on to do exactly that.

In front of a near capacity crowd at the KC, City's inaugural top-tier starting XI boasted a satisfying mix of old regulars and new faces. Summer signings Anthony Gardner, Geovanni, Boateng and Marlon King (a late replacement loanee brought in to fill the gap left by the unattainable Fraizer Campbell) joined Ashbee, Barmby, Dawson and co to make Hull City history.

We started the game brilliantly, taking the game to our opponents and giving them an early scare when Geovanni's header forced a brilliant save from Schwarzer. The atmosphere was electric. Chorus after chorus of 'Can't Help Falling In Love' boomed around the packed stadium as our, quite frankly piss-poor, preseason was forgotten about.

Nevertheless, it wouldn't last. After just eight minutes the bouncing atmosphere would momentarily deflate when future City player (and panto villain) Jimmy Bullard crossed for Seol Ki-Hyeon to head past Myhill.

'Shit. Maybe it is going to be a long season after all. That was far too easy,' Dad murmured, defaulting to his customary pessimistic mode, as a worried KC Stadium fleetingly and collectively contemplated a long and painful season. For the next ten minutes or so it looked as though Roy Hodgson's men could run away with the match. Indeed, even I, at this point a shining light of optimism for all things City-related, was concerned.

Then, seemingly out of nowhere, Hull City announced themselves as a Premier League club. With 22 minutes on the clock, Geovanni latched on to a loose ball just inside Fulham's half, raced away from Zoltan Gera, and curled a spectacular left-footed shot into the bottom corner. I remember thinking how City fans couldn't have asked for a better goal to launch the club's Premier League offensive, yet in hindsight this was in fact one of Geovanni's more modest goals that season. Fulham looked shell-shocked. At this point, I like to imagine a room full of national sport hacks tearing up their naturally presumptuous half-written, 'relegation-bound Hull City' headlined, match reports in disbelief. It was 1–1 and very much back in the balance. Maybe Hull City wouldn't be the worst team in Premier League history after all.

The goal not only drew us level but injected both the players and the crowd with a much-needed boost, proving we could compete in this division, as the remainder of the first half saw the Tigers look a much better side.

It soon became obvious to the 24,500 people at the KC that day that if Hull City were to have any chance of avoiding relegation, the little Brazilian Geovanni would play a huge role. When he was on his game he was simply a class above, and he was unquestionably at the races on his competitive debut for City.

The second half began very much in the same manner as the first. Fulham came out of the blocks raging, with Gera and Bullard both missing decent opportunities to put the visitors back in front. Yet slowly but surely Brown's men found their feet again. Chances for Turner and Geovanni came and went as the clock began to wind down. But this match was never going to end a stalemate.

In the end it was a defensive cock-up that handed City their opening Premier League win at the first time of asking. Future Liverpool full-back Paul Konchesky was caught in possession in his own box and somehow managed to fall over his own feet before substitute Craig Fagan robbed him of the ball. Fagan squared to Folan who tapped in the winner with less than ten minutes remaining.

As the final whistle sounded, the KC erupted. After a wait of 104 years, Hull City had won their first ever top-flight fixture. A strange feeling of relief, not the usual one of joy I felt after a City win, instantly washed over me. Indeed, after the initial celebrations had ended and the stadium began to empty, the atmosphere momentarily changed. It was a victory celebration like no other I had experienced at a City match before. The collective feeling of ecstasy that came with winning our first Premier League game was briefly, but curiously, combined with an air of caution. For just a few moments as Dad, Steph and I made our way towards the exit, it almost felt as though we had no right to be celebrating in this fashion – as though us Premier League new boys should be showing more respect to an established club like Fulham. But this uncomfortable atmosphere was not to last. As the three of us walked back down Anlaby Road towards Dad's car, parked near the half-demolished Boothferry, reality hit.

'I've just thought,' Dad said, turning to Steph and I with a little smile spreading across his face. 'We made up more than a quarter of Derby's entire points tally for last season with just one win today. "The worst team in Premier League history" my arse!' he roared.

Steph and I grinned.

'I told you we'd win today,' I replied. 'Easy this Premier League lark, isn't it!'

All of a sudden, the club now had the feel of being a dangerous unknown quantity and the fans were determined to enjoy every second. Relegation was of course still on the cards at this point as we entered uncharted territory. Hell, the possibility of a lower points tally than Derby was also still very much on the table. However, this vital first Premier League victory provided the belief that City could, and *would*, at least compete.

In his post-match interview, Phil Brown once again stressed Hull City were not in the Premier League just to make up the numbers. Prior to this season opener the national press could barely hide their amusement when confronted with this brand of Phil Brown optimism. Now, momentarily at least, Brown had silenced the patronising clan of hyenas.

That night I turned on BBC One to watch *Match of the Day*. Of course, as a football addict, this programme had been a staple of my Saturday night schedule for years and remains so to this very day. Yet, this episode would be special. It would be the first in my lifetime to feature full highlights of a Hull City league game. And a Hull City Premier League win at that! I was giddy with excitement and was not disappointed. After a slot relatively early in the running order and fair praise from Gary Lineker and his accompanying two pundits, I was overjoyed. But, it will be the final few seconds of the broadcast that will always remain etched into my memory. Looking directly into the camera and broadcasting to an estimated 3.7 million viewers, Lineker uttered the immortal line:

'Hull City: the only side in the history of the Premier League with a 100 per cent record. Goodnight.'

Halifax Town at Boothferry in Division Three suddenly felt a very long time ago.

London 0 Hull 4

Arsenal 1–2 Hull City – 27/09/2008
Tottenham Hotspur 0–1 Hull City – 05/10/2008

DURING the first few months of the 08/09 season everything changed. Hull City, the most unfancied team in Premier League history, started winning games. Not only were we upsetting the odds and competing at the top end of the so-called *best* league in the world, we were also playing some of the best football I have seen a City side play.

Phil Brown's men went on to win six of their opening nine league games, astoundingly going joint top of the Premier League table at the end of October. On top of solid away victories against the likes of Newcastle United and West Brom, before the end of November City had also recorded famous wins against Arsenal, Spurs and West Ham which, when added to the Fulham victory, combined to generate a dream headline for the tabloids. *London 0 Hull 4* was splashed across every national newspaper by Halloween, in homage, of course, to the 1986 classic Housemartins album. It's said that the band's frontman Paul Heaton was referring to his assertion that Hull had four great bands at the time, compared to none from London. For this very short space of time City fans could also claim their home town was superior on the football pitch, as well as in the indie charts.

Naturally, the media – so quick to write us off as relegation fodder before the season had even began – now started labelling us as one of the most successful promoted clubs in Premier League history. They were linking our players with January moves to top European clubs, and suggesting September 2008's Premier League Manager of the Month, Phil Brown, could be the next big thing in English coaching. Of course, this wouldn't continue, once again highlighting the fickle nature of the British football media. Nonetheless, the Tiger Nation was determined to enjoy every second while it lasted.

As summer transitioned into autumn and I began to struggle at school once again as the first of two GCSE years commenced, City's remarkable form provided a welcome distraction. My obsession with football, and City specifically, acted more and more as a much-required sort of escapism. Indeed, the autumn of 2008 would prove one of the most challenging periods of my upbringing in terms of my school life, but this was offset by the most surreal few months to be a fan of Hull City.

Up until this point I had enjoyed my time at high school. During my first three years I had progressed beyond all belief academically and had completely caught up with my classmates in practically every subject. English and Maths were still providing my toughest challenges, yet I was more than sufficiently coping with the workload as I happily chose my GCSE options during the first half of 2008. My almost constant sporting schedule, which by this time consisted of rugby and football training four out of five weeknights and competitive matches on Saturday and Sunday, was also keeping me extremely busy. It was a non-stop three years, but an enjoyable period of my adolescence. Though, things were to change when I started year 10 in September 2008. As it had when I had started a new school in 2002, my confidence started slipping once again. The step-up to GCSE-level classes, and the increased workload in every subject that came with it, hit me like a brick wall. For the first time in years, school was making me miserable again.

As an adult it's difficult to recall just how unhappy and depressed some aspects of school life could make you. Once you have a full-time job, rent and electric bills to pay, many people often say they would kill to relive their school days, but not me – there is too big a risk I would have to relive my GCSE years. Between September 2008 and May 2010 I woke up every morning dreading the thought of catching the bus and heading to school.

I had chosen my ten GCSE subjects carefully and I thrived in about half of them, but the other half saw me struggle badly. By the first half-term of the year in October, I remember sitting down with both Mum and Dad and trying to express just how certain I was about my ever-strengthening feeling that I was going to flunk these subjects. The all-too-familiar sensation of being a phoney soon returned and I once again felt cripplingly anxious about my academic abilities.

Business Studies, History, PE and Resistant Materials were all subjects I had specifically chosen and felt as though I had a vested interest in. I enjoyed most of these classes and my solid to good grades throughout the next two years reflected this.

Maths, Physics, Chemistry and Spanish, on the other hand, had all been compulsory subjects, and I loathed them all for different reasons. Maths and Chemistry were those subjects I was always told I just needed to 'learn, not necessarily understand', as I had no realistic prospect of continuing either subject at a higher level after my GCSEs. This was a concept I always thought sounded good and reassuring, but in practice doesn't exactly help too much. The penny eventually dropped with both of these classes prior to my exams in the summer of 2010, but I struggled severely for much of the two years.

I enjoyed both English Literature and English Language at this time; it was just that my slow reading pace and terrible spelling and grammar made for poor grades initially. Like Maths and Chemistry, I would eventually go on to achieve decent grades in both of my English examinations, particularly after my eventual dyslexia diagnosis in early 2010, yet I struggled to keep up with my classmates for much of my two-year course.

It was Spanish and Physics I hated the most. This was not because I was particularly terrible at either, but because I didn't get on with the subjects' respective teachers. One of my most unpleasant school memories comes from my Spanish mock oral exam in January 2010. I had to prepare a ten-minute Spanish presentation on anything I wanted, and obviously I chose the life and times of Geovanni. After the presentation I then had to answer ten Geovanni-related questions posed by my teacher, who incidentally was perhaps the only human being on the face of the planet capable of speaking fluent Spanish with a gloriously broad Hull accent.

As I left the exam, fully aware it hadn't gone well, the teacher called me over and said, 'Bloody hell, Whitaker, asking you to speak Spanish is like trying to get blood out of a stone!'

Safe to say this is not something a 16-year-old lad just three months away from the biggest set of exams of his life so far needs to hear.

Don't get me wrong, I was to go on to love sixth form where I would study four personally chosen subjects in which I knew I could prosper. Yet I was in for two frustrating school years before I could enjoy such academic liberation. Indeed, the autumn of 2008 represented the start of a fairly miserable couple of years for me personally. All I could do was get my head down, continue to enjoy my sport both in and out of school, and, most importantly of all, release any pent-up frustration going to the football. With Phil Brown's gonzo City side riding unfathomably high in the Premier League – something I never thought I would see, even in my wildest dreams – I couldn't have chosen a better period to rely on my oldest vice and obsession to cheer me up.

It's almost impossible to choose the one most influential match from this period that best sums it up. Most City fans would opt for that unbelievable Saturday evening at the Emirates, I'm sure. Arsenal 1–2 Hull City. The fantastic last-ditch Andy Dawson tackle on Walcott. *That* sensational goal by Geovanni. And Daniel Cousin's headed winner. Truly a classic match in Hull City's modern history. However, I can't choose this match exclusively. It's one of only a handful of games that season I couldn't attend. To my absolute horror, just a few weeks before the match, I had discovered I was due in North Yorkshire for a school rugby fixture I couldn't get out of, meaning I had no chance of getting down to London in time for the late evening kick-off. Unsurprisingly, I was gutted. I was, of course, even more heartbroken after the match, knowing I'd missed one of *the* great City moments. Luckily I was to experience a repeat display at White Hart Lane a week later, but at the time feeling as though I had missed perhaps the best City result of all time made me feel physically sick.

Despite not travelling to Arsenal, I do now have positive memories of watching this game. The match was being broadcast live on the ill-fated Setanta Sports, which meant I could at least watch the entirety of the game and not be restricted exclusively to the *Match of the Day* highlight package. This was clearly a bonus, but on its own was not enough to improve my mood after being forced to miss a key away game. Naturally though, as soon as the game started I perked up.

As the game kicked off, I remember Dad muting the TV and instead putting on KCFM's commentary of the game to accompany the Setanta broadcast.

'It's bad enough we can't be there,' Dad said, 'I'm not going to listen to those patronising, Arsenal-loving stooges drone on!'

It turned out to be a great decision. The genuine passion and ultimate delight of local radio pundit Alex Burgess painted a picture of the game that Setanta's rent-a-former-pro couldn't have possibly matched. Indeed, as Cousin rose above Arsenal's static defence to head home the winner, it sounded as though Burgess was struggling to hold back the tears. Weren't we all?

As the final whistle went, I remember thinking it could not possibly get any better than this. City were not only in the Premier League, but beating Arsene Wenger's mighty Arsenal on their own patch. Yet, the evening had one final twist. Minutes after the full-time whistle had sounded and while the whole family were still dancing around the lounge, Steph suddenly turned the radio volume as loud as our small stereo would allow and ordered us all to be quiet. Her beloved Ian Ashbee, City's Captain Marvel, was about to be interviewed. This was a common occurrence in our household whenever the City captain appeared anywhere near a TV camera or radio mic. It was as though Steph had a sixth sense for it. What she didn't know, however, was that on this occasion the topic of conversation would quickly (and surreally) progress from the most famous win of Ashbee's career so far to 'a certain young lady's' apparent infatuation for the City stalwart.

Steph and her mates had got talking to Alex Burgess in a local pub a few weeks before the Arsenal game. Looking for an expert's analysis, the lads Steph was out with soon began to discuss City's chances that season with the ITK Burgess. Evidently before long Steph got involved, eager to put across her view that Ian Ashbee is, and always will be, the greatest Hull City player of all time. The conversation stuck with Burgess who, to our absolute amazement, gave Steph a live shout-out mid-interview.

'Some people thought I wasn't good enough for the old Third Division,' Ashbee began when asked about his role in the side. 'I know I'm not an eight or nine out of ten every week, but the manager has faith in me and knows I can do a job, and I think I'm doing that job at the minute,' he added in his broad Brummie accent.

'Well, I was speaking to one particular young lady who certainly has faith in your ability; I think she's your biggest fan ...,' replied Burgess, who was cut off mid-sentence.

'Have a bit of a soft spot for me, did she? Well, she's not made of wood, is she?' Ashbee chuckled.

'Ha ha, she'll be absolutely delighted after tonight's result – her name is Steph – can you make her evening and say hello?'

'Of course! 'allo Steph! Where are ya?' Ashbee roared down the microphone.

Indeed, I don't think I've ever seen Steph happier. She wrote to KCFM the next day to request a recording of the interview. They obliged, sending a CD recording of the full match commentary, post-match interviews and the following fan's phone-in. I'm pretty sure Steph still has that CD, although, I'm not too sure her husband, Mike – coincidentally enough, an Arsenal fan – allows it to be played too often.

I speak from first-hand experience when I say, it's hard to see something like this happening in the now almost-clinical environment of a post-match Premier League press conference these days. All managers and players are media-trained within an inch of their lives and, in the top few divisions in England at least, have seen their level of visible personality, character and fan engagement shackled by press officers and in-house PR machines – a perfect example of the sanitisation that has swept through modern football over the past few decades. This was a lovely *human* moment from a City legend and a man who had represented a hero figure for both Steph and I for half a decade.

Depressingly enough, it was also probably the last example of the old, fan-centric image of football fandom Hull City had created during my early years following them. The next few years, perhaps even months, saw the club 'modernise' and 'commercialise' in an attempt to keep up with the Premier League behemoths. Sadly, somewhere along the line the family atmosphere that had kept the club going through some of its darkest days appeared to be lost in the process. But more of that later.

Just over a week after City's best result of the season so far, we were travelling back to north London to face an underperforming Spurs side languishing at the wrong end of the table. Driving down the A1, I vividly recall feeling a twinge of guilt knowing I had had to pull out of that morning's Sunday league fixture in order to make the trip, but after missing one contender for game of the season eight days earlier, there was no chance I was missing this away day.

The match was unusually scheduled for Sunday afternoon, meaning we had to set off early to ensure we would arrive at White Hart Lane with plenty of time before the early afternoon kick-off. I was unsurprisingly excited to finally see City face one of the Premier League's 'big boys' in the flesh, yet for some reason I was not feeling particularly hopeful that we would see a repeat of the previous weekend's performance. Despite City going into the game sitting quite miraculously in third place in the Premier League table, while a free-falling Spurs side were residing in the relegation zone, I had a bad feeling. I was conscious that the bubble was going to burst at some point and, as Dad reminded us on countless occasions during our journey down to the capital, wouldn't it just be sod's law if Spurs loanee Fraizer Campbell was the man to put an end to City's purple patch. As it turned out, I was worrying over nothing.

The journey was an easy one and after parking the car somewhere in Hertfordshire – I forget where exactly; many of these journeys to London away days have merged into one – we got the train into central London and then the London Overground to White Hart Lane. With around 30 minutes to go until kick-off, we wandered around north London in earnest looking for a cafe or chippy to grab some food. To our great surprise and disappointment, every single cafe, greasy spoon, chippy and takeaway on our walk towards the ground was shut. It was Sunday lunchtime, yes, but with 30,000 hungry football fans heading to the match we were amazed.

'A meat pie it is then!' Dad said, rubbing his hands together as we reached the ground.

White Hart Lane wasn't at all what I expected. It was not only much smaller than I had imagined it, with all four stands very compact and beginning just metres away from the pitch, but also the stadium's surroundings were far more urban than I had anticipated. As a kid, thinking of football teams located in London, you assume Big Ben, the London Eye or Tower Bridge are all just a stone's throw away from each stadium. Of course, when you start visiting these grounds, you quickly learn London is in fact quite a large place.

Nevertheless, like all my favourite football grounds, White Hart Lane had a real sense of history and prestige, while at the same time also owning an air of being just about modern enough to not appear shabby or run down. As we climbed the stairs to our seats in the upper tier of the South Stand, two iconic features of the old ground immediately caught my eye. Firstly, the famous THFC club emblem and bronze cockerel sitting proudly on the roof of the East Stand – features I had seen all too often on *Match of the*

Day and Sky Sports. The second sight, and rather less poignantly, was the bizarre police control box, which best resembled a UFO from a corny 1980s film set, which was suspended right in the eye line of the travelling fans on the roof of the South West corner.

However, after our prolonged search for sustenance outside the ground, and a subsequent ten minutes stood in line for a pie in the away end concourse, we didn't have long to take in our surroundings before the match got under way.

The game started as a very open affair with decent chances at both ends of the pitch. Gareth Bale had the first opportunity of the game with a headed chance right in front of the 3,000-strong travelling support, but City quickly responded with George Boateng and Geovanni both going close at the other end. It took less than ten minutes for City to grab the only goal of the match, and what a goal it was. If Dean Windass's Wembley winner is the best goal I've ever witnessed live, this goal runs it incredibly close.

I remember the entire incident so clearly. Marlon King won a free kick 35 yards out, which from our vantage point directly behind the ball appeared much closer to the halfway line than to Heurelho Gomes's goal. As Turner and Zayatte pushed up, Geovanni and Dawson stood over the ball. Somehow, despite having no real right to be having a shot from that kind of distance, each one of the 3,000 City fans knew exactly what Geovanni had in mind.

Taking a short run-up, the little Brazilian whipped the ball with his wand of a right foot, sending it curling into the top corner. As it turned out, the travelling City faithful in the upper tier of the South Stand had the best view in the entire stadium of this incredible strike. It was a truly spectacular goal and to this day one of the Premier League's finest ever free kicks. The away end exploded as Geovanni raced away to the dugout to celebrate with his manager. He had done it again, and for the second time in as many weeks City fans were planning a party in north London.

Much of the remainder of the game remains a bit of a blur to me. I remember Bale trying to emulate Geovanni's free kick which forced Myhill into an excellent fingertip save midway through the first half, as well as former Spurs man Dean Marney hitting the post, nearly putting City two up just before the interval. Despite witnessing an equally famous City victory a week earlier, I couldn't believe my eyes as the match approached half-time. The last week had felt like a dream. Indeed, in one of the more surreal moments of my football-supporting life, as the City players jogged off the pitch at half-time they were greeted with chants of 'We're gonna win the League!' from high up in the rafters of White Hart Lane. Incredible.

Of course, there were still another 45 minutes for Spurs to get themselves back into the game, and they predictably came charging out of the blocks in the second period. Chances for Bent and Campbell both came and went without City touching much of the ball. Nonetheless, City's new centre-back partnership of Michael Turner and Kamil Zayatte stood strong, kicking, heading and generally just getting in the path of every meaningful attack Spurs could muster. Geovanni may have scored the remarkable winning goal, but any man of the match award must surely have gone to Turner.

City offered little going forward in the second half, but as I remember it we didn't need to. As 'City 'til I Die' rained down from the South Stand, the rest of the stadium was becoming impatient. Boos from the home support rang out with 75 minutes on the clock when Aaron Lennon, by far Tottenham's biggest threat throughout the entire game, was replaced by Giovani dos Santos.

'Strange one, that,' Dad reacted, 'I think we're going to see this out – they've resorted to bringing on a cheap imitation of our Geo!'

Notwithstanding an injury-time scare, when Bale put a free kick just inches wide of Myhill's unspoilt goal, Dad was right and City did hold out for yet another famous north London victory. From eight days in which most City fans would have accepted simply not being embarrassed by two Premier League stalwarts, little old Hull City had gone and won six vital points, and they had done so with two very different performances. The first, an

attack-based fightback to shock a genuine title contender; the
second, a mightily impressive defensive display after going ahead
early. This week was to represent the high point of City's first spell
in the Premier League, but what a high point it was.

As we left the old ground and headed for White Hart Lane
station in a sea of bouncing black and amber, the party began.

'DON'T WANNA GO HOME, DON'T WANNA GO
HOOOOOOME. THIS IS THE BEST TRIP I'VE EVER BEEN
ON!'

By the time we got to the station and City fans finally began
to disperse, an unfortunate group of Tottenham supporters who
had been caught up in the celebrations finally emerged. As we
entered the station and looked for our platform, I will never forget
the immortal line angrily whispered by one particularly annoyed
Londoner.

'Hull facking City fans singing and dancing darn the facking
street? Do me a facking fava!'

The three of us stood in silence as we waited for our train to
arrive, all contemplating what had just happened. In the space of
eight days Hull 'fucking' City – who just six years earlier could
be found propping up the bottom of the fourth tier of English
football – had beaten both Arsenal and Tottenham Hotspur
away from home to go third in the Premier League. What a
preposterous concept. Indeed, when City's inaugural spell in the
Premier League is discussed in hindsight and compared with
other seasons from this period, the phrase that often crops up is
something along the lines of 'the journey was far better than the
destination'. I couldn't agree more, it absolutely was. However, for
these first few months of the 2008/09 season, City's journey felt
as though it may just continue a little while longer.

Almost heaven, Barcelona

Barcelona 2–0 Manchester United – 27/09/2009

WHEN I was a kid I had a Marks and Spencer's VHS tape imaginatively entitled *A History of Football*. As far as I can remember, I was given it as a Christmas present when I was about eight years old. Throughout my childhood I would sit and watch this video over and over again, soaking in the old grainy footage, desperate to learn as much as possible about the beautiful game. Thinking back, the only reason I stopped watching it was because by 2010 we no longer owned a VHS player. Anyway, as I would sit and watch as presenter and football commentator Alan Green chronologically narrated the history of football, telling the stories of all the best teams to ever play the game and describing the supreme talents of each of football's greatest players, I often wondered what team and which individuals would be next. Who would be the Brazil 1970 or the Manchester United 1999 side of my generation? Which team would next change the way in which football is played forever, à la Cruyff's Ajax or Sacchi's Milan? And which individual would step up to the plate and be remembered as one of the greatest, up there with the likes of Pelé, Di Stéfano and Maradona?

Initially, as I began to take an interest in world football, I was convinced the first incarnation of Real Madrid's Galacticos would be *that* team. They would be the first team of the 21st century that would go down in history as the side that changed the face of football for my generation. Indeed, I even had my pick from a choice of several spectacular Madrid players who could go on to be the next Pelé. However, for one reason or another, this theory never panned out. Yes, it goes without saying that Zidane, Figo, Raul and Ronaldo will all go down in history as some of the most talented players of their generation and, yes, Real Madrid did enjoy a certain amount of success during this period. But, in 2009 I witnessed the rise of a football team that would go on to eclipse the Galacticos and change football forever, alongside a player that is now considered one of the greatest of all time. After a defensively driven period of football, signified by the successes of Greece at Euro 2004 and Italy at World Cup 2006, Pep Guardiola's Barcelona side, built around the supremely talented young Argentinian Lionel Messi, was about to cause a revolution in world football. This was the side I had been waiting for. This was the best football team of my generation.

If Hull City provided a permanent home for my football obsession, and the 2003 vintage of Real Madrid had demonstrated that football could be an art form and not just a sport, then Pep Guardiola's Barcelona side of 2008 to 2012 illustrated how the game can also be an academic subject – something to be studied, perfected and then mastered. As a (some would argue pretentious) 15-year-old football addict, witnessing the rise of this school of thought, and the incredible Barcelona success that followed, was an absolute pleasure. Indeed, I would go as far as saying that the emergence of this great team genuinely impacted my entire life.

All teenagers go through different trend-driven, and typically embarrassing, phases during their high school years. Most of my generation chose between an awkward emo phase, an obnoxious jock stage, or an annoyingly ostentatious arty phase. I didn't fit into any of these subgroups. I enjoyed my music, but not to the point where I would let it dictate how I would dress or what I would do with my hair. Similarly, although I loved my sport, as a fan of football in a school dominated by rugby I was never going to be a jock, and I wasn't clever enough to fit into the arty scene.

Instead, influenced by the emergence of Guardiola, combined with my already existing view that my encyclopaedic knowledge of football made me the chief football aficionado at school, during my GCSE years I invented my own subculture and went through a phase of my own – the pretentious 'student of football' academic stage. Some would say I never got over this phase.

It's not difficult to understand why a young football fanatic was so influenced by Pep's Barca. The style of football was like nothing the professional game had ever witnessed before. Although Hull City were in the Premier League at this point – meaning instead of being subjected to the stereotypes of lower-league football each week, I was seeing the likes of Cristiano Ronaldo, Wayne Rooney, Frank Lampard and Steven Gerrard live in the flesh on a weekly basis – Barcelona were something else during this period.

Guardiola's style of play, referred to as 'tiki-taka' to his great annoyance, is built upon a team's ability to maintain possession, work the ball through specific channels, and short, quick pass and move tactical manoeuvres. As the former Spain international famously said, '[in football] there is only one secret: I've got the ball or I haven't. Barcelona have opted for having the ball ... And when we haven't got the ball ... we have to get it back.'

Naturally, this blew my mind. I needed to know more about it. After literally months of research, ironically enough taking up time I should have spent learning my GCSE Spanish vocab, I absorbed all the information I could find about the history of Barcelona and specifically the developments and influence of the Johan Cruyff era of management.

While Barcelona began to dominate club football during this period, the Spanish national side also benefited from this style of play and would go on to win three successive international tournaments between 2008 and 2012 – the first team in history to achieve this feat.

However, the relentless march of progress in football cannot be halted, and tiki-taka is not immune from this. Today, the age of tiki-taka is coming to an end, with different styles of play such as the gegenpress favoured by Jürgen Klopp, Sarri-ball introduced by its namesake Maurizio Sarri, and even a resurgence of the Italian catenaccio style, preferred by former Juventus and Chelsea manager Antonio Conte, all becoming more prominent. But while football has moved on, Guardiola's Barcelona sides of 2008–2012 have already secured their place in history as some of the greatest football teams of all time. After winning two Champions League titles during this period – 2009 and 2011 – with two marginally different manifestations of Guardiola's project, there will always be debates over which side was better. For me, this is a futile argument and one this book will never be able to settle. Both incarnations represent different stages of Guardiola's and Barcelona's development and both hold their individual merits. When I think of tiki-taka and Guardiola's Barcelona, however, I will always reflect on the early days and specifically Pep's first treble-winning season at the helm. One game naturally stands out for me ahead of any other – a game that significantly influenced how I will view football forever.

The occasion was the final of the 2008/09 Champions League. The stage was the Stadio Olimpico in Rome. Guardiola's Barcelona, the freshly crowned champions of Spain, were looking to complete a famous treble. Valdes, Puyol, Yaya Toure, Pique, Sylvinho, Xavi, Busquets, Iniesta, Messi, Eto'o, Henry – each and every one of these players is now considered a legend, true greats of the game. Yet, as a team, they hadn't announced themselves on the world stage just yet. Standing in their way were the reigning champions of Europe, Manchester United. This was a final for the purists – Guardiola v Ferguson, new v old, Spain v England, tiki-taka v the hairdryer.

Although not always considered a vintage Barcelona performance per se, watching this match with my United-supporting mate Tom was the first time I sat up and noticed what was going on at the Camp Nou. This was a Barca side still climbing to reach their remarkable peak – which is likely best represented by their 2011 incarnation and the height of tiki-taka – yet even at this stage in their development Pep's men were able to dominate one of the finest, Ronaldo-inspired, Manchester United sides of the past few decades. It was almost frightening to watch.

United started the better of the two teams on the night, with Cristiano Ronaldo dominating all aspects of the match in the opening few minutes, highlighting some early nerves from the Catalan side. But it didn't last long. Samuel Eto'o's goal on ten minutes settled Barca and set the precedent for the remainder of the match. From this moment on, the imperious midfield duo of Iniesta and Xavi controlled the game, starving United of possession and frustrating Messrs Rooney, Scholes, Ronaldo and Giggs. This was tiki-taka executed to perfection.

'I've never seen another team so easily keep the ball away from United,' Tom complained, as the chants of 'Olé!' began to rain down from the Barca end midway through the second half.

He wasn't wrong. A side that looked as though it was still only operating in third gear was outclassing United. As we watched, I remember thinking to myself just how incomprehensibly big the gulfs in quality at the very top end of professional football really are. Just three days earlier, I had sat at the KC Stadium, biting my nails to the knuckle, as what can only be described as a Manchester United reserve XI beat Hull City 1–0 courtesy of a Darren Gibson screamer. After an astonishingly bad second half of our maiden season in the Premier League, City had only just survived relegation by the skin of our teeth, thanks to results elsewhere on the final day. If you can't recall this game, just think Phil Brown singing 'Sloop John B' by The Beach Boys on the KC pitch after the final whistle – an image you can never unsee.

'If your reserves can beat City's strongest team 1–0, and now your strongest XI are being given the runaround by Barcelona, just think what Barca would do to my poor old Hull City,' I responded thoughtfully.

But Tom didn't have time to answer. Just seconds after I finished talking, Xavi almost doubled the Catalan's lead with a 20-yard free kick. United were spared on this occasion, as the midfielder's curling effort rebounded off the post, yet this was to prove a short period of respite. With 20 minutes remaining,

Proof that I was not always a sceptic of modern football. Here I am in 1996, a walking advert for the Premiership.

The match that started it all: Germany 1–5 England. Note Hull-born Nick Barmby in the starting line-up (bottom left).

'Fer Ark' as I remember it. The spiritual home of Hull City AFC.

The original and best: Brazilian Ronaldo, here, moments before he received a rare standing ovation from the Old Trafford faithful, April 2003.

Sliding doors: England players look on during their Euro 2004 quarter-final, as Darius Vassell steps up for his crucial penalty. He would go on to see his effort saved.
If the 'golden generation' was to win a tournament, Euro 2004 surely represented their best opportunity.

Block E5, Seat 151: Dad and I sat in our long-lasting East Stand seats during a home fixture against Luton Town in 2005. We truly did make some friends for life during our 15-year stint in E5.

Back to back: City, led by captain fantastic Ian Ashbee, celebrate a second promotion in two years and a return to the second tier of English football. Pound for pound my all-time favourite Tigers team.

The red mist descends as Rooney is dismissed in Germany, 2006.

Daring to dream: Ian Ashbee scores an iconic header at Oakwell, as City gun for the Premier League.

Steph and I stood in the ageing away end at Ipswich Town's Portman Road, May 2008. A defeat would consign City to the play-offs, but we didn't mind a bit.

Ninety minutes from the promised land: soaking up the atmosphere before the biggest match in Hull City's 104-year history.

Just a fat lad from 'ull: No one alive can tell me a better goal has been scored at the new Wembley. Take a bow, Deano.

Hullo Premier League: Dad, Steph and I, along with Phil and his two sons Luke and Oliver, sat in our usual seats during City's historic first ever top-tier fixture against Fulham, August 2008.

Geovanni celebrates scoring one of the great Premier League goals, as little old Hull City stun the mighty Arsenal.

The greatest of all time? Guardiola and his Barca side celebrate their 2009 Champions League triumph.

(*Top, left*) *Celebrating a fourth promotion in ten years on the hallowed KC turf. Even by 2013, I was still fanboying Nicky Barmby.*

(*Top, right*) *Dad and I enjoy a drink outside Wembley before City's chaotic FA Cup semi-final against Sheffield United. Note the brand-new 'City Til We Die' scarf.*

(*Right*) *The closest I'll ever come to lifting the FA Cup: On press conference for* **SHOOT!** *just days before City's 2014 Cup Final.*

Ecstasy: Curtis Davies celebrates after putting City 2–0 up in the Cup Final. It wasn't to be in the end, but what a day.

The Greatest: A weary Steve Bruce lifts the winners' trophy after gaining promotion back to the Premier League in 2016. His final game in charge.

A breath of fresh air: Southgate's England and their 2018 World Cup display rejuvenated a nation of apathetic fans.

man of the match Xavi crossed for Messi, the shortest player on the pitch, who rose up and headed home a stunning second for Barca, after finding himself in acres of space in the United box.

'It's 2–0! It's Messi! He's scored against an English club now!' Martin Tyler boomed, as Messi wheeled away.

And with that, the game was won.

Ferguson had warned his side prior to the match that Iniesta and Xavi had the ability to put United's midfield 'on a carousel' with their ability to maintain possession and their passing skills, not to mention the mercurial talent of Messi, and a combination of the two threats was precisely what cost his side the final. Not only had Barcelona won a famous treble to welcome in the brave new era of tiki-taka, but Messi had landed the first blow in the decade-long subplot that would develop between himself and Cristiano Ronaldo. This passive aggressive rivalry would soon become tedious in the years that followed as the commercialisation of football, and its most marketable individuals, rapidly increased thanks to social media, but at the time it seemed new and exciting. Indeed, in an era of club football dominated by these two individuals, I have watched every Champions League final since, but I struggle to think of one which inspired me more than that of 2009.

Indeed, it's true to say that in many ways 2009 represents somewhat of a tipping point for me. It arguably signifies the peak of my love for football. A cocktail of technical advancements, changes in how fans consume football and a shift in the balance of power in favour of the players, rather than the clubs (or, God forbid, the fans), among other things, would gradually start to chip away at my love of the sport over the coming years.

However, as I watched Carles Puyol lift the famous old European Cup, I was blissfully unaware of what was to come. As far as I was concerned, my love and obsession for football was to continue to develop indefinitely. Besides, after nearly a decade of fandom, I was still desperate to learn all I could about the beautiful game. I was still fanatically researching the history of the game in more detail than ever before, as well as consuming as much live football as was physically possible. As Real Madrid had in 2003, Pep's Barcelona took my obsession to yet another level – one that saw my most loved hobby become an academic subject that I was determined to master. The transformation from modest hobby to something that more closely resembled a religion, or a philosophy to live my life by, was nearing completion. Yet, as my fixation, and maybe even dependence, would continue to grow, my *love* for the game was about to encounter the first stages of apathy, frustration and disenchantment. With Pep Guardiola's phenomenal Barcelona side at the vanguard, modern football as we know it today was beginning to take shape, and with it football fandom was changing forever.

Modern football is rubbish

Hull City 1–4 Burnley – 10/04/2010

I have a theory that you can accurately date when a football club completed its transition into what we now know as modern football simply by looking at past shirt sponsors. It works for pretty much every football team in England. The Manchester Uniteds and Liverpools of this world were the first to make this transition, securing sponsorship deals with huge international conglomerates such as *Sharp*, *Candy* and *Carlsberg* as early as the late 1980s and early 90s, paving the way for a new era of modern football.

Naturally, modernisation was a longer process for smaller clubs and one that can be impeccably documented by the brands advertised on their playing strips. Think about it – as a Manchester United side with *Sharp* blazoned across their players' chests went on to win five Premier League titles, a handful of FA Cups and a European Cup in the 1990s, for much of this decade, fellow top-flight sides West Ham and Newcastle were still sponsored by local firms *Dagenham Motors* and *Newcastle Brown Ale* respectively. However, the 2000s saw this process of commercialisation universally embraced in the top echelons of English football, and by the end of the noughties gone were the days of *Sanderson, Draper Tools* and *Fisons* splashed across Premier League shirts, replaced instead by the likes of *Fly Emirates, Samsung, Etihad Airways* and *LG*. Fast-forward to 2009 and even Hull City were getting involved.

My developing apathy of modern football and its ramifications on modern life can be perfectly summed up by this seemingly niche aspect of Hull City history. For the majority of the first decade of following City, local electronics firm *Bonus* sponsored the club's shirt – a successful local business supporting their local football team – idealistically at least, exactly what football sponsorship should be all about. By 2009, after two successful seasons on the pitch wearing *Kingston Communications*-sponsored shirts, the Tigers decided they needed a more recognisable, national brand to step up and make commercial partnerships a more lucrative aspect of the club. Indeed, I remember buzzwords of this nature being used by Paul Duffen with pride as it was announced that UK-based high-street bookmaker *Totesport* would become City's kit sponsor for the next two seasons. This was the moment I first remember thinking that Hull City, my team, was being discussed as a business rather than a football club. Naive of me, of course – all football clubs are businesses, yet I don't remember a moment prior to this point in which an owner so brazenly discussed *my* football team as a commercial operation ahead of a family-oriented club. Since 2009, the club have gone on to wear shirts with *Cash Converters*, *12Bet* and *Flamingo Land* unashamedly pasted across the chests, and now, currently heading into the 2019/20 season, City are sponsored by *SportPesa* – a Kenyan bookmakers with absolutely no connection to the city.

While I understand the relentless march of progress cannot be halted, no one can tell me this is a positive form of progress, regardless of the stupid sums of money this has seen generated for my club. City jumped on the national sponsorship bandwagon a decade ago, embracing the commercially driven riches of modern football, and have never looked back. It was, of course, a necessary step that was required to enable the club to challenge financially and keep up with similar sized clubs at the time. Yet, perhaps even unfairly, I will always associate this period with City's transition into modern football, and the moment we sold our soul to the devil.

Nevertheless, if the Tigers were ready to embrace modern football by 2009, a cruel twist of fate was just around the corner. The 09/10 season would prove a disastrous one for the club, ending in financial peril and the first relegation I had suffered as a Tigers fan. We had dared to dream and enjoyed two of the most incredible seasons in the club's history. But this dream was about to become a nightmare.

Funnily enough, after a dreadful finish to the previous campaign that had seen us stay in the league by a single point, the new season didn't start off too badly. After appearing in the Premier League's Asia Trophy in Beijing during preseason, and strengthening the squad with the likes of Steven Mouyokolo, Seyi Olofinjana, Stephen Hunt, Kamel Ghilas, Jan Vennegoor of Hesselink and Jozy Altidore, who joined Jimmy Bullard and Kevin Kilbane, who had signed the previous January, expectations were high. Despite facing both Chelsea and Spurs in our opening two fixtures, City earned an encouraging four points from our first four games. The rut Brown's men had found themselves in at the back end of the season before appeared to be over, and it seemed the perfect opportunity to now kick on and become an established Premier League side. But the optimism was short-lived, as it soon became clear that all was not right at the club behind the scenes. A usually cool, calm and collected Brown became increasingly, and uncharacteristically, short-tempered with the press, and by the time the incumbent player of the season, Michael Turner, was sold to relegation rivals Sunderland for a suspicious 'undisclosed fee' at the end of August, the cat was out of the bag – something was wrong.

In 'typical City' fashion, it wasn't long before these small warning signs evolved into a full-blown crisis. By early October, City had taken just eight points from 11 games and were now languishing once again in the Premier League's relegation zone. It was at this time, just prior to a 2–0 defeat away at Burnley, that Paul Duffen resigned as chairman, taking responsibility for City's horrific form throughout 2009, just days after City's accounts – released five months behind schedule – showed borrowings of over £20 million. Almost entirely out of the blue, City were in trouble. Previously silent majority owner Russell Bartlett finally spoke up and moved quickly to reappoint former chairman and City favourite Adam Pearson to steady the ship.

'Something fishy is going on here,' I remember Dad saying, as the two of us listened to the BBC Radio Humberside's *Sports Talk* programme on the day of Duffen's resignation. 'There is no way Duffen would walk without being pushed. We're deeper in the red than anyone is letting on, and relegation could be the least of our worries, I tell you!'

Dad was right. As City continued to struggle on the pitch, with what appeared to be our best hope of survival, Jimmy Bullard, crocked once again, the full extent of City's financial problems became painfully apparent by Christmas. With Duffen having resigned in October, City began proceedings against him in the December, accusing the former chairman of spending company money for private use during his time in charge, as well as alleging that Duffen's business had received payments from agents in exchange for the opportunity to negotiate transfers on the club's behalf. As these allegations were being made, it became evident that City – a football club that had no debt when Duffen took charge in the summer of 2007 – could be just months away from administration. As fans, we may have just witnessed the greatest few years in the club's history, but it had come at a heavy price. Behind the scenes, City had been living well above its means in an attempt to keep up with the 'big boys', and now our deal with the devil looked to have us staring into the abyss.

With relegation looking a near certainty come March, Pearson decided on one more roll of the dice. After only managing six league wins in his past 51 games in charge, Brown was sacked. Well, I say 'sacked' – rumour had it at the time that due to increasing financial difficulties City couldn't afford to actually fire Brown, meaning the most successful manager in the club's history up until this point was placed on 'gardening leave' until the end of the season. It was a sad end to an unforgettable spell in charge. I remember vividly being sat in a Maths lesson at school when I received the text from Dad telling me the news. I was confused and angry. This was the man who had taken Hull City to the Premier League for the first time in our history, and as far as I was concerned, he had the right to take us back to the Championship and have a go at rebuilding the side himself. But looking back now, the fact that Brown was even afforded the time he was, especially considering City's woeful form over the previous 12 months, was a miracle in itself. In the end, replacing Brown was a required risk – a difficult goodbye, but a necessary one. Pearson's gamble was one that had to be made, but unfortunately, it was executed abysmally.

Former Crystal Palace manager, and Sloth from *The Goonies* lookalike, Iain Dowie was appointed City's new 'football management consultant', tasked with keeping the club in the Premier League. Dowie was given nine games to save City and it's safe to say, after picking up only six points from a possible 27, the gamble backfired spectacularly. City were mathematically relegated with one game to go.

For whatever reason, there is only one game from this dire period I remember clearly. Perhaps this is because this was the game every City fan knew the jig was up – the only game that really mattered during the Dowie era. It's true, it wouldn't be until a 2–2 draw with Wigan on the penultimate weekend of the season that City would be officially relegated. However, a home defeat to fellow relegation contenders Burnley in what was only Dowie's fourth game in charge all but sealed City's miserable fate.

After the bleak situation I have just described it seems hard to believe that Dad, Steph and I went into this game thinking we still had a real chance of staying up. Walking in the glorious sunshine through West Park towards the KC Stadium, fish and chips in hand, I believed the great escape would begin that day. After all, a win would have put City within just one point of safety with five games still to play, while at the same time pulling ourselves further away from Burnley and cutting them adrift, along with Portsmouth, at the foot of the table. Even though Burnley had got the better of City at Turf Moor in October, on paper at least they were the weaker team and one City had the beating of. In reality, however, the hardworking and honest Lancashire side deserved their double over us that season.

The match itself played out as an almost perfect analogy for City's shambolic season as a whole. Dowie's men got off to a great start early on when an unmarked Kevin Kilbane nodded USA international Jozy Altidore's floated cross past Brian Jensen. The KC erupted as 20,000 City fans began to dream of a second survival party in as many seasons.

'Hold on for this victory, and I think two more wins might do it,' I said, as the theme tune of *The Great Escape* began to ring out around the KC Stadium.

'A win today, three points at Birmingham next week, a draw against Villa, and wins against Sunderland, Wigan and Liverpool – easy!' Dad replied sarcastically.

'Now shut up, you're jinxing it!'

I chose to ignore Dad's pessimism. Besides, for the first half hour of the match City dominated the game. As the first half wore on, Altidore and Bullard both had chances to kill the game, the young American forcing a decent save from Jensen, while Bullard volleyed over the bar. It seemed just a matter of time before we scored a second. However, with 35 minutes gone, and against the run of play, Martin Paterson slid the ball under Myhill to equalise for Brian Laws's side. The chants of 'You're going down with the Burnley!' soon followed, taunting a home crowd that had been so full of optimism just moments earlier.

Just as City's entire season had started to fall apart at the first sign of trouble in October, Dowie's men began to collapse as our opposition grew in confidence. The Hull City faithful could only watch in disbelief as things went from bad to worse when their side gifted the visitors two penalties in just over five minutes. It almost goes without saying, Burnley stalwart Graham Alexander dispatched both with ease. 3–1.

'Going down, going down, going down!'

The three of us sat in our East Stand seats, shell-shocked with the collapse we had just witnessed.

'See, you did jinx it,' Steph sighed, as we waited for the referee to put us out of our misery.

But I didn't have time to reply. With six minutes of added time already played, Burnley's Wade Elliott added insult to injury, finding the top corner of Myhill's goal with a stunning inswinging free kick.

4–1 Burnley. City's Premier League survival hopes lay in tatters and relegation was now surely a formality.

'Well, it's been a hell of an adventure and one we never expected when we were sat at Boothferry, ay Greg,' Dad pointed out stoically as we trudged back to the car. 'We turned up back then and we'll do the same again next season ... if there's still a club to come back to, that is!'

Steph and I simultaneously shot him daggers.

'I'm joking! The club will sort itself out. We'll be walking back to our seats come August, trust me. I for one can't wait. I think I prefer the Championship to this entitled Premier League bollocks anyway!'

Of course, Dad was right, we did still have a football club to return to come the following August, though it was a very different Hull City to any we had got used to over the previous decade. City would return to the Championship after two seasons in the big time with an additional £35 million worth of debt now hanging over the club. Despite hankering after the job on a permanent basis, the club's first and only 'football management consultant' left by the end of May and City had the summer to scrape together a squad, and find a new manager, capable of at the very least surviving in the Championship.

And that was that. The Tigers first ever spell in the top flight was over. There was a, not entirely unreasonable, feeling among most City fans that despite the memories created, and the national media's portrayal of the club as a plucky underdog always destined for relegation, we had wasted a huge opportunity. Top-tier football was something the club had fought tooth and nail to achieve for 104 years and after finally attaining it, in the end, it was surrendered without a fight. Too many players hadn't tried hard enough to fix obvious problems, and management, both on the playing side and at boardroom level, had foolishly begun to believe their own myth. Indeed, in just two years the club had gone from one built on the sturdiest foundations of sound financial management and level-headed executive decisions to the brink of administration. And from a squad made up exclusively of modest, hardworking, honest professionals, to one dominated by a group of overpaid mercenaries, has-beens and never-weres.

The Premier League had corrupted my beloved Hull City. The greed, self-indulgence and borderline sleaze induced by modern football had caught up with the club and in this moment, as always, the fans had to take the brunt of the fallout. The good times would come again to the KC Stadium, in reality far more quickly than the club could have reasonably expected, or deserved for that matter. Yet, going to the football was never quite the same. Hull City's first venture into the top tier of the English football pyramid will always be celebrated as an incredibly special two years, and it was. But I will also remember the subsequent downfall for another reason. Relegation from the Premier League and financial peril would signal a new chapter for the club, and with it the first generation of Hull City I had come to know and love would have to come to an end. Indeed, for the first time in nearly a decade of support, a new and near-unrecognisable cohort of players, led by an unfamiliar manager, would emerge after an uncertain summer in 2010. This, combined with a takeover and new owners just six months away, confirmed that a new phase in the club's history was certainly about to commence. I would be equally addicted to this new era, but ultimately it would represent a new Hull City I could never love in quite the same way.

Vuvuzelas and disillusionment

Germany 4–1 England – 27/06/2010

IT is quite remarkable how many unique ways football teams can find to make their loyal supporters miserable. Just when you believe nothing new could surprise you, your team discovers a fresh and innovative new method of causing you despair. The England national team are masters at this. They are notorious for going 1–0 up in a crucial quarter-final and throwing it away. Renowned for heading to international tournaments having not dropped a single point in qualifying, only to then go on and lose their opening game at the finals. Without fail, they will con an entire nation into believing that 'this year' will be different and then, naturally, they will crash out in the first round. Even as a well-educated and seasoned 16-year-old football fanatic in the summer of 2010, I thought I was falling for the same old guff. I didn't think we could win the tournament, confirming I was not quite as deluded as in previous years; however, part of me did buy the hype and was expecting at least a quarter-final finish for the Three Lions. Indeed, Capello's England – a side demonstrably weaker than their '02, '04 and '06 incarnations – travelled to South Africa having once again hoodwinked an entire nation. And, it goes without saying, once again they found new and uninspiring methods of inflicting misery. My GCSEs may well have been out of the way, and I had a summer of football,

171

parties and holidays to enjoy, but yet another memory of a shoddy England World Cup performance would blemish an otherwise perfect summer.

I still think of it as a near perfect summer because that's exactly what it was. After a two-year slog at school completing my GCSE courses, not to mention a terrible season for Hull City, the holidays could not come quickly enough. When they did arrive midway through June, signalled by my last exam (History – medicine through time), my full attention turned to the World Cup. I was finally free, and my first month of freedom would be spent watching World Cup football around the clock with my mates, drinking beer and enjoying the longest summer of my adolescence. There is not a lot more a 16-year-old lad could ask for. Hell, it still sounds like a pretty perfect summer even now.

Naturally, England tried to spoil the party early.

Three days before my final exam, England had kicked off their tournament in Rustenburg against the USA. Fortunately, England's opening game had fallen on a Saturday, meaning instead of being cooped up at home watching the match over a half-opened book of history revision notes, I was able to go to Tom's and watch it with a few friends. With the novelty addition of three crates of Budweiser in the fridge – don't judge, we were only 16 – and clad in our England shirts, we thought a momentous opening victory would set the tone for the rest of our summer. It wasn't to be that simple, of course.

Despite a perfect start to the game, marked by Steven Gerrard's fourth-minute goal, a USA side, coincidentally spearheaded by City flop Jozy Altidore fresh from his spell at the KC, was about to remind my mates and I that all the joys of summer had not quite arrived just yet. With 40 minutes gone, a daisy-cutter of a shot from Fulham's Clint Dempsey was fumbled by Robert Green who, appearing to do his best impersonation of Massimo Taibi, saw the ball squirm over the line. Both Heskey and Altidore wasted opportunities to win the game for their respective sides in the second half, but ultimately the game ended in a stalemate. An underwhelming result but not one that would dampen my spirits. On paper at least, the USA represented the toughest game in England's group, and with Algeria and Slovenia still to play, a draw appeared a half-decent result.

'No more bastard exams and a 4–0 battering of Algeria next week then, please!' I said, as the USA game ended and our attention turned to a hastily thought-up drinking game as that day's World Cup highlights began on the BBC.

Nevertheless, my optimism was to be short-lived. My exams ended and I was surprisingly pleased with how the month-long period had gone academically, yet on the football front an England side symbolised by its talisman Wayne Rooney was about to let me down badly. As I settled down to watch the Three Lions' second game of the tournament at home in front of the TV with Mum and Dad, I was confident England would record big wins in their next two group games. Indeed, in the previous few days since my exams had ended, I had been buoyed through watching shock defeats for both Spain and Germany, both of which only furthered my belief that England's opening result had in fact been a good one, and that our fate would be decided on the strength of our Algeria and Slovenia results. As it turned out, I was correct – England's fate would be decided on these results, yet instead of victoriously storming into the second round with ease, the national team proceeded to bottle it once again.

With the constant annoying drone of vuvuzelas providing the soundtrack, as it did for the entire tournament, the England players walked out of the tunnel in Cape Town apparently full of confidence, ready to kick-start their tournament. Less than two hours later, Wayne Rooney would be snarling down a television camera as his side were jeered off the pitch by their own supporters following a quite pathetic performance.

'Nice to see your own fans booing ya!' Rooney hissed, as a nation sighed. It was happening again. England were in meltdown at a major tournament.

0–0 against a poor Algeria team and England had only taken two points from a possible six. As has become a predictable biennial tradition, it was at this point the wave of disappointment hit me. But this was a different type of disappointment. Realisation once more that the hype had all been for nothing and this England side would again fail to reach expectations. Indeed, this time I felt more disappointed in myself for buying into the excitement than with England for failing to deliver.

Capello's men needed to redeem themselves five days later in Port Elizabeth against Slovenia, and they just about managed it. England claimed their only win of the tournament courtesy of Jermain Defoe's 23rd-minute close-range strike, confirming their place in the last 16. As it turned out, this unconvincing win against poor opposition represented England's depressingly uninspiring high point at World Cup 2010. Besides, even this victory was tainted when Landon Donovan's late winner for the United States against Algeria meant England were pipped to the post and would only manage a second-place finish in Group C, setting up a daunting clash with arch-rivals Germany in the first knockout round. Great.

'I'd rather be playing Germany than Ghana anyway, I think,' I recall Dad saying thoughtfully after the Slovenia game.

'How'd you work that one out?' I replied.

'Well, you know, if we're gonna be knocked out, I'd rather it be against one of the big boys – a potential championship-winning team. Know what I mean?' he chuckled.

'That's the spirit,' I responded, rolling my eyes.

As it happened, the closer to the game it got, the more I came to agree with Dad, but not for the same reasons. The thought of England against Germany just had more of a World Cup feel about it. A classic fixture in world football and one so perfectly set up for this huge stage that it was impossible not to feel excited about it. Then, of course, I had the memories of that glorious night in Munich nine years earlier. The game that had first got me hooked on football. A decent result for England that September night had been equally unexpected – why couldn't we have a repeat? After all, I wasn't asking for a 5–1 victory on this occasion – I wouldn't be greedy – a narrow 1–0 would do. With a likely quarter-final meeting with another old enemy in Argentina on offer, I was allowing my mind to get ahead of itself, but I didn't care. By the time I woke on the morning of the game, I was positive England were going to announce themselves at this World Cup and stun an up-and-coming young German side. As it happened, the game would go on to become a memorable World Cup classic, but for England it would be for all the wrong reasons.

As I had for the USA game, along with a big group of mates and armed with several crates of Budweiser, I went round to Tom's house to watch the match. Tom's family had the largest TV at the time, and we were determined to make the most of it. As we nervously sat watching the pre-match build-up, conversation predictably turned to the two sides' starting elevens. As a group, we universally agreed that, on paper at least, England just about had the stronger of the two sides. This would be a conversation my mates and I would come to look back on with a combination of hilarity and borderline embarrassment. How naive we were.

If researching past matches for this book has done one thing, it has highlighted the fact that time can do funny things to once strongly held opinions. Heading into this match I was convinced that the two starting line-ups were more or less equally matched – if anything England had the stronger of the two squads. Of course, it must be remembered that the vast majority of Germany's youthful starting XI were still very much at the beginning of their successful international careers, while the majority of England's squad had previous tournament experience. However, even with this in mind, today I find it truly bizarre how evenly matched my group of friends believed the two squads to be. To put this into a little context, the likes of David James, Matthew Upson, Emile Heskey and Shaun Wright-Phillips turned out for the Three Lions that day, while, with only four exceptions, the entire German outfit that faced England would go on to win the World Cup for 'Die Mannschaft' just four years later. With the wonderful gift of hindsight, it's easy to say there's no wonder we lost. Though, it is fair to say, the game's 4–1 scoreline did not paint an accurate picture of the game.

Unusually for an England game from this period, and especially one in which the consumption of beer accompanied my viewing experience, I remember the entirety of this match. The Germans went 1–0 up after 20 minutes when Terry and Upson were both caught flat-footed as a Neuer goal kick found Miroslav Klose who slotted past James in England's goal with ease.

'Don't worry lads, we went 1–0 down in Munich as well! Plenty of time yet,' I said in the most confident voice I could muster, trying to convince myself more than anything else.

My confidence was not to be rewarded though. Podolski doubled Germany's lead on 32 minutes, giving Capello's men a mountain to climb. Yet, just five minutes later the aforementioned Upson made amends for his early mistake when he pulled one back for England, heading home from a Gerrard cross. England were back in it. Cue manic dancing and chanting in Tom's lounge, as the room went mad.

'Here we go! The comeback's on!' my friend Will announced, as Germany kicked off.

Buoyed by Upson's goal, England now had their backs up and were, for the only time in the match, on the front foot. Then, just two minutes after the restart, the moment that defined the game and one that still haunts me to this day. Picking up the ball at the edge of the German box, Frank Lampard sees Neuer off his line and beautifully volleys past the outstretched arms of the Schalke goalkeeper.

'LAMPAAAAAARD ... BRILLIANT! ... That surely crossed the line!' Guy Mowbray thundered, as an entire nation held its breath.

The ball struck the underside of the crossbar and clearly crossed the line by at least a yard as it bounced, before being seized on by Neuer, who sheepishly bowled the ball back into play. Somehow this was enough to fool Uruguayan referee Jorge Larrionda, who was perhaps the only individual in the whole stadium not to see the ball cross the line.

'It's not been given! SURELY that was in!' Mowbray raged, as an incensed Mark Lawrenson groaned in the background.

'CHEATING BASTARDS!' I yelled at the screen, as the atmosphere in the lounge soured.

'That was the moment,' Charlie proclaimed, slapping his hands against his thighs. 'We've been shafted here!'

Charlie was right, that *was* the moment. Had the goal been awarded, England would have likely gone in at half-time with the score level at 2–2 and the momentum firmly behind us after a slow start. Instead, Capello's men trudged in, still trailing 2–1, appearing dejected and justifiably so.

Indeed, although not exclusively responsible for the defeat, this one moment would go on to define the match.

England tried to regroup and take the game to Germany in the second half, but the damage had been done. When Müller scored twice in the space of four minutes midway through the half, the game was up.

4–1 Germany – England's biggest World Cup defeat to date – and the suggestion coming from the German camp that justice had finally been served 54 years on from Geoff Hurst's controversial second goal in the 1966 final. Incidentally, Lampard's 'goal that never was' would go on to play a key role in the IFAB's decision to implement new rules allowing the gradual introduction of goal-line technology in football in 2012. Of course, this provides little solace, and to this day even the sight of Manuel Neuer induces a short, but very real, pang of anger in the pit of my stomach.

Another World Cup over. Another controversial moment. Another England failure.

By 2010 I had learnt that England were not the best team in the world, far from it in reality. I had also taught myself not to allow the hype, instinctively generated prior to England appearing in a major tournament, to get the better of me quite in the same way as it had in the past. As always, I would go on to watch the entire remaining stages of the tournament, which in 2010's case signifies without a doubt the worst World Cup I have watched in my lifetime in terms of the quality of football, but still I enjoyed it greatly. However, this tournament will always symbolise a turning point in my relationship with supporting England. At the time I hadn't quite figured it out yet, but South Africa represents a very significant milestone in my story of football addiction. Whilst prior to this moment I had looked forward to each England fixture with bated breath, craving my own 1966, Italia 90 or Euro 96 moment to look back on, by this point I had given up almost without even realising it. I still watched every England game but, upon reflecting on it in the immediate months afterwards, did so out of a feeling of duty rather than one of enthusiasm or enjoyment. This was a new sensation that slowly but surely developed into a private inquiry that consumed me during the last few months of 2010. I didn't understand it at this point, but England had just provided the first symptom indicating my love for football could well be transitioning into an addiction – something I *needed* rather than something I chose to enjoy.

It wasn't long before the glaringly obvious truth hit me like a brick wall. Despite adoring football and everything that came with it, including the national team, it turned out that, well, I had come to absolutely hate watching England.

The more I thought about it, the more there was to dislike. Friendly games – although typically easy victories – were usually dull and unwatchable affairs. Some of the world's greatest players, for one reason or another, became uninterested drones as soon as they pulled on the Three Lions shirt. And the national media, so influential and entwined with British life, made the whole sorry thing one big unlikeable circus. Modern international football – what is there to like?

This realisation frightened me. International football used to be the pinnacle of the sport – 1966, Italia 90, Euro 96 and even Munich 2001, all pay testament to this. But by 2010, corrupted from the top down by the plague of modern football, watching England had become a chore – something that all football addicts like myself knew they must do to feed their habit, but equally something they recognised they would ultimately resent.

The subculture and hobby that had become such an integral part of my existence was becoming infected, I could feel it. I knew I could never give up on football – the fear of missing out would be absolutely unbearable and I would likely fall off the non-fandom bandwagon before you could say, 'Who are ya!' – but somewhere around this time, the enjoyment I used to receive from international football began to diminish.

To paraphrase the great Eric Cantona, 'You can change your wife, your politics [and] your religion, but never, never can you give up on your favourite football team.'

Well, by 2010 I was fed up with England, and the next decade would see my relationship with my oldest love, Hull City, stretched to the limit. But King Eric was right – ultimately my addiction wouldn't allow me to give up on either my club or country. After all, I might miss something.

The simple game I used to love, the one I watched on fuzzy television screens and on dilapidated old terraces, was starting to become something I was struggling to recognise. Watching England had become a necessary evil rather than the once enjoyable experience it had been, and by the autumn of 2010 I was praying the same fate would never come of my beloved Hull City. Of course, modern football had other ideas.

The grass isn't always greener

Sheffield United 2–3 Hull City – 26/12/2010
Hull City 2–1 Leicester City – 03/12/2011

AFTER a decade of practice, by 2010, I knew the drill. England would typically let me down in a major tournament, which would be followed by a football-less few weeks in which I would go on holiday with my family and read the latest book by Jonathan Wilson or Barney Ronay, before the sweet relief of preseason would come to ease my football cravings. But the summer of 2010 was different. Not only had England's woeful display in South Africa, and everything that came with it, had me reassessing my relationship with the beautiful game, City's dire financial situation and subsequent relegation back to the Championship had me dreading what the new season would bring.

The rebuild, as I came to view the 2010/11 season, actually got off to a promising start. With 'football management consultant' Iain Dowie firmly out of the door, Adam Pearson's streak of always finding a way to follow a bad managerial appointment with an inspired one looked to continue when former Southampton and Leicester City manager Nigel Pearson was given the task of steadying the ship. Though, just weeks after his appointment, and with little to no transfer business completed heading into preseason, it was reported that a block on transfers had been set by the board, limiting which players could be brought in to strengthen the squad until the club's near £40 million per year wage bill was drastically cut. Cue one of the biggest squad overhauls in the club's modern history. Over the course of the summer, out went the likes of Myhill, Mendy, Hunt, Marney, Mouyokolo, Geovanni, Cousin, Gardner, Olofinjana and Ghilas, who would be followed by club legend Ian Ashbee, Folan, Zayatte, Duke and Fagan before the season was up. Despite the severe financial difficulties, Pearson bought shrewdly during the summer, bringing in the likes of Jay Simpson, Nobby Solano, Liam Rosenior, James Harper and Robert Koren, on top of loan signings John Bostock, Anthony Gerrard, Daniel Ayala and, later, Vito Mannone, to name but a few. A quite phenomenal rebuilding of the squad and one that would continue under Pearson following a club takeover in the winter of 2010 – an aspect of Pearson's time in charge that is often overlooked.

Perhaps predictably, considering the sheer scale of the overhaul of both management and playing staff, not to mention the financial turmoil off the pitch, we got off to a poor start to the season. The horrific away form continued, and the season didn't get going until we won our first away game in more than 12 months against Norwich City in the September. This kick-started a run that saw Pearson's City go on to achieve a club record 14 consecutive games unbeaten away from home, but even this wasn't enough to banish the fears of a second consecutive relegation. Yet, just a month later, a chink of light could be seen at the end of the tunnel. After months of speculation, it was announced part way through October that Egyptian-born local businessman Assem Allam, along with his son Ehab, had begun negotiations to take over the club.

It was a strange moment. I remember asking Dad just who this family were, as the news was announced on a midweek edition of BBC Humberside's *Sports Talk* programme. Although he had heard of the Allam family and their local firm *Allam Marine*, which manufactured and sold electric generators, there appeared little else to know. The family had never been involved in football or sports ownership before, and generally had kept a low profile around the city. However, with the family worth a reported £150 million and with Assem announcing publicly that he wanted to rescue the club and take it back to the Premier League, the deal almost sounded too good to be true.

'I have been here for 42 years and have built my business in the area. I think it's time to pay it back – Hull City are important to the area,' the Egyptian stated modestly, as the negotiations began.

What could possibly go wrong?

By the time the takeover was completed midway through December, with the club exchanging hands for just £1, the feeling that City were on the decline rather than on the up began to dissipate. With the Allam family now in charge and promising to invest £30 million, starting with the upcoming January transfer window, I was filled with optimism once again. The blip was over. Hull City could return to the successful, financially sensible and family-orientated football club that had seen us thrive for the best part of a decade. In reality though, it would only take another couple of years before modern football, using the Allam family as a conduit, returned with a vengeance as the 'Hull Tigers' name-change saga began.

Sure enough the investment came immediately, with Aaron McLean, Matty Fryatt, James Chester and Cameron Stewart all coming through the KC's constantly revolving door in January, with future transfers Corry Evans and Jack Hobbs joining on loan. This sparked a strong second half of the season and even a late push for the play-offs, though this would ultimately prove a little too much to ask. Funnily enough, the most memorable game of the season for me came just before our busy January transfer window, when we travelled to Bramall Lane for a Boxing Day clash with Sheffield United.

On that freezing cold December afternoon, buoyed by the recent takeover and finally feeling optimistic for the future once again, the away end was bouncing. Goals from the previously stalling Jay Simpson put the Tigers 2–0 up, greeted by the festive chant of 'He used to be shite, but now he's alright, walking in a Simpson wonderland!'.

But we did our best to throw it away. Ched Evans scored twice to pull the Blades level, before City sealed the win in added time. A quick throw from Mannone in the Tigers goal set Cameron Stewart racing down field, gleaming in that season's handsome white and 'collegiate gold' Adidas away strip. The former Man United youngster charged into the box, and saw his shot well saved by Simonsen, only for Jimmy Bullard to hit home the rebound to snatch the late win. Thinking back, this was one of just a handful of positive memories I have of Bullard in a City shirt, but what a moment it was. Cue pandemonium in the City end and one of my favourite ever away days. The city of Sheffield had been good to me in this regard.

Marching in a tightly formed police escort, with around 2,000 fellow City fans, I will never forgetting singing 'Jingle bells, jingle bells, jingle all the way! Oh, what fun it is to see Hull City win away!' all the way back into Sheffield city centre. It had been a wretched 12 months – the worst in my blessed time as a City fan, but it felt like the worst of it was over and the club would now get back on track.

Despite our late push for the play-offs and subsequent mid-table finish, the 2010/11 season will not be remembered as a classic in terms of on-the-pitch action. Indeed, after ten seasons this was probably the first for me as a City fan in which the side hadn't realistically been either battling for promotion or against relegation going into the final few matches of the season – a campaign of mid-table mediocrity in the middle of an otherwise golden decade for the club. What a novelty. Though, looking back, this season was key in Hull City's future. A campaign that had started with the real threat of a second successive relegation and even potential administration had been rescued by the appointment of a sensible manager, and the investment of new owners. From the brink of a financial meltdown to a real belief that a Premier League return could well be on the cards in the following few seasons, the future seemed bright once again. Consequently, I loved the 10/11 season and, momentarily at least, forgot all about my own existential crisis that had secretly begun with my own relationship with football. However, under the Allam family's ownership of my beloved City, this feeling would rear its ugly head again and the next time I would struggle to overcome it.

Lifted by the strong finish to the previous season, and without an England failure to question my love for football in the summer of 2011, the 11/12 season could not begin soon enough. Quite apart from the football, this was also a period of my life I loved for very different reasons. Not only had City got themselves back on their feet, but also I was thriving at school. By the summer of 2011 I had completed my first year of sixth form and, despite suffering from a terrible bout of glandular fever during my AS-level examinations just months earlier, had achieved the best results I had ever had. Boosted by finally receiving an official diagnosis of dyslexia and subsequently accepting the extra exam help I needed, I had gained an A and four Bs, studying History, Politics, Business Studies, Product Design and General Studies. This put me in a much stronger position than expected ahead of applying for university places during the coming academic year, and for the first time gave me a much clearer picture of what I saw myself doing after I left school.

As with everyone of this age, my personal life also changed drastically. Having passed my driving test in June 2011 and being fortunate enough to have been bought a car by my parents for my 17th birthday – a glorious 2003 black seat Ibiza – I was experiencing more independence than ever before. Nights out with my mates every weekend – going to the famous Welly Club on Beverley Road, the ill-fated Pozition nightclub on George Street and the nearby Napoleons Casino – became as normal as going to the match with Dad every Saturday. This was also the first time I started to take any real notice of the opposite sex. Prior to sixth form I had had no real interest in going to the pictures with a girl or asking someone out for a date. Besides, with away days every other weekend and trips to the KC during the Saturdays I actually remained in Hull, I hadn't really had time for them. However, I met my first real girlfriend, Nia, on Bonfire Night

2010. Nia attended a different sixth form, but knew a few of the lads I played football with each Sunday, which facilitated this first chance meeting. As with the majority of sixth-form couples, we wouldn't last much over 18 months, with the strains of a first 'long-distance' relationship taking its toll as soon as we both left Hull for university in the autumn of 2012. Besides, having never managed to convince Nia to attend a City match with me, the relationship was perhaps doomed from the start.

Along with this new-found personal independence came a seemingly exciting new era for Hull City. As the 2011/12 campaign approached, there was once again a real buzz around the KC, with a push for promotion very much on the cards thanks to the Allam's investment and Nigel Pearson's sensible, but effective, management style.

Deadwood such as Jimmy Bullard and Nobby Solano were released and replaced with the likes of Paul McKenna and exciting young United loanee Robbie Brady. The balance between experienced Championship players and young up-and-coming talent, along with the goalscoring abilities of Matty Fryatt, all pointed to Pearson having got the squad just right. The former Boro and Wednesday defender had now had a season to rebuild City, and the results were there for all to see. But come November it was all change at the KC as our new-found stability faced its first challenge.

It's funny. City would go on to be promoted under Steve Bruce one year later with a much changed and, it must be said, stronger squad. However, I maintain that I do believe Pearson would have taken City to the play-offs in 11/12, had he not left.

With a game in hand by the middle of November City were sitting just one point outside of the play-off places when Pearson decided he wanted out. Somewhat out of the blue as I remember it, he asked City's board for permission to talk to Vichai Raksriaksorn, the owner and newly appointed chairman of Leicester City, with the ambition of returning to manage his former club. Raksriaksorn had sacked manager Sven-Göran Eriksson just three weeks earlier after an underwhelming start to the campaign for the preseason favourites for promotion, and Pearson was the Foxes' number one target. A few days later, that was it. Nigel Pearson's tenure at the KC was over and a sense of being back to square one temporarily descended on the KC.

It is undeniable that he left Hull City in a much better state than he found us 18 months earlier, yet the nature of Pearson's departure left a very bitter taste in the mouths of Hull City fans everywhere. Not since Terry Neill in 1974 had a City manager departed to join another club midway through a season, and never before had a manager left for what was seen as such a sideways move. As fate would have it, just 18 days after his departure, Pearson would return to the KC with his new side, making for one of the most hostile environments I can recall experiencing at the KC. Naturally, the club and its fans had a point to prove and, with a little help from the Slovenian wizard Robert Koren (ironically a Pearson signing), East Stand chants of 'You should have stayed at a big club!' complemented a glorious 2–1 victory for the Tigers. Surely the most memorable result at the KC Stadium during this strange post-Brown/pre-Bruce era.

Indeed, the match itself had everything. City, under caretaker manager and club legend Nicky Barmby, went into the match as firm underdogs, with many smartarses in the press predicting Leicester's expensively formed squad combined with Pearson's intimate knowledge of their opposition put the Foxes very much in the driving seat. Dad was equally pessimistic.

'Watch the bastard rub it in today!' he said, as the two of us had a pre-match pint at the Brickmakers Arms on Walton Street, minutes away from the KC. I had turned 18 just two days earlier and was enjoying my first legal pre-match pint with my dad – a lovely moment that somehow Nigel 'Judas' Pearson was finding a way of spoiling.

'Oh, shut up!' I responded. 'At least we don't have to put up with the negative football any more, or his sarky drone during the post-match interviews with Burnsy!' I added, as if trying to cheer up a mate after a nasty break-up.

'Come on, let's have another one in here and then go and get a bet on before kick-off – I fancy Koren to score first.'

As we reached the stadium and found our way to our usual East Stand viewing point, the game was just about to get underway. It was just as both starting line-ups were being announced over the stadium's tinny public-address system that Pearson appeared. A crescendo of boos and vitriol from 18,000 City fans unsurprisingly followed, setting the tone for the entire match. Arrogantly strutting out of the tunnel and characteristically resembling a drill sergeant from a 1980s Vietnam war film, the veteran centre-half swaggered over to his former team-mate Barmby, grinning wildly. Come five o'clock that grin had been wiped from his face.

The game got off to a lively start with decent chances at both ends and full-blooded tackles flying in from each side. It had the feel of a derby game about it, and as with this type of match both sets of supporters knew the first goal would be vital. It came half an hour in when former Fox Matty Fryatt converted from the spot after Matt Mills had been sent off for a last-man challenge on Aaron McLean. 1–0 City and the chants of 'you're getting sacked in the morning!' and 'we're not boring any more!' turned up a notch.

But it all proved a bit premature. Former Liverpool defender and hero of City's first ever Premier League victory over Fulham three years earlier, Paul Konchesky, exorcised his KC demons when he slotted past Péter Gulácsi in City's goal late in the first half. A groan rippled around three sides of the stadium as Nigel Pearson's sneering face appeared on the North Stand's scoreboard.

'Typical!' Dad moaned. '1–0 up against ten men and we find a way to let them back in!'

'Still a long way to go – they'll tire,' I replied impatiently. Dad's pessimism at the football is something that has always bugged me.

Sure enough, Pearson's men were stretched in the second half as City took advantage of the extra man. McKenna, Stewart and Dawson all had good chances to win the grudge match for the

Tigers before Robert Koren settled it in the 88th minute. Looking back it was a classic Koren goal. Quite remarkably, the former West Brom midfielder went on to make 143 appearances for the club, scoring 28 league goals, after joining City on a free transfer in 2010. And if I had to guess, 20 of these goals were likely 'goal of the season' contenders – the man loved a screamer. In one of the greatest decades for the club there are numerous players that must be considered Hull City 'legends', and for one reason or another I think Koren is often overlooked. The Slovenian, who would go on to captain the club, helped stabilise the squad in a time of crisis in 2010 and ended his Hull City career at Wembley as part of the City's one and only appearance in an FA Cup Final in 2014. What a man. Yet, without a doubt, his best remembered moment in a black and amber shirt will be this winning goal against Nigel Pearson's Leicester in 2011. Up there with Ashbee's Yeovil screamer and Windass's Wembley winner, picture the scene: McLean picks up a loose ball just outside Leicester's box with two minutes of normal time to play. Under pressure he finds Rosenior, another sensational free transfer acquired by Pearson, on the right angle of the penalty area. The right-back looks to take on his man before squaring the ball across the edge of the box to the onrushing Koren. Hitting it first time, while 20,000 fans inside the KC hold their collective breath, the ball tears past the diving Kasper Schmeichel, nearly bursting the net in the process.

'WHAT. A. GOAL!' Dad roared, as three sides of the KC Stadium erupted.

As it had after Konchesky's equaliser, Pearson's face flashed up on the giant scoreboard, his smirk now firmly transformed into a contorted grimace.

Chants of 'Who are ya!' rained down, as the ostrich-hating Pearson slinked back to his dugout seat.

The final whistle sounded and the stadium exploded once more. Hull City 2–1 Judas was the narrative, and while it was perhaps a petty and predictable one, a City win really did taste just that bit sweeter that afternoon. As the players made their way off the turf, and the big screen focused on the two managers shaking hands, a wry smile could be seen creeping across Nick Barmby's face and seconds later, a new terrace favourite was born: 'Barmby Army!'

My love for football had faced its first real challenge in the summer of 2010 following yet another miserable showing from England, and knowing a season of financial turmoil at the KC was just around the corner. I knew, as I still do to this day, that a fear of missing out, or an *addiction* if you will, foretold I could never cut football out of my life entirely, but the first seeds of modern football-inducted apathy and disenchantment had indeed been planted.

Having said this, I now look back at this period of my Hull City supporting life with a great deal of fondness. Two mediocre mid-table Championship finishes imply these were two of the worst campaigns blotting the copybook of a phenomenal decade or so for the club. Yet, it must be stated, they also represented two of the final few seasons in which the entire Hull City fan base was universally happy and unified – a hugely underestimated commodity in modern football.

At my time of writing, the club are more or less in exactly the same position in the football pyramid now as we were during the 10/11 and 11/12 seasons. But to compare now and then has become a pointless excursion, and one that makes for depressing conclusions. I will come on to this later.

Good times, even some of the greatest times in the club's history, were now visible on the horizon for City fans, thanks in no small part to the local family that came to the club's rescue in the winter of 2010. Nevertheless, knowing what I know now, half of me still wonders if I wouldn't now be a happier football fan sitting back in League Two or lower, supporting a club without two pennies to rub together, and as far away from supporting a 'modern' football club as it's possible to be. I guess I'll never know.

Ups, downs and the one German that misses penalties

Hull City 2–2 Cardiff City – 04/05/2013

ASK any of my family or friends and they'll tell you I am not a particularly optimistic individual. Although I would describe my outlook on life as my own special form of realism, the reality of the situation is the glass is always half empty for me. As long as I can remember I have always had something to worry about. It's true, I have a nagging worry in the back of my mind as I write this very sentence, but I couldn't tell you a specific reason for why this feeling exists, it's just always there. I think it's a hereditary thing. Mum displays a similar outlook on life, while my grandma Peg is the most hilariously pessimistic human being I know. However, in the summer of 2012, for the first and perhaps only time in my life, I felt truly optimistic about the future.

I was 18 years of age and had just left school surprisingly confident with how my all-important A-level examinations had gone. At the start of the year I had received offers from all six of the universities I had applied for, and knowing I only had to achieve three B grades to get into my first choice – Brunel University to study politics – I was feeling good. I was also set to go on a lads' holiday to the Greek island of Zante with a group of my best mates to celebrate the end of our school careers, followed by a two-week break in Spain with my family before I received my results midway through August. I was about as content as was possible to be. Little did I know that before the year was out I would discover this rare feeling of optimism had been misplaced, as I found myself at the bottom of the worst bout of depression I have ever suffered.

Looking back, sometimes all you can do is laugh at the little ironies life provides. As I went from feeling on top of the world in June 2012, to my lowest ever point, in terms of my own mental health at least, in early 2013, the 12/13 season that ran parallel produced a perfectly mirrored set of contrasting emotions for City. You see, just as I was finishing my exams and enthusiastically looking forward to one of the best summers of my life, the Allam family – just months before branded as the local heroes that had saved Hull City – made the first of many hugely unpopular decisions with the double sacking of Nick Barmby and Adam Pearson. Paradoxically, fast-forward just a few months, and while I was at my lowest ever ebb, under a new charismatic manager and our strongest squad for several years, City were storming their way back to the Premier League. It goes without saying, I have some very conflicting memories about this time in my life.

It all started in May 2012. My exams were in full swing and following Nigel Pearson's sudden exit the November before, City had finished the 11/12 season in a respectable eighth position in the Championship under the stewardship of Nick Barmby, seven points below the play-off places. After the unexpected upheaval and little squad investment, Tigers fans were more than content with this finish. With the expectation that Barmby would be backed and the squad strengthened during the summer to come, there was every reason to be optimistic. Yet these hopes were dashed just weeks later.

After less than six months in charge, and without real warning, Barmby was first suspended and then sacked as Hull City manager by the end of May. The official line coming from the club was that the former England international's position had become untenable following comments he had made in the media about the club's transfer strategy a few weeks prior. To add insult to injury, the news had come after the announcement that

Adam Pearson, the legendary City chairman and acting head of football operations, was also set to leave the club following the termination of his contract.

I vividly recall the moment the news broke of Pearson and Barmby's exits. Months of fantastic work and goodwill built by the Allam family destroyed with just one extremely poorly written press release.

'What the bloody hell are they playing at?' I raged as we first heard the news while watching BBC Look North. 'Pearson and Barmby are the only two people at the club who know anything about football!'

'What are they up to? I can't work it out,' Dad replied thoughtfully. 'They had better have a game plan now,' he added, 'they'll have to go some way to find a replacement for Barmby that will appease the fans. As for Pearson leaving – let's just hope it's not a case of the lunatics taking over the asylum!'

After the apparent shocking mistreatment of two club legends in Pearson and Barmby, in the eyes of the fans at least, Dad was right – the Allam family would have to go some way to find a manager capable of pacifying a riled fan base. Remarkably, they did just that. Experienced Championship and Premier League manager, and former Manchester United captain, Steve Bruce was named as Barmby's successor in early June and, with the promise of money to spend, scrutiny was (temporarily at least) shifted away from Assem and Ehab Allam. Football fans are a fickle and short-sighted breed, after all.

The ownership stayed true to its word and Bruce was able to bolster his squad with the likes of Eldin Jakupovic, Abdoulaye Faye, Nick Proschwitz, Sone Aluko, Alex Bruce and Stephen Quinn in the summer of 2012, with Robbie Brady, David Meyler and Ahmed Elmohamady initially joining on loan before signing permanently at later dates. Looking back this was an astonishing transfer window for the club. With the exception of Proschwitz – bizarrely the most expensive signing of the summer at £2.6m – each of these individuals went on to play key roles in this promotion campaign and represented the club admirably in the Premier League during the few seasons that followed. Bruce's managerial pedigree was apparent from the off, and by the time the squad jetted off to Portugal for preseason training, the whispers of a title challenge were already starting to ripple throughout the city.

Meanwhile, as Bruce prepped his new side for another long and arduous season in the Championship, and England disappointed once again, this time crashing out of Euro 2012 at the quarter-final stage – think Pirlo's Panenka finishing Joe Hart's international career – I was preparing myself for more independence and university life. I was confident that I would achieve the grades I needed to confirm my place at Brunel University down in London, but as 16 August, results day, got closer and closer, the nerves began to hit me. As I mentioned, I needed to achieve three B grades or better from my four subjects to guarantee my place. Having been predicted two B grades and a C – a prediction that formed the basis of my application process – I knew it would probably be tight, but I had faith I would just about manage it.

Waking up on the morning of results day, I logged into my UCAS account to great news – Brunel had confirmed my place. I had done it!

After a teary hug from Mum and a handshake from Dad, all that was left to do now was go to school and collect my results formally. Naturally, knowing my place at my first choice university was confirmed, I couldn't really care less about my actual grades at the time. Besides, if I needed three Bs to confirm my place, surely this is what I must have achieved. Imagine my surprise then, when upon opening the big brown envelope handed to me by my form teacher at school, I found the grades A, A, B, C. Not a particularly special set of grades at my school, but meaningfully higher than I had expected from myself, and a lot better than many teachers had predicted of me. The significance of overachieving wouldn't hit me for a few months, and for the rest of the summer I felt on top of the world as I got ready to move down to London. Ultimately these grades would go on to change the path of my entire life, and drastically influence a number of huge life choices I would come to make over the next few years. However, at the time, with results day out of the way and the process of being readied for university life well and truly underway, during the end of August and throughout September my attention turned firmly back to football.

Knowing the amount of home games I would be able to attend was about to drastically decrease following the move to London, I was determined to make the most of the start of the new season, and I did just that. Out of the Tigers' first eight games of the league season, I attended six, as Bruce's new-look City immediately announced themselves as promotion candidates. Memorable home wins against Brighton, Bolton and Millwall had me missing the KC Stadium before I had even left Hull, before a magnificent 3–2 away victory at Elland Road provided the ideal away day memory to leave for uni on. Little did I know I'd be back attending every home match come Christmas.

It's funny I suppose – when I first arrived at Brunel everything seemed great. I was placed in a modern block of student halls and shared a flat with a great group of people. But after a few weeks something didn't feel right. Initially, I put this feeling down to homesickness. I was four hours from Hull, with no school friends at the same university and a strange feeling that I was the only northerner in a sea of southerners. Indeed, it soon became a running joke in my block of flats that I was 'so northern, I was practically Scottish'. Very witty, southerners, you know.

But it wasn't simply homesickness. The lectures I attended seemed basic and poorly planned, nights out with my flatmates felt more like intense episodes of *Skins* compared to fun, laid-back nights I was used to back home, and, as pathetic as it sounds, I missed going to the football with Dad more than I ever thought possible.

I only lasted a month and a bit in the end. Thoroughly ashamed and more miserable than I had ever been in my life, Dad came and collected me and my things one Sunday morning halfway through November. Both he and Mum were brilliant, to be fair. They knew I hadn't been happy and reassured me that it was a situation I could easily remedy. Although I appreciated the support, at the time I didn't believe them. I had messed up and now had near-on 12 months to dwell on my mistakes.

'At least I still have City,' I thought, as a year home alone without my friends or girlfriend beckoned.

As City continued to hover around the Championship's automatic promotion places in the run-up to Christmas, things went from bad to worse in my personal life. Nia came home from university in Birmingham for the holidays a week before Christmas, and detonated another grenade. In hindsight I can't blame her for instigating the first real break-up I had experienced. After only seeing each other on a handful of occasions since the summer, during which visits I had been likely miserable as sin, it was inevitable really. However, just four months on from having my whole future planned out, I was now living at home, friendless, single, unemployed and thoroughly depressed. I think about this period of my life a lot. On the face of it, I often think it makes me sound like a spoilt brat. I admit, I have lived a very sheltered life, relatively speaking, and listing the somewhat juvenile reasons and events that led to this state of depression appears rather churlish sometimes. Sitting in my bedroom alone during these months, I even remember thinking to myself how I didn't have any right to feel this way. People all over the world have *proper* reasons to be depressed and manage to get on with living their lives. Yet, ultimately this frame of thought, and the guilt that came with it, just made the whole situation worse. It's true, I've lived a charmed life with little to no trauma to note, but at the end of the day sadness and depression really does not discriminate, and can strike at any point in your life. I still suffer from bouts of unhappiness from time to time, as we all do, but never have I felt depression like the autumn and winter of 12/13.

During the Christmas period and the start of the new year, even the football was passing me by. Usually I can list the Christmas fixtures for any given City season of the past 15 years off the top of my head, but I struggle with the 12/13 festive period. All I associate with this horrible time is getting out of bed at around 11am, and wanting to go to sleep in the evening at around 8pm. Sleep became my best friend, and I was becoming more reclusive by the day.

Come the middle of January, Mum and Dad held an intervention of sorts in an effort to get me going again. I sulked, complained and even cried, but by the end of what seemed like hours' worth of talking, they had got through to me. Less than a month later, although not entirely back to my normal self, I was getting back on my feet with the support of my parents. I had gone through the university application process all over again, this time with much higher confirmed grades than the ones school had predicted me a year earlier, meaning new universities and courses were now available to me. I also started picking up small jobs here and there to give me a little money to spend, and after the only blip in 12 years I chucked myself head first back into supporting City. Depression had quelled my cravings for football for a few months, yet the addiction was still very much alive. With Steve Bruce's special strain of Hull City there to be enjoyed, it wasn't long before I was hooked once again.

After the worst few months of my life, by Easter 2013 things were starting to look up. Completing the UCAS process in March, I had been offered a place to study politics at the University of Leeds starting in the coming September. Not only was this much closer to home, meaning regular weekend visits to the KC were still possible, Leeds also represented a much better university and course than the one I had dropped out of just months earlier – one that was now achievable thanks to my better than expected A-level results. Going to Leeds would ultimately turn out to be the best and most significant decision of my life for many reasons. I achieved two good degrees, made some friends for life, and met Becki, prompting my relocation to the north-west. Sliding doors and all that.

Helping out at a friend's father's law firm, mostly filing reports and making cups of tea, also allowed me to make a little bit of money ahead of the summer, while the return of my friends from their first year of uni was now well in sight and something to look forward to. Perhaps most importantly of all, however, was the fact that Bruce's City were also sitting pretty in the automatic promotion spots, with a return to the Premier League looking imminent.

There is only one match I can choose as the most influential from this period. It's up there with some of the most memorable Hull City matches of the past two decades and is remembered fondly as one of those games that (cliché klaxon) 'had everything'. I also associate this game strongly with the end of a tough period of my life, and the start of what turned out to be a phenomenal few years – both for myself personally and for City. Hull City 2–2 Cardiff City.

After a missed opportunity to seal automatic promotion at Oakwell during the penultimate game of the season the weekend before – a wretched 2–0 defeat I witnessed dressed in a full tiger onesie, and one of the worst City performances I have ever seen – it all came down to the final game of the season at home against the already-crowned champions, Cardiff City.

The Tigers' fate was in their own hands, knowing a win against the champions would ensure automatic promotion. Any slip-up and a Watford side facing Leeds at Vicarage Road could take advantage and consign City to the play-offs. As ever, 'typical City' wouldn't do it the easy way but the most dramatic way. What an atmosphere, what a game, what a day.

In the glorious sunshine and in front of a sellout crowd at the KC, Dad, Steph, Mum (who was making a rare appearance at the KC) and I arrived at the stadium early with our fish and chips, nervously discussing the several different outcomes resulting from different scorelines. I wasn't feeling confident. After the Barnsley performance seven days earlier, the Cardiff visit had bad news written all over it.

Nevertheless, it was City that made the better start of the two sides. George Boyd, who had signed in the January, and Robbie Brady both caused Malky Mackay's men problems early on, before loanee goalkeeper David Stockdale was forced to save well from Jordon Mutch's good effort.

As the chants of 'Come on City!' rained down from three sides of the stadium, suddenly a collective quiet shot around the stadium. Seconds later the stadium erupted. News from Watford had reached the KC – Leeds had just taken the lead.

'I never thought I'd be happy to see Leeds winning!' Dad boomed, as a stadium-wide chorus of 'We are going up, say we are going up!' thundered around the KC.

'A City goal would settle the nerves, though!' I replied, trying not to get ahead of myself.

I was right not to get carried away. A serious injury to Watford's second-choice keeper Jonathan Bond midway through the first half resulted in the game being delayed for 15 minutes, and academy stopper Jack Bonham having to step up to the plate.

Two variables City fans were not counting on. Almost predictably, the Hornets levelled before half-time in their match, just moments before former City hero Fraizer Campbell, on as a half-time substitute, put Cardiff ahead with a neat run and an even better finish in front of the North Stand. The former City striker's mocking 'oopsie' celebration that followed incensed the City faithful, creating an almost hostile atmosphere for the first time that season.

'He's annoyingly good, the bastard, isn't he?' Dad sighed, as the KC momentarily deflated.

But the feeling didn't last. City looked for an immediate response and got one; just 15 crazy minutes later we found ourselves ahead and heading towards the Premier League.

Almost comically it was the one striker that couldn't score goals for City, Nick Proschwitz, that scored the first. The lumbering German bundled in a good cross from Quinn to score the most important goal he would ever score in the famous black and amber. The second goal was a much more memorable affair. With just over an hour on the clock, City cult hero Paul McShane found himself on the end of an inswinging Brady corner, diverting the ball past future City stopper David Marshall to put the Tigers in the driving seat.

Pandemonium ensued at the KC. Not since Caleb Folan's goal against Watford in the 2008 play-offs had I experienced such a great atmosphere. Still, there was more drama to come. In the final minute of normal time Cardiff were reduced to ten men when Andrew Taylor was shown a second yellow for a block on Elmohamady. Minutes later and deep into time added on came the moment an entire stadium thought City had sealed the match. Picture the scene: David Meyler, through on goal, is bundled over clumsily by the big frame of Ben Turner in the blue of Cardiff, and the Tigers have a late penalty to put the result beyond all doubt. As thousands of City supporters begin to filter down to the bottom of the stands ready to invade the pitch, and Steve Bruce covers his eyes arm-in-arm with his son Alex on the touchline, Proschwitz steps up and ... SAVED by Marshall.

Cue the immortal line 'Oh, for Christ's sake! Trust Hull City to buy the one bloody German that can't score penalties!'.

Inexplicably, it was to get worse just seconds later. After clearing the ball from the aforementioned penalty, the Bluebirds were unbelievably awarded a penalty of their own after the ball struck the imperious Abdoulaye Faye on the hand as the big Senegalese international fought to clear the ball.

The KC was stunned into silence. From having the win and automatic promotion to the Premier League guaranteed moments earlier, a draw and the disappointment of the play-offs loomed.

Maynard duly smashed the penalty past Stockdale and that was that. As the final whistle sounded, an uneasy murmur rippled around the ground. A few hundred fans invaded the pitch, but with 15 agonising minutes left at Vicarage Road this seemed premature. Dad, Steph, Mum and I stayed put in the East Stand, nervously awaiting updates. A goal for Watford and it would be the play-offs for City. What felt like hours past, checking for updates on mobile phones and crowding around supporters with portable radios. Finally, just as the tension was reaching almost unbearable levels, a huge roar made its way around the KC. Ross McCormack had scored for Leeds at Watford, taking the Hornets out of the race for automatic promotion! Tentative at first, the

City faithful exploded seconds later when City's promotion was confirmed on the scoreboard. As thousands of fans flooded on to the pitch and the City players emerged from the KC's directors' box wielding bottles of champagne, I turned to Dad and burst into tears.

The four of us would join the thousands of City fans on the KC's hallowed turf moments later, chanting, dancing and celebrating what was only City's only second ever promotion to the top flight in 109 years. Yet, for a moment I just stood in my place – Block E5, Seat 151 – and drank it all in. My relationship with football had started to go through a challenging period prior to this point, and I had questioned whether I still *enjoyed* the sport that I felt compelled to follow religiously. Nevertheless, in this moment it felt like nothing had ever happened and that the good old days were back again. This wasn't just because City were winning – far from it – it's the same feeling I had when I was sat in the cold at Boothferry witnessing City lose 1–0 to Huddersfield Town in the LDV Vans Trophy, or when we were on the never-ending drive back from Ipswich after a painful 1–0 defeat – a feeling of belonging and togetherness. Dishearteningly, despite further success on the pitch during the following few seasons, I don't think this feeling of unbridled joy and unity – the one which makes football fandom the best pastime in the world – has been experienced at the KC in quite the same way since. Add to this the fact that the previous 12 months had been the worst of my life up until that point, in which I had felt lows I pray I will never feel again, and the positive memories of this afternoon become doubly poignant. For all its faults, of which there are many, modern football still has this wonderful ability.

As 'Can't Help Falling in Love' boomed out over the KC's speaker system, I joined 22,000 fellow City fans singing at the top of my voice. I felt truly happy for the first time in months.

Why I dislike Kieran Gibbs

Arsenal 3–2 Hull City AET – 17/05/2014

I remember once when I was in the car with Mum, possibly being ferried back to university in Leeds one Sunday afternoon after a weekend at home, listening to some philosophy-themed talk show on BBC Radio Four. The theme that particular day was self-importance and ego in the human psyche. I forget who was presenting the show, but what I do remember is them being as mind-blown as I was when the specialist guest said something along the lines of 'It's human nature to believe you are the "star" in what could be described as The Truman Show that is life'. This struck a chord with me. I came to realise that until one year earlier, in which my life had temporarily gone to shit in the wake of dropping out of university, I had always thought of myself as unique – different from the rest of my friends and classmates and destined for a slightly more extraordinary future. Of course, I now understand that every teenager believes this. The more I thought about this concept of human arrogance, however, the more I applied it to my own relationship with football. If there is a way to link something back to football, I'll find it.

I contemplated about how when I was growing up I had always supposed it strange that Hull City's success and failings had nearly always mirrored the fortunes of my own life. What I mean is, while over the previous decade the club's fortunes had gone from strength to strength, so too had important aspects of my own life, particularly concerning my educational development and self-confidence. By the age of 19 I knew such a correlation was nonsense, yet I couldn't help but believe that the 2013/14 season and my first proper year at university, which ran parallel, echoed one another perfectly. Obviously, I was the star of my own life in what turned out to be a stereotypically life-changing first year at university, while Steve Bruce's City were the surprise package of the season and everyone's second team in the FA Cup. Coincidence? Surely not.

It's funny. In all the time I have been on this football-obsessed little planet, only eight different teams have won the FA Cup. Five of these sides come from the apparently entrenched 'big six' that has emerged during the Premier League era, made up of Manchester United, Arsenal, Chelsea, Manchester City, Liverpool and Spurs. During this time, 25 full seasons have come and gone, with only three winners – Everton in 1995, Portsmouth in 2008 and Wigan in 2013 – managing to disturb the status quo. It's for this reason alone that when I was growing up a devoted Hull City fan, it would be a lie to say I even dreamt of seeing City win the world's oldest national football competition. After all, before 2014 the deepest the club had ever managed to progress in the tournament was the semi-final stage, and even that was out of living memory by this point, taking place in the spring of 1930. Now, don't get me wrong, I was never one for buying into the pundits' 'the FA Cup has lost its magic' nonsense – I loved the tournament as a kid. It's just as a lower-league football fan during the noughties you came to expect that the best you could achieve was a decent cup run that included ties against a few top-tier clubs, before being inevitably knocked out by one of the big boys in the later rounds. In fact, I was more than happy with this arrangement during City's ascent up the Football League. This was, of course, until the magic of the FA Cup descended on Hull during the 2013/14 season.

I had moved to Leeds in the October of 2013, by which time City had made a solid start to life back in the 'big league' as Bruce insisted on calling it, taking 11 points from our opening seven matches. With significant additions having been made to the squad during the summer, notably Tom Huddlestone and Jake Livermore from Spurs, as well as Allan McGregor, Curtis Davies, Yannick Sagbo, Maynor Figueroa and Steve Harper, I was far more certain of Premier League survival than during City's previous two top-tier adventures.

Living in Leeds was perfect. I could travel back to Hull within an hour to ensure I didn't miss a minute of any home game that season, while at the same time being able to easily return to Leeds and not miss any classes or any of the stereotypical fresher activities with a new group of friends. It was the ideal situation. However, it wasn't just the location that suited me. The moment I moved into my halls of residence in Leeds I knew this was the right place for me. Other than the football team, of course, I love everything about Leeds. The city is vibrant and buzzing, yet just small and compact enough not to feel overwhelming, the people are fantastic, and the university is unique. Unlike 12 months previously in London, I threw myself into everything I could during my first year at Leeds, determined to take every opportunity. Before my first reading week midway through November, I was captivated with each of my four politics modules, was playing five-a-side football for two separate teams twice a week, and had discovered an unexpected passion for writing through joining the university newspaper, initially as a sports writer. I was in my element. Just as my first visit to Boothferry Park with Dad had brought with it an overwhelming feeling of belonging, during my first few months in Leeds I just knew this was where I was meant to be.

By the end of the year I was the happiest I think I had ever been. Not only were my studies into British and US Politics going well, I was fitter than I had been in a few years thanks to the return of a near non-stop football schedule, and for the first time in my life I also knew what I wanted to do. I had had my first taste of writing and journalism and I had well and truly caught the bug. Within just months of starting uni, I was writing two or three pieces a week for *Leeds Student* (now *The Gryphon*), the University of Leeds's award-winning student newspaper, on a range of different subjects, for a variety of different sections. From sports to news, films to books. I was hooked.

Once again, I tried to link my new passion with my oldest love, football, and just after Christmas, thanks to hundreds of ambitious emails to every football publication I could think of, I started working as a freelance football writer for *Shoot!* magazine. Having been an avid reader of both *Shoot!* and its biggest competitor *Match* as a kid, I couldn't believe my luck. A year earlier I had been struggling to get out of bed each day knowing all my schoolmates were having the time of their lives at university; now I was making up for lost time. City were looking solid in the Premier League, I had made a bunch of new friends in Leeds, my studies were going well, and I was writing for a national football magazine. What a difference a year can make.

By the beginning of 2014 it looked as though City were going to survive in the Premier League. A steady, if not spectacular, first half of the season saw the Tigers start the new year safely lodged in mid-table, and after two notable home wins in December – 3–1 against Liverpool and 6–0 against Fulham – confidence was high. Though, something else happened during this period which would go on to drastically change my relationship with Hull City, and ultimately shake the foundations of the entire club. A few weeks before Christmas, the local press in Hull reported that Assem Allam had formally asked the FA to change the club's name from Hull City AFC to 'Hull Tigers' from the start of the 2014/15 season. After weeks of fan uproar and confusion, the eccentric owner confirmed the news midway through January, stating that following the local council's decision not to sell him the KC Stadium, additional sources of revenue needed to be found. He argued that a name change from 'City' to 'Tigers' would be enough to open new markets for the club in the Far East, and that should the FA reject the change he would walk away from the club 'in 24 hours'. Protest groups formed, most notably the 'City Till We Die' group – of which I was a part – and for the remainder of the season, an uneasy cloud began to form above the club. The FA Council went on to reject the name change in April

2014, unwilling to set a dangerous precedent, yet this was to be far from the end of the matter. Unsurprisingly, the Allam family didn't walk away following the decision, and the name-change saga would depressingly become the most salient issue at the club for the next few years.

As trouble and unrest began to stir amongst the fan base and behind the scenes, paradoxically something special started happening on the pitch. With Premier League survival looking assured, wins in the third, fourth and fifth rounds of the FA Cup, against Middlesbrough, Southend and Brighton respectively, saw the attention of all City fans turn to a well-deserved distraction in the form of a rare cup run. However, it wasn't until City's sixth-round victory at home against Sunderland that I started to get excited. Prior to this game, I struggle to recall any great FA Cup memories I have had supporting the Tigers. A thrilling 4–3 defeat away to Middlesbrough in 2007 and a 1–0 defeat at home to Villa a year earlier being the only two occasions I remember City even playing top-flight sides. Yet on a gloriously sunny day in March, goals from Curtis Davies, David Meyler and Matty Fryatt sealed a famous win and only a second ever FA Cup semi-final in City's history. With the name-change issue momentarily put to one side, City fans united for what was only to be a second visit to Wembley in 110 years. To add an extra cherry on to the cake, City's semi-final opposition was to be League One side Sheffield United, meaning the prospect of a first ever FA Cup Final was now a real possibility. As the chants of 'Que será, será! Whatever will be will be! We're going to Wembley!' began, the reality of the situation hit me – only ten years after the first promotion that kick-started Hull City's revolution, the Tigers, under Steve Bruce, had perhaps the best opportunity they would ever have of reaching a domestic cup final. It goes without saying that 'typical City' would not go on to do it the easy way, yet despite all the chaos beginning to kick off behind the scenes, it appeared City's meteoric rise which had begun a decade earlier was showing no signs of stopping just yet.

In what felt like a carbon copy day of our last visit to Wembley six years earlier, Dad, Mum, Steph and I walked down Wembley

Way for the semi-final in glorious sunshine, feeling nervous but expecting a comfortable win. In reality the match was an emotional rollercoaster. Despite the remarkable 5–3 scoreline, other than the goals themselves along with an almost overpowering feeling of dread and worry for much of the match, I remember little of the day overall, particularly when compared to the final a month later. What I do remember is being sat much higher in Wembley's upper tier for this match, feeling much further from the pitch than 2008 or indeed the upcoming final. I will also never forget Dad's reaction as Blade Jose Baxter poked home the opening goal 19 minutes in.

'Bloody hell, City! This is our one chance to reach an FA Cup Final and you're throwing it away to a bloody Third Division side!'

I am usually one for shooting down Dad's pessimism so early on in a match, but it was difficult on this occasion. From this moment until half-time, the match really did have a 'typical City' feel about it. Even when City equalised through Yannick Sagbo on 42 minutes there wasn't enough time to get too excited before United hit back immediately, this time Scougall arriving late into the box to finish from Murphy's cross. As the City players trudged in for half-time, I thought we'd blown it.

Bruce rang in the changes at half-time though, bringing on Fryatt and Aluko for Boyd and Figueroa – attacking changes which would go on to define the match. Inspired by terrific second-half performances from Aluko and Huddlestone, City scored twice early following the interval – first a tap-in from Fryatt, before man of the match Huddlestone charged into the box after a tidy one-two with Meyer and curled the ball past Mark Howard in the Blades goal. A brilliant goal.

For the first time that afternoon City were ahead and the black and amber half of Wembley erupted.

'Never in doubt!' I sniggered, as Dad shook his head in disbelief.

'Why can't we ever just do it the easy way!' Dad replied.

But the drama wasn't over just yet. City went on to make it 4–2 when former Blade Stephen Quinn headed home with 25 minutes left to play. Finally, the City half of Wembley felt as though the party could start.

Still, there was to be one more twist in the tale of this remarkable tie. With 90 minutes on the clock, the slim prospect of extra time reared its ugly head once more as Jamie Murphy's volley made it 4–3. An anxious period of added time beckoned, prevented when a breakaway Meyler goal three minutes later sealed the victory and sent 35,000 travelling City fans into raptures.

Hull City were in their first ever FA Cup Final. Just ten years after I watched our promotion from the old Division Three on a large screen in the Vulcan Arena in Hull, I was to return to Wembley to see my beloved City take on the mighty Arsenal in the oldest, most respected domestic tournament in world football. Madness.

The following month was a blur. The league became a secondary concern as the entire city of Hull came down with cup fever. As a result, City's Premier League form suffered with Bruce's men losing four and picking up just one point from our last five matches. Yet, as predicted, the Tigers finished the season in a club record 16th position, securing Premier League football for another year.

A few days after our final league game of the season against Everton, and just days before City were due to travel down to London ahead of the final, quite out of the blue I was emailed by *Shoot!* asking me to attend the club's pre-final press conference at the KC Stadium on behalf of the magazine. Suited up and with the famous old FA Cup just metres in front of me, the opportunity to ask questions to Hull City players and management just days before the biggest match in the club's history was an absolute honour and one I will never forget. Curtis Davies, David Meyler, James Chester and, of course, Steve Bruce all faced the assembled media and were all confident of causing an upset. Their positivity and passion settled my nerves both as a fledgling journalist at my first press conference, as well as a lifelong Hull City fan days before a historic match, and the resulting match preview I wrote for *Shoot!* remains to this day one of my favourite pieces I have ever worked on.

I think it goes without saying that final day itself was one of the most memorable days of my life. With Steph living in London, Dad, Mum and I travelled down to the capital the day before the game and stayed at her Balham flat. As we had six years earlier, only this time with the addition of Mum and Steph's Arsenal-supporting fiancé Mike, much of the day was spent plodding around London in full City attire, stopping at a few pubs, having a bite to eat and generally killing time before a 5pm kick-off. When we arrived at Wembley Park tube station and made our way down Wembley Way in a sea of black and amber, and red and white, excitement started to build in the pit of my stomach. Due to a strange ticket allocation quirk the five tickets we had bought for the final were split. This meant while Dad and I were sat together in the lower tier slightly to the left of one goal, Steph, Mum and Mike were in the next tier up, located on the other side of City's seating allocation. As we said our goodbyes and settled on a meeting point for after the match, Steph said confidently, as Mike rolled his eyes, '2–0 City – shock of the century, you watch!'

As we split up and found our respective turnstiles, I thought about what Steph had just said. Usually before City faced Arsenal I would have laughed it off. 2–0? No chance. But something felt different today. Regardless of City's awful finish to the league season, I felt that we might just witness something special. After all, the so-called 'magic of the FA Cup' is built on 'cupsets' (cringeworthy football cliché klaxon #42).

I have only physically cried at a City game on a handful of occasions, all of which are documented in this book. However, perhaps the most irrationally emotional I have ever felt at a football match was when the traditional pre-match anthem, 'Abide with Me', along with the national anthem were performed just before City's only ever FA Cup Final kicked off. Hearing such an iconic hymn before a match featuring little old Hull City felt significant. I can't explain it, but somehow this moment felt like the pinnacle of anything I could possibly experience as a City fan. Leicester City are perhaps the exception that proves the rule. As a Hull City fan it is extremely unlikely, if not impossible, that I will ever witness my side winning the Premier League title or the Champions League – this is just the reality of modern football – but whatever happens I will always have the experience of watching my side line up against one of English football's giants in a major final.

Due to a plethora of injuries and cup-tied players, Bruce was limited when choosing his starting XI for the final, but ultimately opted for a 3–5–1–1 formation, made up of McGregor, Chester, Bruce, Davies, Elmohamady, Livermore, Meyler, Huddlestone, Rosenior, Quinn and Fryatt – to date the only 11 men to start a major cup final for the Tigers, and names that will forever be etched into my memory. Arsenal, on the other hand, had an embarrassment of talent to select from and with the exception of Fabianski in the Gunner's net, were all first-team regulars and full internationals. Little did they know they were about to get the shock of their lives.

'Here we go, pal!' Dad whispered, as a roar greeted kick-off.

'Stranger things have happened – after all, we've never lost at Wembley,' I reminded him. 'Come on you 'ull!'

In a whirlwind first few minutes, City started much the stronger side and had Arsenal on the back foot from the very off. An Elmohamady cross set the tone of the opening ten minutes, landing on the roof of the net with Fabianski in a state of panic, and seconds later City had forced the first corner of the day before Arsenal had even ventured into City's half. From this resulting corner came one of the most famous goals in Tigers history.

The redheaded Quinn looked for Huddlestone at the edge of the box who tried to strike the ball first time back towards goal, channelling his inner Paul Scholes. The former Spurs man uncharacteristically scuffed the volley, and the hideous pink FA Cup ball looked to be heading well wide before James Chester stuck out a foot and diverted the ball past Fabianski into the bottom corner. 1–0 City after four minutes and absolute mayhem in the Tigers end.

'What did I tell ya?!' I shouted at Dad as the chant of 'Who are ya!' started from 35,000 ecstatic City fans.

Dad raised his eyebrows and grinned. He wasn't getting excited yet.

But, it was to get even better.

Before the overjoyed City faithful had even sat down following Chester's opener, Curtis Davies miraculously doubled our lead. The tenacious Quinn picked up the ball on the left, tricked his way past Aaron Ramsey and chipped into the box for Alex Bruce to head against a combination of the post and Fabianski's hand. The ball rebounded perfectly for captain Davies to smash home from a narrow angle.

As Davies wheeled away, creating his own Marco Tardelli moment, the black and amber half of Wembley totally lost it. Drinks flew everywhere, shirts were removed and thrown into the air, and the noise levels reached new heights. Not since Windass's 2008 winner on the same hallowed turf of Wembley had I witnessed such jubilation.

As I looked on, I was too stunned to form a coherent sentence. Celebratory screams of 'COOOMMMEEEONNNN!' were all that would come from my mouth, as my whole body went numb with excitement. Hull City were 2–0 up after just nine minutes in an FA Cup Final, with the two goals coming from two centre-backs. I quite literally pinched myself several times. Surely, I was still asleep on the sofa of Steph's Balham flat, dreaming of the perfect final? This could not be happening.

Yet, as the players finally ran into position after what felt like minutes of celebrating, and the game resumed, a telltale sign of reality struck – Dad chipped in with a pessimistic comment. It's quite impressive to be fair to him; only my father could say the following with a straight face when Hull City are 2–0 up against Arsenal in a major final.

'Too early. I don't like it. I feel uneasy.'

'Oh, shut up! We're 2–0 up in the cup final!'

Of course, deep down I knew he was right. Could there be a more 'typical City' thing to do than go two up in a cup final only to go on to lose it?

Even Dad nearly cracked a smile moments later, however, when a third goal from a third centre-half was just inches away. Son of the manager – and a much better player than he is ever given credit for – Alex Bruce must have thought he had scored, along with 35,000 giddy City fans, when his looping header floated over Fabianski as the entire stadium held its breath. Unfortunately, Arsenal full-back Kieran Gibbs was on the line to provide a game-changing clearance, which would go on to serve as a much-needed wake-up call for Wenger's men.

I have spoken about sliding door moments both in football matches and in my own life, and this is one of the biggest I can remember witnessing first-hand. I believe if Bruce's header had found the back of the net, City would have won the cup that day. Bloody Kieran Gibbs.

As it happened, this clearance was indeed to provide the kick up the backside for Arsenal I so dreaded and with 17 minutes on the clock they pulled one back.

This goal has never sat right with me, though. What I have always considered the softest of Bruce fouls on Santi Cazorla saw the Spaniard half the deficit with the resulting free kick from 25 yards out. I will never be convinced it was a legitimate foul, for one, and heartbreakingly, it must be said that Allan McGregor should have saved it.

Despite a barrage of Arsenal pressure, somehow City made it to the interval still 2–1 to the good.

However, Cazorla's goal had irreparably changed the mood inside the ground. As the second half went on, City dropped deeper and deeper into our own half and Mesut Özil and Aaron Ramsey began pulling the strings from the Arsenal midfield. As much as it pains me to say it, it would be churlish not to admit an equaliser had been on the cards for some time when Laurent Koscielny bundled in from a corner with 20 minutes to go.

'Shit. What now?' Dad asked as a dejected and exhausted-looking City XI lumbered back into position. 'Go for it with 20 minutes to go, or sit back and play for extra time?'

As it played out, a tired City committed to neither strategy full-heartedly, instead pushing our luck defensively while failing to press forward for a potential winner. Chances came and went for Gibbs, Giroud and Sanogo, before referee Lee Probert blew for full time.

But the final whistle provided little respite for Bruce's men. More of the same came during the first period of extra time with Giroud striking the bar with a fierce headed effort early on, while the Tigers out on the pitch appeared dead on their feet. After 108 minutes of courageous resistance came one of those awful moments that still haunts me to this day. It's true, I have woken up in cold sweats on more than a few occasions during the past five years, seeing in my mind's eye that clever back-heel from Giroud which was then perfectly poked home by Ramsey for the dramatic winner. Agonising.

Late chances fell to Sone Aluko, and on two separate occasions the entire City end thought the Nigerian had equalised, with both efforts close – but not close enough. Moments after the second of these opportunities, Probert's whistle sounded, and that was that. My beloved City, the perennial underdogs, had caused Arsenal all kinds of problems but in the end it just wasn't enough. The Gunners had broken their duck and Wenger had led them to their first trophy in nine years.

Typically a football fan is furious after seeing their side throw away a two-goal lead, especially in a game of such importance, yet somehow it was impossible in this instance. Each and every player dressed in black and amber was sensational that day, while the occasion itself was everything an FA Cup Final day should be. Perhaps unsurprisingly and regardless of the result, it will remain one of the greatest City matches I have had the pleasure of attending.

As Dad and I watched the entire Arsenal squad, including several 'players' clad in red and white I have never seen before or since, climb the 107 steps to the Royal Box, a sudden feeling of melancholia struck me. Just over ten years previously I had watched City struggle to overcome a non-league Morecambe side at the KC in this very competition. Now, a decade later, my club had taken one of the best teams in the land into extra time, giving the mighty Arsenal the shock of their lives. The club may have blown their greatest opportunity of winning the famous old competition, but at least we did so in style.

Indeed, City may not have managed to go the whole way and win the cup, and the toxic behind the scenes activities were continuing to chip away at my love for football, but regardless of this I cannot deny just how special the 2013/14 season was. Not only was the campaign an overall success on the pitch, it was also the last time I viewed the club with complete love and devotion, and provided the last set of players I can look back on with total fondness. It was a club not yet divided and torn apart by a universally despised ownership. A side built around honest and hardworking professionals which, together with a great manager, created a team much greater than the sum of its parts. It was not yet a club with a revolving door policy highly detrimental to squad development, hamstrung by the pig-headedness and greed of spiteful owners. It was a club that still cared about their fans. Not one that appeared to reward decades of loyalty with nothing but price hikes, insults and patronising incentives. Cracks had started to appear with the initiation of name-change proceedings months earlier, yet this was to be nothing compared to the deep chasm that would rapidly form between Hull City's owners and their faithful fans during the immediate years to come. No wonder I began to fall out of love with the beautiful game.

Nevertheless, nothing can ever take the memories of this wonderful season away. A club record league finish in one of the greatest and most competitive divisions in the world and a narrow defeat in a thrilling FA Cup Final, in which we led for much of the 90 minutes. It may sound unambitious, but the truth of supporting a traditionally lower-league football club dictates that this might well remain the most successful season I ever witness as a City fan. But, do you know what? I'm okay with that.

Generations of Tigers fans endured a century of relative mediocrity with nothing but a burning passion for the club keeping them going. If nothing ever tops this season, I am just grateful I was a part of it.

2014–2019

Apathy, addiction and rehabilitation

European blues

Hull City 2–2 KSC Lokeren – 28/08/2014

AS much as I think about it, and I think about it a lot, I can never pinpoint the exact moment when my love for football transitioned into something that more closely resembles an addiction. I have never been able to identify that one moment that tipped me over the edge. The simple explanation of this is because, as documented throughout this book, this moment has in fact come about as the result of a gradual process and attempting to find one match or specific moment of change would be oversimplifying an overtly complex situation. That being said, there is a season in which I knew my relationship with football, and City specifically, had irreparably changed forever.

Regardless of the fact that Hull City's best season on record was just months behind me, the climax of summer brought with it feelings of frustration and annoyance I had never experienced before. For the first time, I found myself resenting aspects of a game I once had loved unquestionably. I now recognise that the issue had been bubbling under the surface for a few months, but it wasn't until this dreadful realisation came to a head on one miserable evening in August 2014 that I began to understand the full extent of the problem. The location was the KC Stadium. The event was Hull City – or 'Hull Tigers' as all of the appalling Allam-conceived marketing around this time would have you believe – squandering a once-in-a-generation shot at progressing into the group stages of a European competition.

Thinking about this night still makes me feel sick.

It's important to note first, however, that away from football I had a great summer in 2014. After finishing a wonderful maiden year at university in the May, I travelled down to London and moved in with Steph for a two-month adventure in the capital. On top of writing for *Shoot!* and *Leeds Student* over the previous eight months, my newly discovered passion for writing had seen me branch out, freelancing on both a casual and paid basis for dozens of online sites. One of these websites was *Urban Times*, a London-based social content publishing platform that was still going through its infancy. I had been providing *UT* with regular content since the turn of the year, before, quite out of the blue, I received an email from one of the platform's founders Alexander Phillips asking if I would be interested in a two-month internship over the summer. I was asked to intern in a political editor role, sourcing content, managing a small pool of writers, and spending long days in *UT*'s Regents Park office space. Naturally, I couldn't have agreed quickly enough.

Not only did this mean spending summer living in London with Steph, proactively obtaining vital experience in an industry I was now desperate to become a part of, it also meant I would be living in London for the duration of the 2014 World Cup. It does have to be said, somehow still on a downer from South Africa four years earlier and with the uninspiring Roy Hodgson in charge of the national team, I didn't have high hopes for England. Yet I was looking forward to the tournament all the same, and as a spectacle it didn't disappoint.

As it turned out, I was right not to have high hopes for Hodgson's England. In a style in which only the Three Lions can manage, arriving in Brazil without any real expectations for the first time in decades, they would leave the spiritual home of football having miraculously managed to lower national belief even further. Some feat.

England's World Cup was over in just six days. A hard-fought 2–1 defeat to Italy in our opening fixture created an uphill battle from the very start, yet a shocking display five days later against

Luis Suarez's Uruguay saw England fatally go down 2–1, crashing out of the tournament before it had even got going. Embarrassing, but predictable.

A decade earlier I had wept when a Ronaldo-inspired Portugal had knocked a brave England side out of Euro 2004 at the quarter-final stage. As I sat in the Green Man pub just off Great Portland Street watching England's meaningless final group fixture against Costa Rica with my London-based university mate Art, I felt nothing but apathy for England. Everyone knew we would disappoint at Brazil 2014; it just turned out this inevitable disappointment came a few rounds earlier than usual. I was almost happy, as it goes. As Art and I watched on as England bored us half to death, while Luis Suarez bit Italian Giorgio Chiellini in Group D's other concluding match, a feeling of relief struck me. An early England exit meant my full attention could turn to enjoying the rest of the tournament as a football-loving neutral without worrying about supporting a shambolic England side. This is exactly what I did. And with the one exception of Russia 2018, which I will come on to, I don't think I have ever enjoyed a World Cup more. Messi's spectacular stoppage-time winner against Iran, classic World Cup goals from James Rodríguez, Robin van Persie and Tim Cahill, and, of course, the unbelievable image of Brazilian fans applauding the Germans in the second half of a semi-final that saw the hosts smashed 7–1 by the future winners. What a World Cup.

My internship came to an end in late July and I returned to Hull, my passion for writing hitting new levels and, despite a woeful England showing, my love for football temporarily restored after a wonderful summer of football. Luckily, I didn't have to wait long before I could get my teeth stuck into more competitive football.

Thanks to Arsenal qualifying for the Champions League the season before, City had qualified for the Europa League third qualifying round as FA Cup runners-up – providing Hull City with a first taste of European competition in 110 years. As such, the 2014/15 season was to start early for the Tigers with an away trip to Slovakian side AS Trenčín kicking off a long and arduous season. I didn't travel to Slovakia for the match on 31 July – a 0–0 draw that saw Huddlestone miss a penalty as Bruce's men looked somewhat rusty. Though I did attend the second leg at the KC a week later. In this game City didn't appear too much brighter, to be honest, having to come from behind with goals from Elmohamady and Aluko ensuring City progressed into the next qualifying stage.

This time City were drawn against Belgium side Sporting Lokeren, again with the first leg to be played away. With Mum and Dad home from their annual holiday in Spain the week before City's second European tie, Dad and I were set to travel to Belgium for a midweek break to support City and sample a few Belgian beers before my return to university the next month. Alas, it wasn't to be in the end. Upon returning from Spain, Dad had fallen ill and was practically bedbound for three days before he was taken into hospital with a high fever and severe back pain. A few months later the source of the mystery 'episode', as one doctor that August described it, was solved when at only 61 he was diagnosed with kidney failure. I remember being gutted at the time – heartbroken that I was to miss what turned out to be my only opportunity to watch City play away in European competition. Of course, in hindsight none of that seemed to matter too much.

One week later, as Dad continued to recover in hospital, I attended the second leg of the tie alone. Although I always much preferred going to the football with my dad, 11 years of sitting in the same seat in the KC's East Stand had seen us make plenty of friends in the E5 vicinity – a group of close friends that remained together until the inception of the dreaded 'membership scheme' a few years later – another Allam family failure.

City had lost 1–0 in Belgium, the only goal of the match coming from a McGregor error, but there was still all to play for. The only issue being, City would never take the tie or the opposition seriously and ultimately wasted a unique opportunity in the club's history. Indeed, Bruce made six changes to the team that had played in the Premier League just days before, indicating from the off that the Europa League was a secondary concern.

Before the match even kicked off, I remember a strange atmosphere lingered around the KC. Although the Premier League season was underway by this point, there was still an overriding air of preseason surrounding this game. Nevertheless, City got off to the perfect start when Brady scored just six minutes into the match, bundling in a Figueroa cross. 1–0 on the night and 1–1 on aggregate.

But it was the Belgians that grew stronger as the game went on. McGregor made amends for his mistake in the first leg with a great save from a well-struck free kick from Lokeren's Killian Overmeire early in the second half, but there was nothing the Scot could do about Jordan Remacle's powerful effort that came from the resulting corner, leaving City needing to score twice to progress thanks to UEFA's away goal rule.

Brady gave us City fans hope just six minutes later when his penalty kick put us within touching distance of the Europa League's group stages, but it wasn't to be.

When Yannick Sagbo was sent off with 20 minutes to go, we lost all momentum.

'That's it,' I remember saying to Gary and Jamie – a father and son that had been sat in the row in front of Dad, Steph and I for a decade, 'the only chance we'll ever have of seeing City play in Europe and we've blown it. Typical City.'

Gary nodded sombrely, as the little atmosphere that had been created inside the KC evaporated.

Tom Huddlestone, City's key man who should have started the game, predictably made a positive impact coming off the bench late on, but it wasn't enough, and City's fate was confirmed just seconds after his late effort was cleared off the line as the final whistle sounded. It was all over.

If the result and City's approach to the game hadn't infuriated me enough, Bruce's post-match comments tipped me over the edge. As I drove myself home that evening, listening to BBC Humberside, I nearly screamed as the former Manchester United man said 'Focus always has to be on the Premier League, it has to be ... It's gone too quick for everyone but it's not to be, so we move on'.

Prior to this second leg, Bruce had stated how excited and proud he was to bring European nights to the KC Stadium as he waxed lyrical about the importance of taking the Europa League seriously for the sake of the fans. Then he selected a starting line-up peppered with fringe players, omitting our best midfielder in Huddlestone and our key goalscorer in Jelavić. The result: a gamble on an unbalanced and disjointed team that *should*, but ultimately *did not*, have enough to beat an ordinary Lokeren side. What a wasted opportunity.

It's interesting. If you were to ask any Hull City supporter worth their salt who is the greatest City manager of all time I wager an overwhelming majority would tell you it's Steve Bruce. This is absolutely the correct response, by the way; the man masterminded two separate promotions to the Premier League, took us to a first FA Cup Final and, in patches, had us playing some of the best football I have ever seen a City side play. But, and it's a big 'but', the 2014/15 season was an absolute disaster.

Indeed, after being unceremoniously dumped out of the Europa League, Bruce spent big in an attempt to build on the previous season's 16th-place finish in the Premier League. The likes of Robert Snodgrass, Tom Ince, Harry Maguire, Andrew Robertson, Michael Dawson, Abel Hernández and Mohamed Diamé all contributed to what must be considered Hull City's strongest ever squad, while Gastón Ramírez and Hatem Ben Arfa also joined on loan. Yet inexplicably the catastrophic 14/15 season still ended in relegation.

In truth City were not one of the worst three sides in the league that year, and relegation did feel unjust. But, as you all know, (cliché klaxon) 'the league table never lies', and negative tactics during the second half of the campaign caught up with us.

I will never forget sitting at the KC at the final whistle of City's last Premier League game that season – a 0–0 draw with Manchester United. As the most expensively assembled Hull City squad in history apologetically applauded the emptying stadium,

I remember thinking what a difference a year could make. Less than 12 months earlier I had been glowing with pride following City's heroic FA Cup exploits and buzzing with excitement for the Tigers' first, and probably only, European adventure. A return to the Championship and the prospect of our greatest ever squad being hastily dismantled was a brutal and depressing return to reality.

As I watched Harry Maguire and Andy Robertson – soon to be two of the hottest players in English football – trudge around the pitch, my mind also wandered back to that second leg against Lokeren and Bruce's post-match comments. 'Focus always has to be on the Premier League.'

'What a savage indictment of modern football,' I thought.

Ultimately a Premier League-centric policy cost a set of supporters, dying to see their side play in a European competition, a chance of witnessing a once in a lifetime spectacle. And for what – one more year guaranteed at the top table? In the end we didn't even get that.

Don't get me wrong. I love Steve Bruce, and he would make amends by returning City to the Premier League just 12 months later, despite dealing with increasingly difficult conditions under the challenging regime at the club. However, part of me will not forgive the great man for failing to take our first and probably last adventure in Europe seriously. This failure stank of modern football – prioritising greed and money ahead of supporter-led passion, romance and sportsmanship – and I hated it.

Deplorably, this was a relatively small step in the grand scheme of changes modern football – that in City's case is epitomised by greed, arrogance and poor ownership – had planned for Hull City. Indeed, from this moment to the present day supporting City has been a slog; I've made no bones about it. I've made it painfully clear that my addiction will never allow me to abandon my decades-old Hull City fandom – the experience of the past four or five years has highlighted this – but by 2015 showing my support was becoming a whole lot more difficult. If City's golden decade had been between 2004 and 2014, the next chapter was to be a much bleaker affair.

The gloomiest promotion

Hull City 1–0 Sheffield Wednesday – 28/05/2016

PROMOTION seasons are wonderful things for lower-league football fans. For the vast majority of match-attending supporters – those of us not 'fortunate' enough to be regulars at Old Trafford, Anfield or Stamford Bridge, that is – promotion is usually the best we can hope for after a long season of following our clubs around the country. 'Going up' creates memories that can never be forgotten – memories like Ian Ashbee's screamer at Huish Park in 2004, Nicky Barmby doing 'the aeroplane' celebration at Valley Parade in 2005, Deano crying his eyes out at Wembley in 2008, and Paul McShane scoring against Cardiff in 2013.

The climax of the 2015/16 campaign – my fifth and final promotion season – would forge a set of new memories of its own, yet these recollections are tainted. Unlike the pure, unadulterated joy generated in past promotion seasons, the 2016 play-off victory will always be a bittersweet triumph. You see, when I think of this season my mind doesn't immediately fixate on Diamé's wonder goal at Wembley or Bruce hoisting up a trophy. No, I think of a fan base split into pro-Allam and anti-Allam camps in the wake of the whole name-change saga, an increasingly dejected Steve Bruce, and, most depressingly of all, my final season as a Hull City AFC season ticket holder. The infection that is modern football had now ravaged the entire club and, as always, the fans were the first to suffer.

More than ever before, it was during the 15/16 season that I felt as though, alongside the vast majority of its once unquestioning fan base, I had been alienated by the club I had adored for well over a decade. As a result, the first horrible pangs of apathy struck. This growing inertia perhaps contributes to why I have vastly conflicting memories and emotions about this year in my life. On the one hand, I was in my final year of my undergraduate university course in Leeds, complete with a fantastic social life. I had just started seeing Becki – the woman I would relocate to Chester with just two years later – and the burning excitement of career prospects were very much on the horizon.

On the other hand, Dad's health was at an all-time low, resulting in frequent hospital visits and a programme of dialysis three times a week, alongside his early retirement – both huge changes in his life that he initially struggled to adapt to. Dad's illness also appeared to have an unforeseen knock-on effect on Mum whose levels of anxiety increased, and with this came memory issues and changes in personality she continues to struggle with to this day. Although Dad did receive a new kidney that would last two years thanks to a successful transplant at the back end of 2015, Mum's health has never quite been the same.

2016 was also the year my own football playing days came to a horrible end. Playing five-a-side on a dark and cold evening in March of that year I tore the ACL in my right knee, meaning at the age of 22, I hung up my boots and the world of football (presumably) shed a tear.

On the City side of things, we looked a dead cert for an immediate return to the Premier League, which made for an exciting season on the pitch. That being said, the whole season was monumentally overshadowed by the lingering aftertaste of an internal civil war between fans and ownership following Hull Tigers-gate. This situation worsened in the April of this season with the announcement that season tickets would be scrapped in favour of a 'membership scheme' – an unpopular decision that to this day makes Hull City AFC the only football team in the top four professional divisions not to offer concession ticketing to junior or senior supporters.

The day loyalty died at Hull City.

Fans that had supported the club through thick and thin for 60 years were being told to 'earn their stripes', while simultaneously having their concession ticket prices taken away, not only making it far more difficult to attend games themselves, but also challenging their ability to bring along friends and family. It's no coincidence that since the introduction of the scheme, attendances at the KCOM have plummeted. To put this into context, in City's 2003/04 Division Three campaign City's average league gate was 16,847. In the 2017/18 Championship campaign, coming just one year after a season in the Premier League, the average was 15,622. And this figure is expected to drop further for the 2018/19 season. Talk about earning your stripes, eh?

Indeed, I remember thinking throughout this campaign that during my lifetime as a City fan, the club has battled for its very survival at the foot of the Football League, yet still as a club felt 100 times more unified than it did during this period. Somewhere along the line the family atmosphere that had kept my club going through its darkest days appeared, to me at least, to be dying, and it was horrible to watch.

Paradoxically, if one focuses strictly on the on-the-pitch activities, Bruce's final season as City manager would have gone down as one of City's finest. Though, of course, football doesn't work like that. There were a few sticky moments during the season, but this campaign is unique as the only one I recall never believing promotion was not absolutely guaranteed. Despite my preseason worries, Bruce had managed to keep hold of a large proportion of the squad relegated the season before, with the only real players of note to leave the club being Brady, McShane, Chester and Jelavić. Indeed, the shrewd summer signings of Sam Clucas, Moses Odubajo and Shaun Maloney, combined with the existing talent Bruce had convinced to stay, unquestionably gave City the strongest squad in the division – a squad that on paper appeared more than capable of finishing comfortably in mid-table in the Premier League, never mind a Championship title challenge. Of course, football isn't played on paper. (Sorry.)

As I made my way through my final year in Leeds, City consistently occupied a place in the top six places of the division, playing exceptionally well on occasions, yet somehow never able to reach top gear. Uruguayan Abel Hernández and Robert Snodgrass, the latter who had missed the entirety of the previous season with a serious knee injury, proved City's key men going forward, while the young Andy Robertson, Harry Maguire and Sam Clucas looked destined for the Premier League whether City were to be promoted or not.

Kitted out in a smart black and amber pinstriped number, ruined by the universally disliked, newly redesigned nameless crest and embarrassing *Flamingo Land* logo plastered across the front, there are a few matches that will live long in the memory from this season. A 2–1 defeat to Charlton in August 2015, my first trip to The Valley and a great away day despite the result, as well as a 6–0 City mauling at the KC in the corresponding fixture, stand out for me. Not to mention the hard-fought 2–1 victory at home to Wolves, and the mass fan protest in response to the announcement of the membership scheme before Brentford's visit to the KC.

However, it's the play-off campaign of 15/16 that defines this season for most City fans. The 3–0 drubbing of Derby County at Pride Park in the first leg, nearly throwing it away at the newly rebranded KCOM Stadium in the second leg, and a third Wembley win in eight years in the final against Wednesday.

Even as a one-off occasion, City's trip to Wembley for the 2016 Championship play-off final was underwhelming. Don't get me wrong, as a fan of a club who waited 104 years to even play at the national stadium, I know a visit to Wembley should never be sniffed at, but there was such a negative feeling around the club at this time, which in many ways poisoned the whole experience. Dad, Mum and I travelled down to London the day before and stayed at Steph's London flat, and after a lengthy breakfast on final day, made our way across London to Wembley in order to soak up the atmosphere early. But when we arrived, something felt off. Our previous three visits brought with them something of the unknown – a first shot at the Premier League, a first semi-final in 84 years and a first ever FA Cup Final – yet this was different. We'd achieved so much more since our last play-off final eight years earlier, and the usual feeling of Wembley excitement was replaced by one of gut-wrenching anxiety and nerves. After all, once the novelty of Wembley wears off, all a play-off final comes down to is one *all or nothing* match. A one-game shoot-out in which, on this occasion, we were heavy favourites to win. I felt sick.

The excitement of the Wednesday fans wasn't helping my mood. For weeks they had taken to social media en masse, describing City as a 'tinpot' club and stressing how they could sell their allocation of Wembley seats ten times over. It was almost as though they had forgotten that City had experienced four promotions, an FA Cup Final and a brief taste of European football during the 16 years since their relegation from the Premiership. Though credit where it's due, the Owls fans were brilliant both inside and outside Wembley that day in stark contrast to the travelling City supporters, embarrassingly surrounded by swaths of empty red seats. Indeed, as I looked around the City end and then across to the Wednesday fans before kick-off, I thought back to 2008 and endeavoured to pinpoint what had changed and why City fans no longer resembled their South Yorkshire counterparts at the prospect of a place in the Premier League. After a while it became obvious. Unlike our opponents that day, us City fans had seen everything we could realistically expect our club to achieve in the space of ten years. We had then seen all of that hard work spoilt by unpopular ownership decisions and petty infighting, and now an anti-Allam boycott movement was impressively gathering momentum. Wednesday and their buoyant fan base, on the other hand, were ready for a return to the Premier League after their strongest league finish since relegation from the top tier in 2000. An Owls win seemed written in the stars.

Unlike 2008, however, the match was not to follow any script. As it turned out, City dominated large sections of the match, limiting Carlos Carvalhal's men to long-range efforts and ambitious Forestieri set pieces. Meanwhile the Tigers' front four of Snodgrass, Diamé, Hernández and Elmohamady, as well as some fantastic wing-back play from both Robertson and Odubajo, controlled the game as City slowly started to turn the screw as the match progressed. Good chances came and went for City with Diamé hitting the post, and Hernández, Dawson and Robertson all going close, before the decisive moment of the match came in the 72nd minute. It was to be well worth the wait.

A long ball wasn't properly dealt with by the Wednesday backline and possession was picked up by Snodgrass. The Scottish international cut inside, looking to find room to shoot and drawing two Wednesday defenders towards him in the process. He nipped the ball to the vacant Diamé on his right who took one look up before curling a right-footed shot past Keiren Westwood. The east end of Wembley exploded as off-the-pitch issues momentarily were put to one side as a goal of genuine quality was celebrated. If Windass's 2008 Wembley winner is my favourite of all time, Diamé's 2016 vintage is a close second.

Wednesday never recovered. Chances to make it 2–0 came for Odubajo and Hernández before Bruce 'parked the bus' with the late introductions of Maguire, Meyler and Clucas. Five minutes of injury time later, and that was it. City were back in the Premier League. Bruce had redeemed himself and returned City to the big time just 12 months after taking us down. The black and amber half of Wembley made sure Bruce knew just how appreciated he was when the manager followed his players up the steps and into the Royal Box. Little did the 30,000 jubilant City fans know that this would be his last competitive match in charge of the Tigers. As the emotionally spent manager wearily lifted the oversized trophy aloft, the greatest manager in Hull City history received the loudest cheer of the afternoon. Yet, even this touching moment was ruined just seconds later, as the trophy was passed along the line of delighted players and handed to a triumphant-looking

Ehab Allam who lifted the trophy jubilantly. Cue a deafening crescendo of boos.

The owner of a side that has just won the so-called most expensive game in world football at Wembley to return to the Premier League being roundly booed by his own supporters – only Hull City AFC could find themselves in such a bizarre situation.

As the five of us walked back down Wembley Way towards the tube station, Dad turned to me and said, 'Well, it's never the same second time around, but an enjoyable day all the same.'

'Let's just hope our Premier League status attracts new owners ASAP,' I replied. 'I'm not sure how much more of this I can take. It might never be the same again, but new owners would be a start.'

I wouldn't get my wish.

Less than three months later, a manager-less City would be labelled the 'worst prepared team in Premier League history', just days before the start of what would become the club's fifth and final top-flight campaign to date.

Rock bottom

England 1–2 Iceland – 27/06/2016

FOOTBALL addicts can only stay mad at the game for so long. It's the nature of being an addict. Despite walking away from Wembley as a fan of the winning side after the play-off final, I told myself I needed a break from football. A detox over the summer was needed to sweep away the apathy and frustration, and come August I would be ready to deal with modern football again. There was only one issue. In the summer of 2016 England were travelling to France for the Euros. Although I promised myself otherwise, naturally I relapsed and watched as many matches as humanly possible. As a supporter of England, and a football fanatic questioning the very nature of his relationship with his biggest passion, this was to be disastrous.

Away from football, the summer of 2016 was a fascinating one. Alongside the European Championships, Europe was also dominating the news headlines with the build-up, and then of course aftermath, of the UK's shock decision to leave the European Union following the so-called Brexit referendum in June. Incredibly, more than three years on, we are still dealing with the fallout of this decision.

My own life also changed significantly in the June with the formal end of my undergraduate life. For a couple of months at least, I was forced into the real world. Along with my flatmate Mark, I started working for a well-known pub chain in the centre of Leeds – it wasn't journalism, but it paid the bills. I didn't much want a part-time job at the time; I was still living off a precarious combination of my student loan, freelancing jobs and an ever-growing overdraft, but with my degree over I needed something extra to keep me going for a few months. I had taken the decision to follow my ambition to become a journalist and had enrolled myself in an International Journalism MA course at the University of Leeds. This seemed the obvious choice at the time – build my skill set and qualification level in an area in which I wished to pursue a career, while staying in a city I loved for another year. But with my MA not starting until the October, I had five months to kill. As it turned out, working behind the bar of a busy pub in the centre of Leeds, with each Euro 2016 game being broadcast live in the background, was a pretty good way of killing time. Looking back, it was a pretty idyllic student summer of 'working', drinking and watching as much football as possible. If only England had got the memo.

As ever, the Three Lions had breezed through the qualifying stages and had even thrown in some impressive friendly victories against France, Portugal and world champions Germany in the lead up to the tournament. It was as though Hodgson's men were teasing fans that this time would be different. Though after England's last three tournaments in which we followed a strict agenda of arriving, doing very little and then crashing out, I wasn't allowing myself to get too excited.

This was a sensible decision.

I was working on the night of England's first Group B match against a poor Russia side, but was able to watch the entire match over the shoulder of thirsty customers while pouring pint after pint. Wales, also in Group B, had recorded a comfortable 2–1 victory over Slovakia earlier that day, meaning a win against the Russians was vital not only to aid qualification to the next round of the tournament, but also for national pride. However, it could be argued that national pride had already been damaged badly at this point following the news of riots involving English fans, Russians and the French police on the streets of Marseille the day before. But that's another story.

Dressed in what is by far my least favourite England strip of all time – a bastardisation of our traditional all-white home shirt, featuring light blue sleeves with darker blue details on the collar and down the sides of the shirt, finished off with the ridiculous addition of cherry-red socks – England blotted it once again. Despite dominating for the full 90 minutes and going ahead midway through the second half through a fantastic Eric Dier free kick, a lack of concentration in stoppage time allowed for Vasili Berezutski's header to level the match. Two points dropped.

England's second match against Wales was a much more enjoyable affair. With a midweek 3pm kick-off, I was able to watch what turned out to be the most enjoyable England match of the tournament on the big screen, with a big group of my mates, at *The Terrace Bar,* Leeds University Union. The place was packed, the atmosphere was electric, and for once, England didn't disappoint. Despite allowing Wales to go 1–0 up thanks to a combination of Gareth Bale magic and Joe Hart incompetence, a battling England comeback restored a little hope and belief into a jaded English fan base. Jamie Vardy – a man still on a high after playing the season of his life for Leicester City – bundled in the equaliser, before England scored a vital injury-time goal of their own when Daniel Sturridge worked his way into the box and poked home at the near post. The union building erupted as the only positive English memory of 2016 was created.

An incredibly forgettable final group game against Slovakia followed in which the Three Lions could only manage a 0–0 draw, resulting in a second-place group finish behind Wales. This match was so dull, it represents a rare example of a tournament game involving England I have no recollection of watching. Clearly, my poor brain deemed it too tedious to bother even storing for future reference. Quite impressive when you think I can't remember a second of this, but I can name the entire starting line-up for City's clash with Stockport County at Edgeley Park in 2005. Strange.

Frustratingly, this typical English slip saw a second-round tie against surprise package Iceland, rather than the weaker

Northern Ireland side drawn by the Welsh. This would prove highly significant.

Although the Scandinavians had impressed throughout qualifying and looked solid enough in a group containing Portugal, Austria and Hungary, England went into the last-16 match as heavy favourites. After all, as the media constantly reminded us, a nation ranked 34th in the world – and with a population of just 330,000 – were surely no match for an English side packed with world-class players in each position, were they?

I watched the match in my shared student house in Hyde Park, Leeds. Stocked up on crisps, sweets and crates of lager, around 15 of us crammed into the lounge of our little terrace house ready for a Euro 2016 party. We watched as Joe Hart barked motivation buzzwords at his team-mates in the tunnel, proclaiming England were the better side, and urging his comrades to use their quality to intimidate their opposition, all the time insisting on a mindset of total focus and concentration. Oh, how ironic this would turn out to be.

Funnily enough, England did look the much superior side during the opening few minutes.

'Could be a big win for England, this,' I said, as Raheem Sterling beat his man twice in the opening few minutes of the match.

Sure enough, with just four minutes on the clock, we got the early goal we were looking for. Captain Rooney was the man to put England ahead, scoring from the spot after the Icelandic keeper Halldorsson brought down the lively Sterling. With flashbacks to Michael Owen scoring the opener against Brazil all those years ago, I sat back down and naively allowed my mind to get carried away. Hodgson's men would now coast into the quarter-finals where they would embarrass host nation France on their own soil to reach a first semi-final since Euro 96, suitably against the Germans. It was at this moment, just as I was picturing a revitalised Wayne Rooney smashing his third past Manuel Neuer, that I was brought crashing back to reality. Within a minute of the restart Iceland had equalised. A dangerous long throw into

England's box – think Rory Delap in his prime – bamboozled Hodgson's backline allowing Ragnar Sigurdsson to tap home from close range.

The goal rocked England. Other than two poor efforts drilled over the bar from Alli and Kane respectively, Iceland began to take control. On 18 minutes, the Nordic pressure paid off and my heart dropped. Kolbeinn Sigþórsson found himself at the edge of England's box with the ball at his feet and in acres of space. The big Nantes striker took two confident strides into the area and fired a tame shot down to Hart's left. The Manchester City goalkeeper, so confident in the tunnel prior to the match, appeared to go down in instalments and, despite getting a flapping hand to the ball, saw it squirm past him and over the line. For the second match in as many weeks a Joe Hart mistake had cost England a vital goal.

'Oh, here we go,' groaned my pal, Niall. 'Surely not even England can balls it up against Iceland – they're a bloody supermarket!'

No one appreciated the humour. England were in trouble.

What followed was without a doubt the most abject and shameful footballing performance I have ever witnessed. While England may have controlled possession for the painfully uncreative remaining 75 minutes of play that followed, we looked totally and utterly bereft of ideas going forward. The result? An hour and a quarter of *the* worst football I have ever seen. And remember, my football-supporting days started on the terraces of Boothferry Park watching Division Three footballers kick the shit out of one another.

Half-chances came and went for Kane, Smalling and Alli, before substitute Jamie Vardy almost grabbed a dramatic leveller in injury time. Yet, an all-important equaliser never came, nor was ever deserved. Indeed, the best chance of the second half actually fell for Iceland's Ragnar Sigurdsson, when his spectacular bicycle kick was palmed away by Hart.

When the final whistle sounded, England's players sunk to the turf, dejected and shell-shocked – an image mirrored perfectly in my downstairs lounge. We could not believe what we had just witnessed.

As a stony-faced Roy Hodgson headed straight down the tunnel and the Iceland players joined their fans in performing their famous thunderclap celebration, an almost disgusted-sounding Clive Tyldesley struggled to make sense of what he had just watched.

'England are out. It's another wretched night for England at a major tournament,' the crestfallen veteran commentator announced. 'Club players who have excelled on European stages in their club colours have repeatedly failed to produce in England shirts at international tournaments, but this is THE most abject failure I can recall.'

He was spot on.

The sad truth of the matter is that England were simply out-manoeuvred, out-thought and ultimately outplayed that night. I had lost hope in England a few years prior to this stain on English football's modern history, and was still recovering from the wounds of 2010 and 2014. But as soon as the final whistle sounded in Nice, I knew this setback was something else.

The media would go on to label the Iceland game English football's 'biggest embarrassment'. This is, of course, nonsense. People forget Iceland are a side that qualified by beating Holland home and away – they are no mugs. Yet, it was the nature of the defeat that irked me, as well as an entire nation of football supporters. It's true that by this time England sides had underperformed, and badly, at each tournament for nigh on two decades, but this was different. Euro 2016, embodied by this one wretched display against Iceland, represented the moment a generation of England fans collectively gave up on their national side. The arrogance, entitlement, privilege and greed that had oozed from every pore of the FA for years was finally catching up with the outdated organisation, as the plight of modern football began to hit home on the pitch.

After a nightmare couple of seasons supporting a deeply flawed club in Hull City, I had once again let my guard drop as I foolishly sought solace in supporting England at a major tournament. What was I thinking?

Luckily, in terms of following my national side, this would represent absolute rock bottom. I suppose it's merely a coincidence that this nadir for England perfectly coincided with my own personal crisis with City. Either way, while the Iceland result would directly lead to an overhaul in the running and mentality of the English national side – and an unexpected revival at the 2018 World Cup would reaffirm my love for the beautiful game – the same could not be said for City, who were about to embark on perhaps the most shambolic and chaotic of Premier League stints in the history of the division. Of course, I would readily watch every second of it.

But, why do I keep doing this to myself?

Well, you know when you're stuck in a traffic jam on the motorway, creeping along at five miles an hour, you can see the flashing lights of police cars and ambulances up ahead, and you can't help but slow down to observe the damage when you finally inch past the accident? This is the best metaphor I can come up with for describing football addiction. No matter what happens – if Hull City and their dreadful owners find themselves in the ninth tier of English football, or England fail to qualify for the next dozen international tournaments – I know I will never be able to stop myself watching.

The final pilgrimages

Hull City 2–1 Leicester City – 13/08/2016

Hull City 1–1 Sunderland – 16/09/2017

HEADING into my 16th full season as a City fan, I was not only dealing with continuing feelings of deep frustration, but also worry. In the two months since our Wembley victory a lot happened, none of it good. Just days after being interviewed by the FA for the vacant position of England manager, Steve Bruce announced his resignation following a meeting with City's ownership. A lack of transfer activity, as well as tiring disputes between the Allam family and the supporters, his rationale. Who could blame him? Assistant manager Mike Phelan took over as caretaker and the circus continued.

No permanent manager, no new signings, despite having a squad of just 13 fit first-teamers, and a sizeable list of long-term injuries. Not to mention the painstaking speculative rumours of takeovers by Chinese consortiums or the former CEO of Goldman Sachs, and the division between fans and the owners larger than ever before. Oh, and to put a cherry on top of this cake of misery, City's opening game of the season was to be against reigning Premier League champions, Leicester City.

It comes as no surprise that City were being labelled the 'worst prepared team in Premier League history'. In reality, the club deserved to be branded much worse.

As it goes, in the end it was not that summer's misadventures that saw Dad and I make one of the toughest decisions of our football-supporting lives. In reality our minds had been made during the final few months of the previous season and the announcement of the new membership scheme. In protest of the way our much-loved football club was being run, and in particular as a response to the abolition of concession ticketing at the KCOM, Dad and I took the decision not to renew our season tickets (or 'membership' as it is now sickeningly known) for the 2016/17 season.

We agreed we would still attend as many away matches as we always had, and go to the KCOM for the odd game here and there, the latter of which would not last, but in all good conscience we could not become part of the membership farce.

The choice hurt – and three seasons later still does, with the Allam family and their concession-less membership scheme still blighting the club – but it's a decision we both stand by. Indeed, as I write this in the late spring of 2019, it's been well over 18 months since my last pilgrimage to the KCOM. What a depressing thought.

Looking ahead to the first season in over 15 years in which I knew I wouldn't be guaranteed a live football match each week, I recognised I needed to find other ways to feed my addiction. In the end I found something that more closely resembled rehabilitation. I threw myself into volunteering with the Hull City Supporters' Trust.

The HCST was created late in 2014 when the successful 'City Til We Die' name-change protest group merged with the long-established Tigers Co-operative, which was set up in the late 90s with the sole objective of ensuring the supporters of Hull City would have their voices heard. After years of conflict between the fans and the Allam family, the HCST, and its ties with both Supporters Direct and the Football Supporters' Federation, appealed to me as the one place I could perhaps start to make a difference myself, and by 2016, after two years of membership, I was ready to offer any help I could provide. Starting with writing the odd article here and there on the website, by the end of the year I was an elected director on the Trust's board, managing

the website and acting as a stand-in press officer. After years of
frustration and apathy, I had finally found a like-minded group
of fans that felt exactly like me, and were proactively working
together to do something about our plight. This work was the
closest thing I could find to replacing the hours of football I
was missing every other week at the KCOM, allowing me to
keep my connection with the club, without supporting a regime
I despised. Unfortunately, my time on the board of the HCST
would be cut short just 12 months later when working for the
BBC created a potential conflict of interests, yet, my Trust
work still represents one of my proudest achievements to date.
Three years on and still under the leadership of Geoff Bielby,
the fantastic work the Trust conducts continues to make steady
progress in achieving all of its aims and objectives, helping to
re-engage what is possibly *the* most disenchanted fan base in
English football.

As the season drew closer and closer, I became increasingly
more anxious. I genuinely thought City were so underprepared
that we might actually break Derby County's unwanted record
low Premier League points tally of 11 from nine seasons earlier.
A horrible thought.

Despite having only just made the heartbreaking decision not
to reserve our E5 seats for another season, Dad and I did choose to
go to City's first game of the new campaign. I was due at a planned
HCST protest outside the KCOM prior to the match that day, and
to not stay for the match after the protest seemed daft. As it goes,
it turned out to be one of my final visits to the KCOM Stadium.

Of course, as with every opening game of the season, I went
to the match full of excitement having been deprived of league
football for a whole summer. Yet, I am not embarrassed to admit
that for the first time in my life, I arrived at a gloriously sunny
West Park believing City had no hope whatsoever of picking up
a positive result. I could not have been more wrong. It appears
'typical City' works both ways.

A depleted City team – containing just one recognised centre-
back, and five academy players on the bench – miraculously

managed to beat the reigning champions of England 2–1, sparking what I think it's fair to describe as the last *great* result in City's recent history.

You couldn't write it. Going into the match, the so-called 'worst prepared team in Premier League history' were not given a chance against 'the Unbelievables' of Leicester City, and rightly so, but from the very first whistle Mike Phelan's ramshackle 11 were fantastic.

Indeed, other than a poor miss from Jamie Vardy in the first half, the champions were comfortably contained by the Tigers, with Curtis Davies and stand-in centre-half Jake Livermore contributing outstanding performances. Incredibly, it came as no real surprise when Adama Diomande's spectacular overhead kick put us in front on the stroke of half-time. The goal only served to better an already electric atmosphere inside the KCOM – the last time I can really recall the entire ground bouncing with excitement. Even during the interval, which usually brings with it a lull in the atmosphere, fans remained in their seats, waving banners and chanting 'WE WANT ALLAM OUT, SAY WE WANT ALLAM OUT' on an endless loop. For the first time in a few years, I felt the same tingle run down the length of my spine that I had first experienced outside Boothferry Park all those years ago.

Riyad Mahrez pulled one back for the Foxes, slamming home from the penalty spot after Demarai Gray was deemed to be trod on by Huddlestone. Replays would show the foul actually occurred outside of the penalty area, but in the end it wasn't to matter. With 57 minutes on the clock, man of the match Robert Snodgrass marked his Premier League comeback with the sweetest of winners, powering a shot into the bottom corner from the edge of the area after the champions failed to clear their lines. The KCOM erupted.

City managed to weather the storm fairly comfortably for the remaining 35 minutes, inflicting a first opening-day defeat on the champions of England since Arsenal lost to Manchester United in 1989.

'Never write off Hull City,' an abnormally positive Dad chuckled, as we wandered through West Park after the game.

'One swallow does not a summer make, though, and I think Phelan will have to be careful now. There's a chance all that result does is disguise all the issues within the club, which we have to sort out before the window closes,' he added, more seriously.

I was impressed with Dad's ability to turn a fantastic result into a glum prediction, although, of course, I knew he was right.

'The Allams probably think the squad is big and strong enough to compete after watching that!' I retorted.

Despite a positive start, our preseason fears soon began morphing into reality, and with City cemented in the relegation zone by January, Phelan was sacked and replaced by a relatively unknown quantity in the Portuguese Marco Silva. A gamble that very nearly paid off. Yet ultimately, a deserved relegation was all but unavoidable.

Relegation was not the fault of either the manager or our squad of players that year. Yes, both managers that season, and our limited squad of players, made mistakes at points, but the buck stopped with the club's owners. From not providing funds for players at the start of the season, to selling our best performer, Snodgrass, in January, the Allam family deserved to suffer relegation for the way they mismanaged the situation. Any manager in the world would have struggled to keep City in the Premier League that season. To use a cricketing analogy made famous by former chancellor Geoffrey Howe, that season felt as though the Allam family had sent '... our opening batsmen to the crease only for them to find that before the first ball is bowled, their bats have been broken by the team captain'.

As always, it's just a crying shame that the fans are the ones who suffer most. A horrific side-effect of modern football.

Since the beginning of that season I had started writing regularly on a freelance basis for *Yahoo Sports UK*, adding to my growing writing portfolio and providing some extra income during the year studying for my Masters. Most of this work concentrated on the Premier League, with a particular focus on the north-east. Having gone back and reread a lot of my content from this time, it's fair to say City's relegation was always expected. However, what I had forgotten was just how much (ultimately misplaced) hope the introduction of Marco Silva provided. Indeed, in my final *Yahoo* piece that season, I wrote:

'From being written off by fans and pundits alike before a ball was even kicked last summer, via a mini revival under an exciting new manager, finishing with the bitter disappointment of relegation following an injection of false hope, it is so difficult to know how to feel, or even how to evaluate the club's season.

'While I would be lying to say I'm not disappointed, it is an expected disappointment on the back of a season I enjoyed far more than I believed possible back in July. The future may well look bleak at this moment in time for the Tigers; however, in the circumstances I believe that, somewhat paradoxically, when the dust has settled, this season of "what ifs" will be looked back on with a certain level of fondness in years to come.'

As ever, it was the hope that killed City fans.

Silva jumped ship following relegation, and was soon predictably followed by a mass exodus of players, leaving the club both manager-less and with only a skeleton squad for the second consecutive summer. With a long and arduous season in the Championship ahead, the devastating prospect of back-to-back relegations seemed a real possibility.

Writing this in the spring of 2019, the following sentence makes me feel physically sick. My final visit to the KCOM Stadium came just a few months later in the September of 2017.

After another suitably chaotic summer in which nine first-team players left the club, former Russia and CSKA Moscow manager Leonid Slutsky was the man tasked with masterminding an immediate return to the Premier League. I will never forget on the eve of his first competitive match as Hull City manager, with a beaming smile of his face, Slutsky gleefully told the assembled media that the opportunity to manage in England was a 'fairy tale come true'. It would only be a matter of months before Slutsky's fairy tale rapidly became a nightmare, as City systematically killed the spirit of the happiest manager in world football.

In a consistently inconsistent start the 2017/18 campaign, made up of a strange combination of big City wins mixed with woeful defeats, the attack-minded Slutsky wouldn't even make it to Christmas. As it goes, the only match I saw at the KCOM that season was during Slutsky's brief tenure – a dismal 1–1 draw with fellow double-relegation candidates Sunderland. I think about this game a lot.

It's funny, when Dad and I decided to buy tickets for this fixture – the first home game we had attended all season – neither of us expected it would be our last. However, by the time we collected our usual fish and chips from Viking and walked through an almost deserted West Park at 2.45pm, we had both individually made up our minds that we would not be returning to the KCOM until the Allam family had left the club. The experience actually made me incredibly emotional. After more than a decade of experiencing vibrant, crowded and truly happy Hull City home games every other week, the sight that greeted us knocked me sideways. We had managed to get our old seats for the game, but were immediately shocked to find swaths of empty seats either side of us – our group of friends we had seen every other Saturday since 2003, gone. The empty seats also brought about a terrible lack of atmosphere, giving the whole game the feeling of a training match. Instead of the non-stop singing and chanting I had become used to after more than a decade in the East Stand, the sounds of players shouting and the high-pitched squeal of the referee's whistle could be heard clearly over the dull murmur of a half-empty stadium.

The game itself was also a stinker. City went one down early on after James Vaughan powered a header past Allan McGregor on 17 minutes. Much of the remaining 75 minutes was dire, aside from David Meyler snatching a late equaliser for the Tigers with eight minutes to go. Yet even this somehow failed to generate much of a reaction from the City faithful.

As the full-time whistle sounded, greeted by an undertone of dissatisfaction, Dad and I sat for a few minutes and watched as the players trudged down the tunnel and fans filled out of the exits.

I felt awful – a horrible concoction of disappointment and anger had hit me. Not with the result – I have seen much worse results at the KCOM, believe me – but by everything else I had just seen. What I just witnessed was not a City home match, not as I remembered, anyway. It was a club, a set of players and its loyal fans simply going through the motions. The passion that I had witnessed at the KCOM, and Boothferry Park before that, every other weekend for 17 seasons was gone. Of course, I already knew this was happening. I had streamed or listened to every home game that season. However, witnessing the deterioration of a once family-orientated, local football club first-hand broke my heart.

'It's dead. They have completely killed it,' I lamented, as we walked back to the car.

'It will never be the same until the club is under new ownership. The heart and soul of the club has been torn out. Today was a horrible reminder of that,' Dad replied.

'Let's stick to away games for now. I don't want to taint the wonderful memories of the KC we have already made, and I resent giving the Allam family even one more penny of our own money,' I proposed, already knowing Dad's answer.

'It's going to hurt, but I was going to suggest the same thing. Sitting in that stadium, seeing the damage that has been done makes my blood boil. I don't want that any more,' Dad agreed.

Thanks to the current regime at Hull City, many loyal fans, usually in the shape of OAPs and under-23s, simply cannot afford to attend home games any more following the abolition of concession ticketing. After nearly three seasons of the membership scheme alone, a situation has arisen in the city in which once diehard Tigers fans simply don't care any more – many have completely fallen out of love with a football club they had supported their whole lives. To put this into perspective, these are fans that supported the club through 104 years of lower-league football. Fans that stood outside Boothferry Park in the freezing cold with collection buckets when it looked like the club was going under. Fans that nearly saw their side fall out of the Football League altogether in 1999. And fans that work all week just to afford to go to the football with their kids or elderly parents each weekend. To disenchant this set of fans takes a hell of a lot, but somehow the current Hull City owners managed it. The Allam family claimed to have saved the club when they took over in 2010, and in terms of finances they did just that. However, in order to save the club again, this time from potentially losing a whole generation of supporters, they must sell the club before it's too late.

As for me, the Sunderland match in 2017 represented the end of the line. The final time I supported my beloved Hull City at home after years of loyal support. Modern football had finally got its own way and forced me to choose between a mutilated version of the game I had once loved and my own set of morals. Dad and I, along with the thousands of other City fans choosing to boycott, have been accused of simply cutting off our collective nose to spite our face, but it is a decision we stand by. Why let years of good memories be ruined by a vindictive set of owners?

Nearly two years on from my final visit to the KCOM, it saddens me to describe myself still firmly teetering between the 'football junkie' and the 'disenchanted former fan' quadrants of my crudely thought-up spectrum of fandom. Though, in my heart of hearts, I don't think I'm going to recover from my football addiction, or my preferred strain of Hull City AFC, anytime soon.

During the 'City Til We Die' anti-name-change campaign a few years back, one fellow member and lifelong City fan said something that has always stuck in my mind. She said 'Players come and go, managers come and go, chairmen come and go. But the club will always belong to the supporters'.

She was absolutely right. You see, long after the current regime at the KCOM is over, and when Dad and I are back sitting in our old E5 seats, I know I will remember why I vowed to love Hull City unconditionally. And I know that despite the unstoppable march of modern football, it will be at this point that my football addiction will once again transition into a genuine love for the game. I can't wait.

Salvation in a blue waistcoat

Colombia 1–1 England AET
(3–4 penalty shoot-out) – 03/07/2018

AT the end of the 2017/18 season I was fed up and disillusioned with football. As well as prompting me to start noting some of these feelings down in a journal that ultimately formed the basis for this book, these thoughts frightened the life out of me. Other than my family, football has been *the* only constant in my life, and the thought of turning my back on it terrified me. What would I do if I stopped liking football? I write about it for a living, while my spare time consists of watching, reading and breathing everything football.

I'd be pretty snookered at this point in my life if I were to abandon my one true passion. But who can blame me for having these thoughts? A godawful Hull City – still a club very much going through a bitter civil war between fans and ownership – had just finished 18th in the Championship, narrowly avoiding relegation thanks to the hard-fought work of the annoyingly positive Nigel Adkins, while an England side that was so mind-blowingly disappointing at Euro 2016 were about to head to Russia for the World Cup with a largely untested manager in Gareth Southgate.

I was aware, as I still am, that there was no way Hull City could provide any solace until a change of ownership had taken place, and with nearly two decades of experience following England at major tournaments, I certainly wasn't getting my hopes up for a Southgate-inspired revival.

But then the unthinkable happened: England over-performed at a World Cup.

Having finished my Masters degree and moved to Chester to live with Becki in the January, I took little notice of the build-up to World Cup 2018. I was still making ends meet freelancing for a number of online publications, and picking up the odd shift on the radio; however, I also began working at a bank, sifting through PPI claims to keep my income healthy. It wasn't ideal, but it served a purpose while I looked to get my foot in the door of full-time journalism.

As ever, England had coasted through World Cup qualification and, after recovering from the Sam Allardyce debacle, Gareth Southgate had gone about his business quietly, significantly making the difficult decisions to drop captain Wayne Rooney and first-choice goalkeeper Joe Hart, instead turning his focus to building a young and hungry side. It paid off.

Going into the World Cup, England's group looked a bit of a mixed bag, with unknown quantity Tunisia, tournament debutants Panama and one of the bookies' favourites Belgium joining the Three Lions. Despite the relative apathy in the weeks and days before a bizarre Robbie Williams appearance opened the Russia World Cup, it would be England's performances in this group that re-engaged an entire nation, me included.

England got off to the perfect start, beating Tunisia 2–1 with captain Harry Kane scoring the winner in stoppage time in Volgograd, preventing a draw that surely would have brought about a feeling of 'same old England'. Six days later, the Three Lions were truly up and running with a dominant 6–1 victory against Panama, Kane grabbing a hat-trick in the process. Wry whispers of 'It's coming home' started to be heard all over England.

A fortuitous 1–0 defeat for a much-changed England against Belgium in the final group game guaranteed Southgate a second-place finish and what appeared, on paper at least, an easier route through the knockout phases compared to what Roberto Martinez's men now faced.

Next up for England, Colombia. In a World Cup of shocks, which had already seen world champions Germany eliminated at the group stage, and Spain sent packing by hosts Russia in their own last-16 match, Southgate had labelled the Colombia game England's biggest for a decade.

It wouldn't disappoint.

By this time a nation was allowing itself to get carried away again, but somehow in a more self-deprecating manner than ever before. 'Three Lions' took over the internet in new vine and meme form, while for a glorious three-week period, the phrase 'It's coming home' briefly replaced 'hello' in the English vernacular. Coinciding with what felt like a never-ending heatwave back in the UK, a nation fed up with years of austerity and the ongoing Brexit farce appeared collectively happy for the first time in years.

I watched the match in my Chester flat with Becki, hoping for the best but still very much expecting the worst. Although I had started to buy into the hype surrounding this England team, I was yet to be convinced anything had actually changed. We had finished second in a group containing Belgium and had beaten Tunisia and Panama to this point – nothing that spectacular yet. Get past an underrated Colombia side and I might start to think differently, I remember thinking.

The match got off to a predictably scrappy start. Without their injured key man James Rodríguez, Colombia's game plan soon became extremely apparent. From the first whistle the South Americans were doing everything possible to frustrate England and prevent us settling into our possession-based game. Each time England looked to push forward, a yellow-clad swarm descended, with persistent fouls and cynical tackles preventing Southgate's men from finding their rhythm. It all came to a head just before half-time when, while jockeying for position in his own penalty area, Wilmar Barrios appeared to headbutt the unsuspecting Jordan Henderson.

'SEND HIM OFF!' I roared at the TV, as Becki looked at me, amused with how seriously I was taking what she saw as just 22 men running around a field.

Shouts for VAR were made, but with no indication that technology had been used, Barrios was shown a yellow card and the match continued. A let-off for the South Americans.

England would take advantage on 57 minutes, however, when Kane coolly converted from the spot after being dragged to the floor when looking to connect with an inswinging corner just moments earlier. 1–0 England and one foot in the quarter-finals.

Though one final echo of 'typical England' would reverberate around the Spartak Stadium before the final whistle went. Directly from a corner in stoppage time, moments after Jordan Pickford had pulled off the save of the tournament to keep England ahead, defender Yerry Mina's header bounced over the head of Kieran Trippier on the far post, and past Pickford. England looked to have thrown it away again.

Thirty painstaking minutes of extra time could do nothing to break the deadlock, meaning 22 years after Gareth Southgate's infamous Euro 96 semi-final miss against Germany, England's current crop – a far less fancied set of individuals – had the chance to put it right for their manager.

As I sat on the very edge of the sofa, struggling to watch, I couldn't imagine a life without football.

However, a few minutes later I was staring once again down the barrel of yet another England shoot-out failure. Falcao and Cuadrado scored Colombia's first two penalties and Kane and Rashford responded with aplomb. However, when Jordan Henderson failed to match Luis Muriel's third for Colombia, England were in trouble.

'That's it. It's all over,' I groaned, to a slightly more interested Becki.

However, my moaning was proven premature after Mateus Uribe spectacularly hit the bar with Colombia's fourth attempt, before Pickford heroically blocked Carlos Bacca's effort to set the stage for Eric Dier to win it for England. The Spurs man bowed his head and waited for the whistle.

'He's going to miss. I just know it,' I murmured, now watching from behind my hands.

He stepped up and ...

'YES! England are World Cup quarter-finalists again! And they've done it on penalties!'

An excitable Clive Tyldesley summed up the feelings of an entire nation, while the England players celebrated. Under the unfancied Gareth Southgate, a young England squad had just won their first knockout match since 2006, recording England's first ever World Cup penalty shoot-out victory in the process.

As I sat back on my sofa, watching a jubilant Southgate, complete with trademark waistcoat, applaud the travelling England fans, I thought back to England's 5–1 drubbing of Germany – the game that first sparked my love for football. And in that moment I remembered why I adore football. Yes, there will be times when the idiosyncrasies of modern football become problematic, making love for the beautiful game hard to maintain. But eventually I realised, once a football addict, always a football addict. I can accept this now.

England would go on to comfortably beat Sweden in the quarter-finals – with Harry Maguire's big head winning me £150 in the process – to progress to a first World Cup semi since Gazza's tears in Italia 90. Ultimately, despite an early Trippier goal, and a 'what if' moment involving Kane and Sterling, a Croatia side lead by the incredible Luka Modrić proved too strong, winning in extra time, ending England's wonderful Russian adventure. England may still be waiting for football to come home after 2018, but at least, during a time in which the nation's population is as polarised as it perhaps has ever been before, a magnificent showing at the Russia World Cup managed to bring a nation together and provide a renewed sense of national pride, if only for a few weeks, anyway. These are the moments us football addicts live for. These are the moments I had not enjoyed for the past few years.

It's curious. I very nearly didn't write this book. Writing about the deterioration of my relationship with football – probably the biggest part of the first 25 years of my life – was always going to be difficult. However, the process was made even tougher when I realised this decline has coincided with a plethora of monumental changes in my life – some good, some bad. From the deterioration of my parents' health over the last five years and a life-changing bout of personal depression, to discovering a new passion for writing, and meeting the woman I want to spend the rest of my life with in Becki. This realisation made the process a highly emotional experience, and not just the cathartic one I had first envisaged.

For many, this book will represent nothing more than a collection of idyllic childhood memories, and on the face of it, that's exactly what it is. Yet for me, it is more than that. It's my entire life in microcosm.

While I have enjoyed revisiting some of my old favourites, as my writing progressed I became worried that documenting the unquestionable decline of this relationship in black and white would somehow force me into a decision I never want to make, and ask questions I don't want to answer. After all, as the past few chapters have acknowledged, the last five years or so had seen me come to resent the two most important factors involved in my love (come addiction) for football. This raises the question: compulsion to never stop watching apart, do I still even *like* football?

Well, when I first began considering the key concepts for this book on the bus home from work just over a year ago, I wasn't too sure. It's true, I had nearly given up on football altogether just months before my affection for the sport came full circle. You see, just as England's famous win in Munich successfully converted me into a football fan all those years ago, it was a new generation of England players that would reaffirm my passion for the beautiful game.

My relationship with football nowadays is perhaps better described as 'an addiction' rather than 'love', there is no getting away from that. And yes, I do believe this is a fate destined for an increasingly large group of football fans the world over as the current vision of 'modern football' continues to profane and bastardise the once simple, working-class sport we have all loved. But somehow all of this fades into insignificance when you find yourself standing on the terraces with a parent, travelling to an away game with your mates, or even sat in front of the TV with your better half, waiting for a match to start. Addiction or affection, in the end, it doesn't matter. When it comes to football, I can't help falling in love with you.